Christian Ethics and Social Policy
Christian Realism
Social Salvation
Christianity and Our World
Christianity and Communism
The Christian as Citizen

CO-AUTHOR OF *Christian Values and Economic Life*

CHRISTIANS AND THE STATE

CHRISTIANS

AND

THE STATE

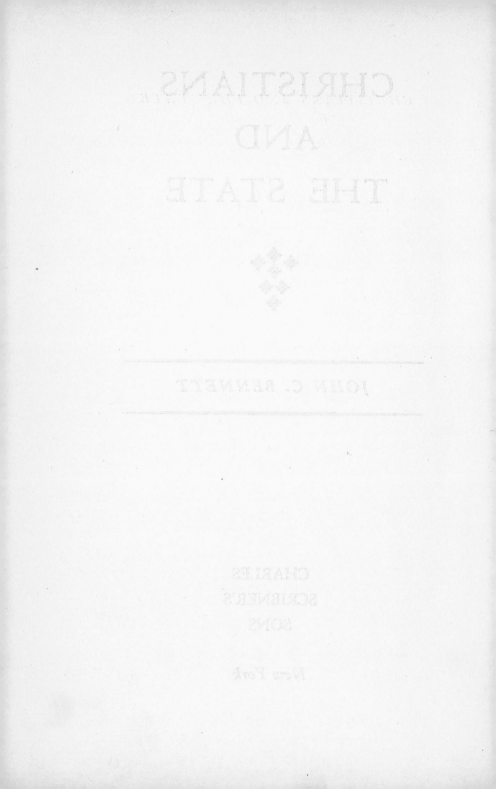

JOHN C. BENNETT

CHARLES
SCRIBNER'S
SONS

New York

CHRISTIANS AND THE STATE

JOHN C. BENNETT

CHARLES
SCRIBNER'S
SONS

New York

TO

Reinhold Niebuhr

AND

Henry Pitney Van Dusen
Friends and colleagues of many years
with deep gratitude

I HAVE chosen the title, Christians and the State, to suggest that this book deals with far more than the problems of Church and State though I have discussed them at some length. I have sought to write a book about the theological basis of the state itself about the state's nature and function, and about the problems of political ethics.

I have written against the background of the institutions and problems of the United States. Recently I wrote a little book at the request of the International Missionary Council about Christian citizenship,* and I was supposed to make it applicable to all parts of the world, especially to the countries of the "younger churches," in Asia and Africa about which my knowledge is very limited. In my effort to carry out this assignment I came to realize how remote generalizations intended to apply to all situations are from many situations. I resolved then to write a book that would deal with some fullness with the problems in the United States with which I am most familiar. Christian convictions can be illuminated best when we move from abstract discussions of them to the consideration of what they mean for one time and one place. When that is done, much that is said may prove to be relevant to other times and places if proper allowances are made for differences in situation.

The reader may be puzzled about my locating the first two chapters at the beginning of the book and setting them off as Part I for they are more obviously related to the material in Part III on Church and State than to the chapters which in-

* *The Christian & Citizen* (Association Press, 1955).

PREFACE

I HAVE chosen the title, *Christians and the State,* to suggest that this book deals with far more than the problems of Church and State though I have discussed them at some length. I have sought to write a book about the theological basis of the state itself, about the state's nature and function, and about the problems of political ethics.

I have written against the background of the institutions and problems of the United States. Recently I wrote a little book at the request of the International Missionary Council about Christian citizenship* and I was supposed to make it applicable to all parts of the world, especially to the countries of the "younger churches" in Asia and Africa about which my knowledge is very limited. In my effort to carry out this assignment I came to realize how remote generalizations intended to apply to all situations are from many situations. I resolved then to write a book that would deal with some fullness with the problems in the United States with which I am most familiar. Christian convictions can be illumined best when we move from abstract discussions of them to the consideration of what they mean for one time and one place. When that is done, much that is said may prove to be relevant to other times and places if proper allowances are made for differences in situation.

The reader may be puzzled about my locating the first two chapters at the beginning of the book and setting them off as Part I for they are more obviously related to the material in Part III on Church and State than to the chapters which im-

* *The Christian as Citizen* (Association Press, 1955).

mediately follow. They do, however, set forth a point of view that is presupposed in the book as a whole, a point of view about the relation of religion to both state and nation and about the relation of Christian faith and ethics to the more broadly based moral convictions and preferences which influence our public life. The decisions of the state depend upon this broad moral consensus. At every point in the affairs of the state Christians cooperate with fellow citizens who do not share their religious convictions but who share with them a common social conscience. Our national life would be a shambles if there were no such consensus on matters of justice and public morality. How we should understand the relation between distinctively Christian ethics and this public conscience is an area of considerable confusion in contemporary Christian thinking.

Any reader with primary interest in the much debated issues of Church and State may easily move from Part I to Part III but I hope that he will browse a bit in Part II where he will find discussed many necessary presuppositions about the state.

My first attempt to organize my thought on this subject took the form of a series of lectures in 1952 at Garrett Biblical Institute on a foundation recently established in honor of its much revered Professor of Theology, Harris Franklin Rall. In 1954 I gave the Fondren Lectures in which I dealt with the same themes at Perkins School of Theology in the Southern Methodist University. In 1957 I gave a series of lectures in the same general area at the Augustana Theological Seminary and at Bexley Hall (Kenyon College). I had a chance in these various series of lectures to try out my convictions on concentrations of Methodists, Lutherans, and Episcopalians. I have also profited by the stimulus of my own students at Union Theological Seminary in a seminar that I have given for several years on the subject of this book.

I am grateful to my colleagues, Professor Reinhold Niebuhr and Professor Robert Lee, for reading the manuscript as a whole and to the Reverend Herman E. Wornom for reading the manuscript of Part III. They are not responsible for the views expressed or for any errors that the reader may discover.

My wife has been tireless in her help at every stage. She has typed the manuscript more than once and her editorial judgment has in many places smoothed the path for the reader.

John C. Bennett

August 15, 1958
Union Theological Seminary
New York City

CONTENTS

CONTENTS

xiii

PART THREE: CHURCH AND STATE

INTRODUCTION

Christian Faith and the Fatefulness of
Political Problems

POLITICAL problems have come to be the most fateful social problems. Three decades ago it seemed that economic problems were primary and Christian writers about society were generally preoccupied with them. Even then economic problems led to questions concerning the role of the state in economic life, which remains one of the most urgent of the political problems. Today, while there is no doubt about the significance of the interaction between economics and politics on many levels, it seems that the greatest threats to man come from the conflict of political ideologies, from political instability within various countries and regions, and from the danger of nuclear war. There are issues of economic justice and well-being involved in all of these threats, but we can no longer assume that all political ideas and forces and decisions are merely reflections of what happens in economic life.

The experience of totalitarianism has shocked our generation into political thought at a deeper level than arguments between political parties which share the same presuppositions about the state. Economic factors have been important in the rise of totalitarian movements but they did not of themselves create the totalitarian doctrines which have been most destructive of human freedom. For example, they did not create the illusion that if the Communists only push through their revolution to its final end, the apparatus of the coercive state will wither away.

The same fatefulness of political issues is apparent in the experience of new nations which must speedily develop their political institutions in order to solve the most desperate economic and social problems; and they must do this under strong pressure to choose the Communist political shortcut to economic progress. Here the economic problems may be in one respect fundamental but the possibility of their solution depends upon a long period of political stability and decisions are as much between political as between economic alternatives.

In the United States the problems which cause most bafflement and anguish are those that are posed by foreign policy, by our dual responsibility to preserve as wide an area of political and spiritual freedom as possible and to prevent the war that could end human hope in this world. The issues here are primarily political as are those which involve the long-range development of the institutions of world community. Foreign economic aid is a major factor in the discharge of our responsibility but its acceptability depends to a considerable extent upon our political stance and its effectiveness depends upon political stability in the countries aided. Also the United States has recently emerged from a period of hysteria which threatened to undermine our freedom and this was caused in part by a serious conflict in our own minds concerning the conditions for both freedom and security.

There are immediate problems in this country in the sphere of Church-State relations. They are likely to be more acute in the next period. There will be intensive debate about them; this debate will have serious repercussions on our educational system and on the relations between our religious communities. I have chosen to devote more than a third of this book to these problems.

Back of the contemporary discussion of these many political

problems there is the whole history of Christian thought. Much of this history that has the greatest relevance to our problems today is more fundamental and broader than Christian political theory. It deals with God's purpose for our life, with the nature of man and society, with the political symptoms of sin, with the direct and indirect political effects of the redemption mediated to us by Christ, with the essential nature of the Church and its role in society. Christian theology and ethics have dealt continually with the problems of justice and order that underlie all political institutions and they have profound implications for political and spiritual freedom. In these areas there has been much clarification in recent centuries.

I have used the word "state" in the title of this book to refer broadly to these political problems. It has not always been the most suitable word to refer to political institutions. This was true in the period of the New Testament and in the mediaeval period of many principalities and of feudal relationships under rather distant imperial and papal authorities. We can learn something from Christian political thinking in such periods that are very different from our own, but the problems of the modern *state* which is the political structure of a *nation* have called for much fresh thinking. The democratic state in which Christian citizens are the immediate source of political authority raises many new problems. Today we should be less concerned to apply to our situation the results of earlier Christian political thinking than to relate Christian faith in its fullness to our political life.

PART ONE

CHRISTIAN FAITH IN A RELIGIOUSLY PLURALISTIC SOCIETY

CHAPTER I
PART ONE

CHRISTIANS IN A RELIGIOUSLY PLURALISTIC NATION

How should Christians who are citizens of a religiously pluralistic nation express their faith that both nation and state stand under the providence, the judgment and the redeeming love of God? On what basis should they cooperate with citizens of other faiths or with those who reject all traditional forms of religion? What is the relation between the Christian faith and the ethic that is derived from it and the moral convictions which Christian citizens share with most of their fellow citizens and which are partially embodied in laws and institutions?

Answers to such questions will not fit many different national situations. Every nation has to begin with the consequences of its own history, and these consequences in American life are unusual, if not unique, in the way in which the following characteristics are combined:

1. Our heritage is in the main vitally Christian although the nation is not committed to any one faith.
2. Church and State are legally separated but the state is friendly to religion and cooperates ungrudgingly with churches and other religious bodies.
3. The pervasive western secularizing influences are strongly felt and yet there is a remarkable revival of religious interest, and religious institutions grow rapidly and show signs of unusual vitality.

One distinctive aspect of the religious pluralism of the United States is that the one non-Christian religion with considerable

CHAPTER I

The Nation Under God

How should Christians who are citizens of a religiously plural-istic nation express their faith that both nation and state stand under the providence, the judgment and the redeeming love of God? On what basis should they cooperate with citizens of other faiths or with those who reject all traditional forms of religion? What is the relation between the Christian faith and the ethic that is derived from it and the moral convictions which Christian citizens share with most of their fellow citizens and which are partially embodied in laws and institutions?

Answers to such questions will not fit many different national situations. Every nation has to begin with the consequences of its own history, and these consequences in American life are unusual, if not unique, in the way in which the following characteristics are combined:

1. Our heritage is in the main vitally Christian although the nation is not committed to any one faith.
2. Church and State are legally separated but the state is friendly to religion and cooperates ungrudgingly with churches and other religious bodies.
3. The pervasive western secularizing influences are strongly felt and yet there is a remarkable revival of religious interest, and religious institutions grow rapidly and show signs of unusual vitality.

One distinctive aspect of the religious pluralism of the United States is that the one non-Christian religion with considerable

3

strength in numbers and influence is Judaism. Judaism shares with Christianity essential elements of the Biblical tradition and faith and it is a strong support for a Biblically derived ethic which, so far as the goals of public life are concerned, is difficult to distinguish from the Christian ethic. This makes for a great deal of moral unity. On the other hand, because of the historical relations between Christianity and Judaism, Jews are naturally more negative about the public use of Christian symbols than are citizens who are religiously indifferent or who are adherents of secular faiths.

It may help to throw our situation into relief if we compare it with that of the British nation. In spite of much erosion of Christian commitment and understanding, Britain claims not only a traditional but also a normative relationship with Christianity. This is not merely to say that England has a state Church and that Scotland has a national Church. It is still natural for the state on behalf of the nation to use Christian symbols and to express in forms of Christian worship the dependence of the nation on God. In recent years we have observed two British coronation ceremonies. In both cases there was among the British people a deep appreciation of the strongly Christian symbolism of the event. People in this country were, I think, on both occasions amazed at the high level of national Christian commitment that was presupposed in the ritual.

It is not strange that many Anglicans still insist, as Alec Vidler does, that the state should recognize the Church "on grounds of truth and not of expediency alone" and that the state should "*profess*" (italics mine) one faith while deliberately providing "full security for dissenting minorities."[1] But it may be surprising to Americans to find that many leaders of the Free Churches no longer call for disestablishment of the Church of England because they fear that this would weaken

[1] *The Orb and the Cross* (S. P. C. K., 1945), pp. 94, 126.

the tie between Christianity and the national life. H. F. Lovell Cocks, a leading Congregational theologian, writes: "Perhaps there is value, after all, in the public acknowledgement of Christ's claim over the national life, provided that in regard to the counter-claim of the state the national church is uncompromisingly non-conformist." He says that if the national church proved to be able to retain its freedom from control by the state over its faith and worship, Nonconformists might return to it.[2]

T. S. Eliot's *The Idea of a Christian Society*[3] could not have been written for this country as Mr. Eliot clearly recognizes and therefore it provides some illumination for us by contrast. It sets forth in very persuasive terms the idea of a society that is positively Christian rather than neutral but it provides for full freedom for non-Christians. It presupposes an established Church to which most of the people belong, but Mr. Eliot emphasizes less the authority of an ecclesiastical hierarchy than the intrinsic influence of a Christian elite consisting of clergy and laity of "superior intellectual and/or spiritual gifts."[4]

American Christians cannot participate in either the advantages or the illusions that go with this formal relationship between Christianity and the nation. Yet our nation or state is not in principle secular or even neutral as between religion and the rejection of it. There is among us an officially recognized theism which appears in many state documents such as the Declaration of Independence and in the constitutions of most states, in the official utterances of national leaders, in the provision made for prayer on many official occasions, especially at meetings of legislative bodies. Twice in recent years two very

[2] *The Non-Conformist Conscience* (Independent Press, London, 1943), pp. 93-94. See also, "The Report of the Commission on Church and State appointed by the Free Church Federal Council in March 1950" (London, 1953), pp. 61-63.

[3] Harcourt Brace, 1940.

[4] *Ibid.*, p. 37.

different Presidents, F. D. Roosevelt and Dwight Eisenhower, thought it appropriate to lead the nation in prayer when they addressed it. A recent decision of the Supreme Court written by Justice William O. Douglas said: "We are a religious people and our institutions presuppose a Supreme Being."[5]

The present situation becomes clearer if we compare those words of Justice Douglas in 1952 with the words of Justice Sutherland in 1931 to the effect that we are a "Christian people."[6] That was, as far as I have been able to learn, the most recent statement by the Supreme Court affirming that as a nation we are not only "religious" but "Christian." It was however in line with what has been said before by that Court and by other American courts and it was consistent with a legal tradition according to which Christian ethics are part of the common law.[7] I do not think that Christians should desire either our courts or other public bodies to affirm again that we are a "Christian people." They should affirm the fact of our Christian heritage but it is only fair to avow our religious pluralism.

What are we to say about this national acknowledgment of God which because of our religious pluralism cannot have more content than a vague theism? It is easy to dismiss it as insincere or as little more than a harmless anachronism or to see special irony in the fact that the words, "In God we trust," appear on our coins, and that the word "God" appears so frequently in political perorations. The association of this theism with current popular forms of religious reassurance and especially with the current desire for religious sanctions for the American way of life has caused many theologians and religious leaders to criticize it very sharply. The soundest criticism is that

[5] *Zorach v. Clauson et. al.*, 1952.

[6] This statement in the Macintosh decision (1931) refers back to *Holy Trinity Church v. U. S.* (1892).

[7] Cf., Anson Phelps Stokes, *Church and State in the United States* (Harper, 1950), Vol. III, pp. 565-582.

in practice we often find ourselves engaged in the ritual of a third faith[8]—not Christianity or Judaism. As Will Herberg says, we have an American religion which may begin as a common denominator of our historic faiths but which becomes in practice a substitute faith.[9] This American faith is often nationalistic and it can become chauvinistic though, for the most part, we have escaped that. It lacks emphasis upon the transcendent judgment of God. It is often a folk-religion with some Christian overtones. The association of the current revival of religious interest with the justification of America as against atheistic Communism, and the fact that this revival of religious interest coincides with great emphasis on social conformity and on material prosperity increase the religious distortion that is involved. So are enhanced our national self-righteousness in relation to the world and our national complacency in relation to ourselves. There are contrary tendencies such as the widespread personal anxiety and emotional distress but, while these disturb complacency, they also tempt us to use religion primarily as a source of reassurance. It is often pointed out that the very popularity of religion is as much temptation as opportunity for the churches because it leads to the dilution of the religion of the churches so that it is often in content little more than the national culture religion.

These criticisms of the vague religiousness of the United States which is expressed in national theistic (or sometimes deistic) symbols are very important. In some contexts major emphasis should be put on them. But they are only a part of the truth.

There is one source of correction for the idolatrous corruption of this public recognition of God in the religious affirma-

[8] Cf., Will Herberg, *Protestant-Catholic-Jew* (Doubleday, 1956). In this context I prefer to think of Christianity as one faith, though in Professor Herberg's sociological context it is meaningful to speak of Catholicism and Protestantism as two faiths.
[9] *Ibid.* Chap. V.

tions of Abraham Lincoln. Lincoln expressed essential elements of Biblical religion though he did not use the Christian symbols which would be divisive in our pluralistic society. He humbled himself before the sovereignty of God as the transcendent God of history, as the God of righteousness and mercy. How different Lincoln's religion was from the worship of an Almighty who is on the side of one's nation or cause! His recognition that good and devout men on both sides of the Civil War prayed to the same God, and that the will of God was not identical with the purposes of either party meant for him that humility and mercy accompanied commitment to the right as God gave him to see the right. This is an authentically Christian outlook even though Lincoln did not use Christian symbols and it is removed as far as possible from the self-righteous religiosity which is often encouraged by our official recognition of God.

A strong case can be made in some contexts for the idea of an absolutely secular state. It is a way of avoiding many religious distortions. Christians in India know that their religious freedom depends upon the fact that India is a secular state. If it were not a secular state, it would be a Hindu state and this would not only interfere with religious freedom for non-Hindus; it would also mean that the endless social ramifications of Hindu custom and law would greatly obstruct social and economic reforms. Prime Minister Nehru, who is the great champion of the secular state, is also the great champion of religious freedom and he also struggles against a conservative Hinduism for social reform and for such things as the full application of medical science to problems of public health.[10] When religion sanctions social rigidity, the secular state is a great step forward.

Religious traditions in this country do not sanction this kind of rigidity and there is no reason to move beyond the idea of

[10] On a visit to India in 1950 I noticed that Nehru had to campaign for the use of inoculations for cholera against opposition even though there was an epidemic of cholera at the time in a part of the country.

a state that is neutral as between the great religious traditions to a state that is avowedly secular. Such a secular state is likely to wrap itself in the mantle of a self-sufficient secularism and to become a secularizing state. It is likely to give the impression that God has nothing to do with public life, that religion is a purely private matter as many American advocates of the secular state believe. When the representatives of a nation invoke the name of God there is a danger that they may seek to use God for their purposes. But, when they are completely silent about God, there is a danger that they may fail to remind themselves that they are under a higher judgment and that the nation may lose all sense of the relation between the private religion of citizens and a transcendent dimension in the light of which the nation and state realize their limits.

I believe that a better approach in this country is to have it clearly understood that the state is neutral as between the traditional faiths, that it is not a secular state or indifferent to the religious life of the citizens or to the relevance of their religion to its affairs, that it does not *profess* a common-denominator religion, that it is in no sense a teacher of religion but that it does use symbols and provides for acts of religious recognition that refer to the Reality which the churches and other religious bodies alone are competent to interpret. When the word "God" is used it should mean to the citizens not some common-denominator idea of deity but what they learn about God from their religious traditions.

There are difficulties in this position as there are in any alternatives. One is the fact that the word "religion" covers such a luxuriant growth of religious movements in this country that its use is misleading. Religious freedom leads to much superstition and idolatry, to tendencies that are so aberrant that, while they ought not to be suppressed, they hardly deserve public encouragement. However, there is sufficient strength in the Christian and Jewish communities to give normative meaning to religion in America.

Another difficulty is the presence of a small but very influential group of citizens who reject all organized forms of religion, who are atheists or agnostics or Naturalistic Humanists. Often they feel that there is discrimination against them in the position that I am advocating here. They reject the traditional religious symbols and feel that the state misrepresents them in adhering to such symbols and in cooperating with historical forms of religion as much as it does. They advocate in this connection an absolutistic version of the separation of Church and State, making it include the separation of the state from all religion.[11]

I offer two suggestions toward a solution of this problem.

One is to recognize without the least condescension that atheistic or agnostic critics of religion make an important contribution to the religious communities themselves. Their criticisms of what they understand to be the meaning of the historical religions are often valid. They represent a challenge to obscurantism and clericalism that is needed. They are often specialists in their concern for particular values which at any given time the churches may neglect or even undermine. There is a stuffiness that comes over all religious bodies when they never have to face this kind of opposition.

My other suggestion is that in this situation we have to weigh the negative religious freedom of a small minority over against the positive religious freedom of the vast majority. In doing so, we should protect this negative religious freedom to the extent that it involves freedom to express opposition to religion. But

---

[11] T. S. Eliot has his way of dealing with this type of dissent. He says: "But a positive culture must have a positive set of values, and the dissentients must remain marginal, tending to make only marginal contributions." *The Idea of a Christian Society*, p. 46. This quotation is not entirely representative of Mr. Eliot's book because he emphasizes the need for freedom and recognizes the temptations which accompany a religious monopoly.

we should not, in protecting it, deny to most of the people opportunities for positive religious expression in the context of their national life. There have to be adjustments here which will not satisfy everyone. They call for restraint and consideration on the side of the minority as well as on the side of the majority.

There is another objection to this approach that is rooted in the strong tendency in contemporary theology to see no place for references to God except those that come through the Christian revelation. It is assumed that, since there is so clear a self-revelation of God in Jesus Christ, there is little or no value in theistic affirmations or acknowledgments that are vaguer or that have less content than the full Christian affirmation of God in Christ. But this view is itself only one Christian position and those who hold it should not seek to limit the freedom of others in the churches and outside.

There is one serious confusion in many theological discussions of this subject. It is one thing to reject a rationalistic natural theology based upon proofs of the existence of God. This seems to me to be justifiable. But it is quite another thing —and to me this is an error—to deny that there is a broad religious awareness of which the traditional arguments for God are expressions (though they are not proofs independent of such religious awareness). The concept of "general revelation" in this sense has importance even if a rationalistic "natural theology" is to be rejected.

The rejection of general revelation represents a theological austerity that denies deep human realities. There are religious responses to God that are broader than distinctively Christian responses. Among us they are conditioned by centuries of Jewish and Christian experience and they have classical sources which, both independently and through their influence on Christianity itself, have had a part in forming our spirits even though we may forget them.

H. Richard Niebuhr in his book *The Meaning of Revelation*,

which emphasizes chiefly the influence upon our minds and our culture of the distinctively Christian revelation and which powerfully warns against man's use of religion to defend his interests and his self-esteem, calls attention to the reality of this broader faith. He says: "Though they cannot therefore be regarded as non-historical and simply rational, our ideas of the goodness, omnipotence and eternity of deity represent the demand of our Western, Hellenized, human reason and come to us in social memories which are not connected with the name of and life of Christ."[12] Professor Niebuhr goes on to show how these ideas of deity are both fulfilled and transformed by Christ. The Christian witness in the nation is to that fulfillment and transformation but it should not begin by denying that there is in this broader religious response something to be fulfilled and transformed.

[12] Macmillan, 1941, p. 182.

CHAPTER II

Christian Ethics and the Moral Consensus

A SECOND problem growing out of our religious pluralism is the relation between Christian faith and Christian ethics on the one hand and the common moral convictions, which are generally shared by Americans, on the basis of which Christians cooperate with their neighbors who are outside the Christian community. This raises the problem of natural law which is so much emphasized by Roman Catholic teaching and which until recently has been the designation of this common morality in the western world. The reality of this common morality has been accented by the contrast between the humanistic ideals which unite many peoples and the amoral ruthlessness of totalitarianism, but this very conflict often has shaken confidence in the common morality which only a few decades ago was sustained by a trend toward universal moral agreement in an emerging world community.

The fact that such a nihilistic morality as that associated with National Socialism could arise in the heart of Europe was a profound shock to that kind of moral confidence and the split between Communism and the free world continues to have a somewhat similar effect. There is an important difference in the case of Communism in that the fundamental purposes which it expresses are in harmony with commonly accepted ideas of justice; the tragedy is that Communism in practice sacrifices most concrete human values to an abstract scheme of social redemption. In the process Communism as a power movement embodied in the Soviet Union and in China subordinates moral goals to a combination of the designs of the party and the ambition of the Communist nations. I enlarge on this in order to emphasize the fact that while Communism in principle is not morally cynical or nihilistic, it has had the effect of creating a deep moral chasm in humanity which makes cooperation on the basis of common moral convictions across the chasm enormously difficult.[1] It uses moral relativism as a weapon.

Unnecessary confusion has been created in the discussion about this common morality by the assumption that we must choose between moral scepticism on the one hand and the claim that there is universal knowledge of the same moral standards on the other. The actual situation seems to be that there are moral convictions in our society which have a much broader base than the Judaeo-Christian tradition though they may not be universally accepted. In western nations the roots of these moral convictions are so intertwined with that tradition that it is impossible to separate them from it. There are classical roots which have their own independence even though they were given Christian baptism and in some measure transformed by the Gospel. But their independence in Plato, Aristotle, Cicero and the Stoics is a fact of great importance about man's capacity for moral knowledge apart from Judaeo-Christian influence.

Whatever be the roots of these moral convictions, they can be defended today by considerations recognized as true apart from Christian revelation. The moral awareness which is nourished by the Christian tradition is confirmed by pressures from contemporary experience. There is an objective moral order—

[1] There is abundant evidence that the attitudes of people in Russia when they are approached as human beings are much less affected by the distortions of morality resulting from the Communist scheme than might be feared. They are kept in line by much talk of peace by their government and by actual social and economic achievements by which they benefit and by bright hopes for the future. They show ignorance of the outside world but no hatred. This situation adds a peculiarly tragic dimension to the moral chasm that divides them from us but it should prevent that chasm from causing basic moral scepticism or cynicism.

and we should think of it in dynamic rather than static terms—which is the expression of God's will for man. I believe that from the standpoint of the Christian revelation this moral order can be most adequately understood, but it presses upon every man and is discerned in part by most men. Theological doctrines which deny this possibility have had only occasional support in Christian history and even Christian theologians who refuse to give a place to natural law in Christian thinking do in practice recognize an overlapping in moral awareness and conviction between Christians and non-Christians.

There are two indications of the existence of this moral order which come from quite different types of experience and I give them here only as illustrations of how the moral order affects us whether we recognize it or not. One is the necessity of moving toward better human relations among the nations if the race is to survive the threat of total nuclear war. Competitive coexistence based upon a balance of terror may work for a time, but there is little hope that it will prevent war for many decades. The other indication comes from illumination of the human soul in personal relationships that has come from modern psychiatry. We know that hostility poisons life and love heals and the love that heals is not merely "eros"; it must include an element of "agape" for it is the love that accepts those who are rejected by others or by themselves. Both of these indications of the moral order belong to ground that is common to Christians and non-Christians.

This conception of the overlapping of the moral awareness and convictions of Christians and non-Christians allows the Christian ethic to have its own grounding in revelation, its own motivation in response to the love of God, its own refinement and expansion through the sensitivity that is the fruit of Christian love. It allows for parallel contexts of faith which support the ethical awareness and convictions of non-Christians.

The converging of many tendencies of thought today in a

common criticism of the tradition of natural law is in large part a desire to avoid a static and rigid legalism which assumes a too detailed knowledge of what is right in all circumstances and which does not allow for changing social needs. Protestant theology[2] criticizes the Catholic natural law teaching on this score; at the same time, secular legal thinkers and judges have been resisting and actually overturning the individualistic inhibitions against social legislation which were embodied in natural law as understood in the American legal tradition. Much of the relativism in legal theory is not a basic moral scepticism, but a revolt against the fixed legal norms which have proved to be inadequate guides for either judges or legislators in a rapidly changing society. There is always a tendency for both moral and legal thinking to become crystallized around the institutions of a society in a particular period or the interests of a particular dominant social group. Moral or legal norms, believed to be absolute, usually reflect those institutions and interests and need to be continually criticized and purged in the light of new situations, of new needs, or of new awareness of old needs.

Whether or not it is wise for Protestants to avoid the use of the phrase "natural law" (I am not sure about it), the phrase does need to be rescued from some elements in its history if it is to be used. But if it is not used, this should not be allowed to suggest moral scepticism or any tendency to deny that Christians and non-Christians do have much in common in their moral awareness and in their moral convictions. We should also recognize that the natural law tradition in the various stages of its history has been a great treasure and that out of it has come much of the humanizing of western society and many gains for human freedom.

The moral standards of most non-Christians in the west have

[2] Note especially Reinhold Niebuhr's *Faith and History* (Scribners, 1949), chap. XI. Emil Brunner who in later writings has a greater place for natural law gives the basic criticism in *The Divine Imperative* (Westminster Press, 1943), pp. 627-633.

the marks of the Biblical revelation upon them. The Ten Commandments, especially the second table (five to ten) which gives in negative form our duties to our neighbors, are not only the summary of Christian moral law that is included in Christian liturgies and that often forms the basis for the elaboration of Christian ethics within the structure of Christian theology, but they are also expressions of the general moral consciousness in our society.[3]

I shall now suggest some of the moral convictions which belong to the area of overlap between the Christian conscience and the broader public conscience and which can be validated by considerations which do not depend upon the Christian revelation.

There is one moral conviction which has such wide support that it cannot today be attributed to Christian influences alone though they have had a central role in its emergence. It is the conviction that there is a real unity in the human race and that all men have a right to equal consideration as human beings regardless of their race or class or nation. It was one of the great contributions of Stoicism to bring this insight to the

[3] There is an illuminating passage in Dietrich Bonhoeffer's *Ethics* (The Macmillan Company, 1955), illuminating in part because the author shares the presuppositions of the Protestant critics of the conception of Natural Law. He says: "But for pagan government the answer is that there is a providential congruity between the contents of the second table (of the Ten Commandments) and the inherent law of historical life itself. Failure to observe the second table destroys the very life which government is charged with preserving. . . . Does this mean that the state is after all based on natural law? No; for in fact it is a matter here only of the government which does not understand itself but which now is, nevertheless, providentially enabled to acquire the same knowledge, of crucial significance for its task, as is disclosed to the government which does understand itself in the true sense in Jesus Christ. One might, therefore, say that in this case natural law has its foundation in Jesus Christ" (pp. 305-306). I do not fully understand those words but I wonder whether it would be different to say that natural law has its foundation in God who is revealed centrally to Christians in Jesus Christ. Bonhoeffer admits the reality that is often designated by natural law but he desires to avoid the idea that this is a creation of human reason and controlled by man.

ancient world and Christianity put it into a context which made it more intelligible and which also provided strong religious motives for its implementation.

There are several important factors in our experience which support this moral judgment which are independent of Christian faith. There is a much clearer understanding than formerly of the actual biological and psychological similarity of men, with individual differences having more importance than racial or ethnic differences. There is the actual experience of mutual friendship across every one of the lines which have separated the usual groups into which humanity is divided. There is also mutual enmity or suspicion but the discovery of the possibility of good human relations across a particular barrier proves something about the people on both sides of that barrier that no negative experiences can refute. If there were any natural human group whose members were incapable of entering into any such friendly mutual relations with any other group, that would tell us something about humanity which would contradict our present experience. The fact that none of the social barriers prevent intermarriage is obvious. There is another fact about humanity which it does not require Christian revelation to establish: all men are bound together by a common fate in this world. This is a part of the divine pressure upon them to find ways of living together with mutual understanding and respect, with justice and with something like what Aristotle called "friendship" which he described as "the greatest good of states" and "the will to live together."[4]

Justice is the key word in any discussion of the social morality shared in common by Christians and non-Christians. Yet it is a word with growing content and the conception of justice generally held among us was long ago transformed by the influence of the Gospel. Its essential formal meaning is that every person should receive his due, that there should be no arbitrariness or

[4] *Politics*, III, 9, p. 1281.

unfairness in dealing with any man or with any group. So much the word as used by us has in common with the word as used by Aristotle. But this formal meaning of justice tells us nothing about what any man's due is for that depends upon the moral convictions in the culture. When slavery was accepted as rational and good, when women were regarded as inferior persons, when the law decreed that petty crimes were punishable by death, when it was assumed that the children of the poor would be excluded from the opportunities for the development of their capacities which were provided for the children of the more privileged classes—justice as applied to slavery, to the rights of women, to punishment, to economic opportunities was a far cry from what it is today when applied to these matters in any civilized community.

Ideas of justice are now combined with the ideas about the unity of humanity. Actually justice has been transformed by love; it has become dynamic and in its name the status and opportunities of all but the most favored human groups have been raised. This has been made possible at each stage of advance by the new articulateness and the new power of groups that had been neglected or exploited. Political pressure from below has provided the power to make many changes but this pressure has also created a new awareness of the meaning of justice which has won the support of a broad public conscience. In this country the experience of the economic depression in the 1930's has destroyed many individualistic illusions which obstructed economic justice, and now minority races are beginning to come into their own. The conception of justice grows whenever any who have suffered from injustice make ther claims felt by the community.

There is a very broad consensus concerning the need of spiritual and cultural freedom, freedom from political tyranny and freedom from social intimidation if the human spirit is to grow to its full maturity and if there is to be justice in society.

Indeed freedom is one of the ingredients of justice because it is a person's due. There must be continuous examination of the exact form and limits of this freedom, of the relation between freedom and order. As Professor Eduard Heimann says, in one of the most illuminating discussions of this subject: "Order can be said to be more physically necessary, freedom more spiritually so . . . Order is more fundamental, freedom is higher."[5]

It is obvious that there is general acceptance of the need of order and peace, especially in national life. Here we have not the highest moral standard, but a prerequisite of social morality in general. What has long been taken for granted in domestic affairs is now as clearly needed for the sake of survival as well as for the sake of good human relations among the peoples. The pressure of the objective moral order upon the nations of the world is as clear as it is fateful. There can be agreement between Christians and non-Christians here even if the policy dilemmas which are involved today in the quest for world order and peace divide Christians themselves.

Another whole range of common moral judgments has to do with honesty and integrity in business, in scientific work, in government, and in everyday personal relations. There may be occasions in which it is right to deceive as when to do so is necessary to save a person from the police of a totalitarian state, but support for such emergency action does not justify lying as a habit. Indeed, part of the revulsion against the totalitarian state is based on the fact that it destroys truth.

Another area of common moral convictions is the sphere of personal discipline. In specifics the differences here are much greater than in the other areas mentioned. But there is very general agreement that there must be discipline in the life of sex, that promiscuity and prostitution and predatory sexual behavior are wrong. Who of any religious faith, or of no faith, does not agree that the stability of family life is important for

[5] *Freedom and Order* (Scribner, 1947), p. 10.

the moral and social health of the community and who does not wish for himself and others that their homes may be held together by affection and loyalty? I think that there is a greater tendency in our society to agree on a morality of compassion than on a morality of discipline but while there may be less willingness to pay part of the cost of discipline than was the case with an earlier generation closer to the Puritan influence, there is recognition that at some stage discipline is necessary to avoid personal disintegration from sexual license and other forms of intemperance.

In attempting to state a view of the vexed problem of the relation of Christian faith to a more broadly based morality, I have been careful to avoid claiming too much. There may be no completely universal agreement on a world scale on any of the moral issues mentioned except that within the limits of all social groups there are parallel moral standards governing behavior within each group. There are individual moral cynics and sceptics, and aberrant movements based upon racial hatred. However, this lack of universal agreement does not mean that there are not widely accepted standards and goals which form the basis for cooperation between Christians and non-Christians, and these standards and goals can be defended by considerations that do not depend upon the Christian faith.

The existence of these elements of a common conscience does not prevent far-reaching differences of opinion but, in political conflicts, these differences cut across all divisions between Christians and non-Christians. They have to do with the weighing of the relative claims of values which are generally agreed to be important, such values as order and freedom, or they grow out of differences of judgment in regard to the effect of a policy. The pressures of class interest, racial and ethnic prejudice, the national hysterias that have their periods of rise and decline distort the judgment and the conscience of people within the Christian community and outside.

I shall conclude this discussion of common moral convictions by making two statements which, on the surface, may seem to be inconsistent with one another but which really belong together.

The first is that selfless and courageous dedication to the goals which are implied in this common morality is often present to a remarkable degree outside the Christian community. Often the churches have to be prodded by the consciences of those who are apparently without benefit of specifically Christian influence. In this whole discussion I have been aware of the contribution of the Jewish people to the common morality and we can say of them that they share with Christians a very important part of the Biblical revelation. In American life they have often been more sensitive than Christians to the problems of justice, both because of their inheritance of the prophetic tradition and because, as a minority, they have never been able to share the complacency that often overtakes the Christian majority. But often beyond the circle of Christians and Jews we find special awareness of the claims of justice and freedom and intellectual honesty. We should admit that the Christian tradition is so rich and capable of yielding so many emphases that one-sided interpretations of it often provide escapes from facing all but the most personal moral obligations and are sources of rationalizations for many unjust social institutions. We may also say that the very success of Christianity as the dominant religion causes the churches to be allied with and the Christian faith to be interpreted by the people in a society who are most satisfied with the *status quo*. These facts about Christianity call for endless self-criticism within the churches, for mutual criticism as between churches.

The second statement, made as it is from inside the Christian community, will not receive as much acceptance outside as the first. It is that the Christian revelation provides the most adequate context for all but the most obviously prudential elements in the common morality. The unity of humanity as I have presented it and as it is widely affirmed is a precarious conviction if all men are not seen in their relationship to God as creator and redeemer. Freedom can be best understood ultimately as the freedom of the person who belongs wholly to no social group, who is a citizen of two cities, who is responsible to God. Christian faith provides not only the most adequate grounding for what is true in the common morality but also the motives for obedience which in the long run are most dependable. When societies become sick there are two kinds of disease which are most virulent: private irresponsibility, and public idolatry. Often the first leads to the second as a false cure that is in fact the more destructive sickness. I do not say that without the dominance of conscious Christian commitment in a nation it must fall victim to either disease but rather that it is the grace and the truth from God, which are best understood and made most fully available through the Gospel, which are needed to prevent or to heal these diseases.

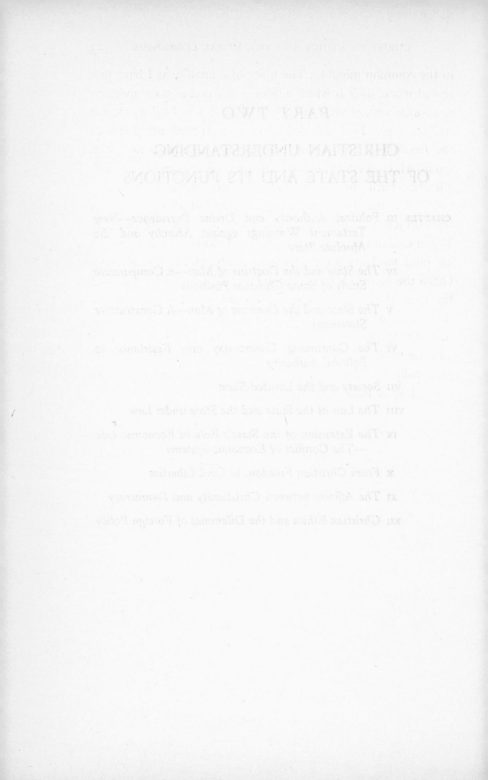

PART TWO

CHRISTIAN UNDERSTANDING
OF THE STATE AND ITS FUNCTIONS

PART TWO

CHRISTIAN UNDERSTANDING OF THE STATE AND ITS FUNCTIONS

Political Authority and Divine Providence—
New Testament Warnings Against Anarchy
and the Absolute State

THE New Testament was written in a period in which the state as we understand it or the political form of a national community did not exist. For the New Testament writers the state meant the authorities of the Roman Empire, the Emperor and his delegates who ruled the provinces. These authorities were distant from and alien to the early Christian community, though Paul's use of his Roman citizenship suggests in a remote way what we mean by participation in the life of the state. Clearly the Christians of the New Testament period had no chance to influence the state, in that sense they were without political responsibility. There can be little in New Testament teaching dealing directly with political life which is relevant to the experience of Christians who live in democratic societies and who themselves share in the authority of the state.

Where Christians live under hostile and tyrannical governments they naturally feel that their situation is close to that which is presupposed in the New Testament. Sometimes under totalitarian regimes they feel the pressure of a hostile state far more than was the case with Christians under the Roman Empire, for the range of conflicts between Christianity and a state based upon an ideology such as Communism or National Socialism covers the whole of life, while one could live as a Christian in many occupations in the early centuries without feeling the

CHAPTER III

Political Authority and Divine Providence—
New Testament Warnings Against Anarchy
and the Absolute State

THE New Testament was written in a period in which the state as we understand it as the political form of a national community did not exist. For the New Testament writers the state meant the authorities of the Roman Empire, the Emperor and his delegates who ruled the provinces. These authorities were distant from and alien to the early Christian community, though Paul's use of his Roman citizenship suggests in a remote way what we mean by participation in the life of the state. Clearly the Christians of the New Testament period had no chance to influence the state; in that sense they were without political responsibility. There can be little in New Testament teaching dealing directly with political life which is relevant to the experience of Christians who live in democratic societies and who themselves share in the authority of the state.

Where Christians live under hostile and tyrannical governments they naturally feel that their situation is close to that which is presupposed in the New Testament. Sometimes under totalitarian regimes they feel the pressure of a hostile state far more than was the case with Christians under the Roman Empire, for the range of conflicts between Christianity and a state based upon such an ideology as Communism or National Socialism covers the whole of life, while one could live as a Christian in many occupations in the early centuries without feeling the full force of the conflict between worship of God and the cult of the emperor. Persecution of Christians in the Roman Empire was intermittent.[1] Also the modern tyrants have methods of thought control which did not exist in earlier periods. But quite apart from that, the early Roman Empire was in intention a state based upon law and hence it was very different from these modern tyrannies.

While the New Testament is not a source for direct political guidance there are two emphases in New Testament teaching which have great importance for our own thinking about the state.

The first is that most New Testament writers saw the state as a God-given institution which was necessary for human life and to which Christians owed obedience. Two very similar passages, Romans 13 and I Peter 2, have been the proof texts for all rulers who sought obedience from their subjects. They have been greatly misused in the interests of tyranny in every century of Christian history. The attitude toward the governing authorities which both passages enjoin is certainly conditioned by the situation in which they were written, but behind that conditioning there lies a permanently valid recognition that God is ordering human life through government and that without government, even bad government, society would fall into anarchy. The warning against anarchy because of the unruliness of men's sin is one of the persistent emphases in all Christian thinking about the state.

This warning against anarchy was presented by Paul and the author of I Peter in the context of a surprisingly positive attitude toward the state. What remarkable sentences about the gen-

[1] "The Christians were thus punished because their religion was believed to be inimical to the interests of the state. This belief was shared by the people and the rulers alike, but only in times of crisis did it become a belief which required aggressive action. Ordinarily Christians were regarded as potentially but not actually dangerous to the peace and security of the Roman empire." Robert M. Grant, *The Sword and the Cross* (Macmillan, 1955), p. 16.

eral nature of political authority are these in any century: "For rulers are not a terror to good conduct, but to bad. Would you have no fear of him who is in authority? Then do what is good, and you will receive his approval, for he is God's servant for your good. But if you do wrong, be afraid, for he does not bear the sword in vain; he is the servant of God to execute his wrath on the wrong-doer. Therefore one must be subject, not only to avoid God's wrath but for the sake of conscience." (Romans 13:3-5)

Professor Oscar Cullmann[2] has helped us to see these words in perspective when he reminds us that they come in the same context with the injunction in the previous chapter that Christians should not take vengeance into their own hands: "Beloved, never avenge yourselves, but leave it to the wrath of God; for it is written, 'Vengeance is mine, I will repay, says the Lord.' " (Romans 12:19) In that context it is clear that one reason for Paul's emphasizing the state in the following chapter is that it is the means by which the wrath of God is made effective in society.

This reminder of the context, which because of chapter divisions is usually forgotten, does help us to understand why Paul speaks as he does in Romans 13 but when we realize how concise Paul's discussions are and how unexpected his transitions, we should not allow this consideration to suggest, and Dr. Cullmann does not suggest it, that the positive elements in this emphasis were unimportant. There is behind it a strong sense of divine providence working through the political authorities and of the Christian's obligation to obey them.

It is often said that Paul wrote those words while he was still having a favorable experience of the Roman authorities. They had helped him to deal with his Jewish opponents and had secured for him his rights before the law as a Roman citizen. Nero was emperor when Paul wrote, but his persecution of

[2] *The State in the New Testament* (Scribner, 1956), pp. 57-58.

Christians was still in the future. However, the Roman authorities took the final responsibility in the crucifixion of Jesus, and Paul could not have forgotten this even though the tendency in the early Church was to put chief emphasis on the responsibility of the Jews for Jesus' death. Also, we have very significant evidence that Christians continued to take this positive attitude toward the Roman authorities in the midst of persecution in the First Epistle of Peter.

This epistle contains a passage (2:13-17) which is in part a paraphrase of Romans 13. The author writes: "Be subject for the Lord's sake to every human institution, whether it be the emperor as supreme, or to governors as sent by him to punish those who do wrong and to praise those who do right." There is here the same optimism about the capacity of the state to distinguish between right and wrong and in a context which makes it clear that Christians had already begun to suffer persecution at the hands of the emperor and his governors.

Dr. John Knox has suggested as an explanation which Dr. Cullmann mentions with approval that a leader of a persecuted church could write these words because he believed that the persecution was based on false charges and that the Roman authorities could be convinced that there was no basis for persecution in the fact that people were Christians. Dr. Knox says:

"The author of I Peter is convinced that once magistrates generally recognize that the only crime of Christians is that of being Christians, the persecutions will cease."[3]

The other side of the New Testament attitude toward the state is movingly expressed in the Book of Revelation. This book was written at a time of persecutions and in a situation where the conflict between the worship of the emperor and Christian loyalty was most acutely felt. The very government which Paul

[3] John Knox, "Pliny and I Peter: A Note on I Peter 4:14-16 and 3:15," *Journal of Biblical Literature*, 1955, pp. 187 ff. (Mentioned in Cullmann, p. 55.)

described as "God's servant for your good" is described as a blasphemous beast which made "war upon the saints." (Revelation 13:7) The positive attitude toward the state which is characteristic of Paul and the author of I Peter is gone. The great words of the apostles in Acts 5, "We must obey God rather than men," which were directed toward the Jewish authorities and not toward the representatives of the emperor, are in line with the spirit of this book. It is quite obvious that the author of Revelation had no thought of political resistance. All that his opposition to the state suggests is suffering resistance rather than participation in idolatrous worship. It is fortunate that this book is in the canon because without it we should not have clear and direct warning against an absolute state with pretensions that have become demonic. We get no political advice from the book but we do learn from it that it is not always true that the Christian should obey the governing authorities.

While it is a mistake to insist on harmony between writings which come from contrasting historical situations and with different problems in mind, we should take account of two things that can be said which prevent Christians from finding an ultimate contradiction between these two approaches to the state in the New Testament.

Dr. Cullmann emphasizes the view that the opposition to the state in Revelation is not to the state as such but only to the state that exceeds its proper bounds. Emperor worship was a mark of the state that makes itself absolute and demands of the citizen what no state has a right to demand. Dr. Cullmann believes that Paul would have taken the same view of emperor worship and mentions his martydom as evidence that there were limits to his obedience to the authorities. He also says that the author of Revelation would not necessarily have rejected the state in so far as it performed its proper functions and that there is no anarchistic rejection of the civil order in his denial of the state's religious pretensions. Dr. Bultmann makes the same point. He writes:

"The hatred toward Rome which breaks out in Revelation rests not upon a rejection of the existing civil order on principle but upon indignation over its demand of emperor-worship, at which Christian obedience naturally draws the line. For that reason one must not regard the attitude of Revelation as contradictory to the general Christian acknowledgment of the civil order."[4]

It can also be said in interpreting Paul that in his description of the state there are implicit standards by which the state should be judged. A state which does not answer to the description that it is "not a terror to good conduct but to bad" can, at least in extreme cases, be condemned as no true state. There may be some question as to whether this was in Paul's mind but it has later appeared in Christian history as the basis for resistance to the state. In the sixteenth century it was John Knox's scriptural basis for resistance to the Queen of Scotland and it underlies Karl Barth's denying of the protections of Romans 13 to the National Socialist state.

For the New Testament as a whole the state, while having a positive role in the providential ordering of society in this aeon, was soon to pass away and Christians were not much interested in it. Paul's references to the courts of justice in I Cor. 6 suggest this attitude of indifference so far as the normal life of the Christian is concerned. He enjoins Christians to avoid recourse to the law courts in settling their quarrels with one another. This involves no derogation of the state's function as the dispenser of justice through the courts, but it does indicate a desire that Christians should remain detached even from this legitimate function of the state. Dr. Cullmann bases upon this passage the general statement that "everywhere the Christian can dispense with the State without threatening its existence,

[4] *Theology of the New Testament*, Vol. II (Scribners, 1955), p. 231.

he should do so."[5] I cannot avoid the feeling that Dr. Cullmann makes too much of this because it was natural that Paul, with the exalted expectations that he had for his converts who had become new creatures in Christ, should feel the incongruity in their having quarrels which they had to call upon heathen law courts to settle. Paul's own appeal to Caesar is hardly consistent with Dr. Cullmann's generalization.

It is, however, desirable to compare the emphasis of Romans 13 with the spirit of detachment toward the state which is characteristic of I Cor. 6. The latter is representative of the early Christian feeling that none of the institutions of this world were very important as compared with the Kingdom which they would soon inherit. They were living at the end of an age and expected God to deliver them from the burdens of this historical existence. They were living after mighty events, the death and resurrection of Christ, and as a result all political powers and all of the various problems of status in this world were of little importance compared with the new status of redemption which had come to them. They belonged to a tiny minority which had no political power and no political responsibility except the responsibility to obey the state in its God-given function of preserving civil order.

The words of Jesus, "render unto Caesar the things that are Caesar's and unto God the things that are God's," well summarize the outlook of the New Testament toward the state. They allow for the positive role of the state but they make clear that there are things which belong not to the state but to God.

The difference between our situation and that on which the teaching of the New Testament was based is so great that neither the emphasis on obedience nor the emphasis on detachment is altogether applicable.

The equivalent of obedience in a democratic society is re-

[5] *Op. cit.*, p. 61.

sponsible participation. The "authorities" do not stand over against the citizens, for the citizens have responsibility for the choice of those who exercise authority, for the laws by which they are guided, and even for the continuance of the political structure which surrounds their authority. The providential ordering of society, which Christians in all societies affirm, takes place through the citizens, through their consent to and participation in the political processes which belong to the substance of the state.

There is no reason to expect a harmony of all wills in the "general will" expressed by the state. Citizens who are outvoted, who belong to a political minority may feel at times that the "authorities" in the particular administration in power do not represent them at all and in a sense stand over against them. But the political minority in a democracy does will to have the results of elections accepted, and its responsible participation includes criticism and lawful resistance and the organizing of an opposition to displace those in power. Its function as opposition is a part of the structure of government and usually it still retains some capacity to influence policy.

At many particular points individual citizens may feel that the authorities are over against them. The most extreme case of this is when a court convicts and sentences a citizen to prison. Even in this extreme case there is in the system of trial by jury a symbol of the fact that no alien government but one in which his own fellow citizens participate condemns him. The convicted man himself may in many cases inwardly accept the condemnation.

There are many occasions on which citizens obey a law because it is a law and not because it is an expression of their own wills, though even in such cases it is often their will that the law as law be obeyed.

Later I shall deal with the question as to whether or not Christians should ever break the law or even, in extreme cases, engage in illegal activity and sometimes violent resistance to the center of authority in the state. In democratic societies this issue seldom arises except in the case of a particular law that may be offensive to the conscience and then the Christian should willingly accept the legal consequences of his disobedience and thus affirm the law's authority.

The basic difference between the first-century situation and that which now obtains in such a country as the United States makes it very important that we avoid the use of any of the passages in the New Testament to which I have referred as texts by which to defend or criticize existing political institutions. The most that we can learn from the New Testament is that there must be political authority, that the Christian should take a positive attitude toward the order-creating functions of civil government because in and through them the providence of God is at work in preserving essential conditions for human life, and that the state should be kept in bounds and not be allowed to usurp the place of God. These things which we do learn from the New Testament apply to our situation, but they are only the beginning of the political guidance which we may gain, not from the specific political passages of the New Testament, but from the Christian revelation as a whole.

CHAPTER IV

The State and the Doctrine of Man—A Comparative Study of Some Christian Positions

THERE is a contrast in Christian thinking about the state between those Christians who regard the state as entirely, or almost entirely, the result of the fall of man, as the divine provision for dealing with the consequences of sin, and those who, while not denying this negative role of the state, emphasize its positive functions as an instrument of human cooperation, as a constructive agency for human welfare that expresses the social nature of man.

The extremes can easily be distinguished from one another but actually there are among Christian thinkers endlessly varied combinations of emphases and nuances, each a part of a particular configuration of thought and experience. Also there is considerable confusion in theology at this point because of differences in the initial definition of the state in relation to the social life of man as a whole. If the state is defined most narrowly as the instrument of coercion and the more constructive social agencies are identified with other aspects of the community, it is natural to say that the state exists only to restrain man's sin.

I shall give some examples of Christian thinking on this issue.[1]

In general, there is a difference between Catholic thought

[1] Recent thought is well canvassed in Nils Ehrenstrom's *Christian Faith and the Modern State* (Willett, Clark, 1937), Chaps. 7, 8, 9.

and the thought inspired by the Protestant Reformation, especially that of Luther. Catholicism emphasizes the Aristotelian idea of the state as an expression of the social nature of man and sees it as governed by the natural law that can be known universally to human reason. The Catholic contrast between the natural and the supernatural is the background for a doctrine of man that exempts man's nature, including his reason, from the worst consequences of the fall and of original sin. Since the state belongs to nature, it shares this exemption. Man is in need of revelation and grace for his salvation but this need does not imply as dark a view of his natural condition as we find in the theologians of the Reformation. Professor Rommen, in summarizing the Catholic view of the origin of the state, says that "the state proceeds by inner moral necessity from the social nature of man for the sake of the more perfect life, the fuller realization of personality for all its members in a working sovereign order of mutual assistance and mutual cooperation."[2] In another passage he says:

"The great thinkers have maintained that the state would have developed out of human nature even in the *status naturae purae*. This doctrine was elaborated especially by late Scholasticism after the Reformation contended that the origin of the state lay in sin. It is true that the masters taught that some qualities of the state originate in sin; for instance, its coercive power. But they taught, too, that in the state of pure nature political authority would have been necessary, though only a directive, not a coercive one."[3]

Luther was at the other extreme. He saw in the political authorities a dark but providential coercive power which exists only to keep man's sin in check, to restrain disorder and anarchy, to be the ultimate social power without which society would destroy itself. The state was for him an agent of God, symbolized chiefly by the sword, with authority to defend

[2] H. A. Rommen, *The State in Catholic Thought* (B. Herder Book Co., 1947), p. 137.
[3] *Ibid.*, pp. 228-229.

society against enemies from without and to punish crime and sedition within. He broke completely with the Catholic contrast between nature and super nature and with the view of nature as little damaged by the fall.

Luther had a dualism of his own which contrasted the pre-serving work of God through coercive political power with the saving work of God through the persuasive power of the gospel. His emphasis upon this contrast hardened into a con-ception of the separation of the Gospel and the Church from the political responsibilities of the secular order which has been a handicap to Lutheranism in dealing constructively with the political problems of justice and freedom, a handicap which has had its most fateful consequences in Germany and from which German Lutheranism is struggling to free itself.

Luther describes the role of the political authorities, con-trasting it with God's redemptive work through the Church in the following passage:

"Since few believe and still fewer live a Christian life, do not resist the evil, and themselves do no evil, God has provided for non-Christians a different government outside the Christian estate and God's kingdom, and has subjected them to the sword, so that, even though they would do so, they cannot practice their wickedness, and that, if they do, they may not do it without fear nor in peace and prosperity. . . . If it were not so, seeing that the whole world is evil and that among thousands there is scarcely one true Christian, men would devour one another, and no one could preserve wife and child, support himself and serve God; and the world would be re-duced to chaos. For this reason God has ordained the two govern-ments: the spiritual, which by the Holy Spirit under Christ makes Christians and pious people, and the secular, which restrains the unchristian and wicked so that they must needs keep the peace outwardly against their will."[4]

Luther not only saw the origin of the state in man's sin, he also found in the state a special embodiment of sin. It

[4] "On Political Authority," *The Works of Martin Luther* (Muhlenberg Press), Vol. III, p. 236.

is ironical that later Lutheranism often became in practice highly complacent about the state, allowing it moral autonomy in its own sphere, but Luther had no such complacency. He says of the princes in words that are often repeated: "You must know that from the beginning of the world a wise prince is a rare bird in heaven, still more a pious prince." He goes on to say: "They are usually the greatest fools and knaves on earth; therefore one must constantly expect the worst from them and look for little good from them, especially in divine matters, which concern the salvation of souls. They are God's jailers and hangmen, and His divine wrath needs them to punish the wicked and preserve outward peace."[5]

This contrast between the two realms which Luther presents here is a subject of continuous discussion among Lutherans and among all students of Luther. On one side it is a vindication of the independence of the Gospel and the Church. These have their own way of working and are outside the sphere of the political power. It is also a way of affirming that God is Lord of the state and that the rulers are responsible to him whether they know it or not. In spite of the scorn which Luther expressed for the rulers, he took for granted that they were within the Church and that they did receive Christian moral instruction from the Church. But the separation of the two realms in explicitly secularized societies left no way by which the Church could speak effectively to the rulers about their responsibility to God. Luther showed no interest in the provision of political checks upon the rulers though he made clear that they are as much a part of the problem of human sin as they are means of restraining it. Luther's emphasis upon order made him strangely indifferent to the problem of justice and the need of defence against the injustice of those who have the political power.

There is validity in Luther's realism about the conflict be-

[5] *Ibid.*, p. 258.

tween Christian love and the necessary functions of the state, between what a man's duty may be in his office and what he would choose to do as a Christian in his private relations with his neighbors, but he separates these two realms so completely that there is no way of keeping the political order under the ultimate criticism of love.

One of the most fateful weaknesses of Luther's approach can be seen clearly in a democratic society in which Christians have political power without being subjected to the particular occupational hazards of Luther's princes which made him so fully aware of their limitations. Luther's distinction between the Christians and the world and the suggestion that Christians —of course he guards himself by saying "true Christians"—do not need to be under government is one of his greatest errors and a curious one in view of his own emphasis in other contexts on the sins of the redeemed. In our society Christians, who are by any test sincerely devout, are among the rulers, as voters or office-holders, and need instruction concerning their Christian vocation as citizens on more complicated decisions than those suggested by the sword or the hangman's rope, and these same Christians represent particular social interests and, with the very sinful blindness which Luther emphasizes as characteristic of sinful man, defend those interests beyond the point of justice. So they need relevant guidance for their vocations and they need to be checked by effective use of power by other citizens who suffer unjustly at their hands.

It is surprising in view of the usual stereotypes of Calvin that, in spite of his harsh doctrine of total depravity, he was closer to the Catholic view than to Luther in his thinking about the state. Underlying his explicit statements about magistrates and political institutions there is a conception of the "common grace" that enables men to live together in civil society. What Calvin says about man's capacity for political order and about his understanding of the moral law is quite remarkable. He says that "man is naturally a creature inclined to society, he has also by nature an instinctive propensity to cherish and preserve that society; and therefore we perceive in the minds of all men general impressions of civil probity and order." He says that "not a person can be found who does not understand, that all associations of men ought to be governed by laws, or who does not conceive in his mind the principles of those laws."[6] Calvin lived before the world was broken, before the deeper moral chasms appeared in what was once Christendom. Today we cannot speak with his confidence about what men actually "conceive," though we may have more confidence than the moral relativist that there is a moral order that can be discerned from many points of view.

Given this view of man's civil capacities it is not strange that Calvin held a positive view of the origin and function of the state. He says that "the authority possessed by kings and governors over all things upon earth is not a consequence of the perverseness of men, but of the providence and holy ordinance of God, who has pleased to regulate human affairs in this manner; for as much as he is present, and also presides among them, in making laws and in executing equitable judgments."[7] When he discusses the functions of civil government he says that it should "regulate our lives and manner requisite for the society of men, to form our manners to civil justice, to promote our concord with each other, and to establish general peace and tranquillity."[8] One can see advantage in Luther's separation of the two realms when one finds that Calvin says that "this civil government is designed, as long as we live in this world, to cherish and support

---

[6] *Institutes of the Christian Religion*, Bk. II, Chap. II, Par. XIII.
[7] *Ibid.*, Bk. IV, Chap. XX, Par. IV.
[8] *Ibid.*, Par. II.

the external worship of God, to preserve the pure doctrine of religion, to defend the constitution of the church."[9]

All Christian thinkers, Catholic and Protestant, are nourished and stimulated by the thought of St. Augustine. His thought is rich and many-sided and his great book, *The City of God*, was written over so long a period that it reveals contrasting emphases within it. It makes some difference whether he is speaking of the pre-Christian Roman state or about the "Christian" empire. There is ambiguity in his view of the relation between the state in its various historical stages and the "Earthly City" which he generally associated with the forces of evil. I think that Augustine shared the positive view of the origin and the role of the state which we find in developed Catholic thought and, to some extent, in Calvin, but that he had fewer illusions about the actual political order. His view of human nature was very dark, with great stress upon the destructive pride and egoism of man, but he was also insistent that man could not exist if he were totally depraved, that the possibility of existence for any beings, including the devil and the evil angels, depends upon the good in them, though it is perverted good. [10] He had a great sense of the transitoriness and relative character of all political orders but he also had genuine appreciation of the earthly peace which they make possible. He says, for example, of the earthly city "which does not live by faith" that "it seeks an earthly peace, and the end it proposes, in the well ordered concord of civic obedience and rule, is the combination of men's wills to attain the things which are helpful to this life. The heavenly city, or rather the part of it which sojourns on earth and lives by faith, makes use of

[9] *Ibid.*

[10] "Vice cannot be in the highest good, and cannot be but in some good. Things solely good, therefore, can in some circumstances exist; things solely evil, never; for even these natures which are vitiated by an evil will, so far indeed as they are vitiated, are evil, but in so far as they are natures they are good." *The City of God*, Bk. XII, Chap. III.

this peace only because it must, until this mortal condition which necessitates it shall pass away."[11]

Contemporary thinkers are much harder to classify than the great traditions which they represent. There is so much interaction between them and they are all so greatly influenced by contrasting historical situations that it is impossible to find pure types among them.

I first became vividly aware of this contrast in Christian thinking at the Oxford Conference on Church, Community and State in 1937. At that time there seemed to be a theological division in terms of geography between Protestants on the European continent on the one hand and the whole Anglo-Saxon world on the other. This was deceptive because there were wide differences among thinkers on the continent but it was true that Anglo-Saxon theologians and lay political thinkers were unanimously on the side of the positive interpretation of the state's origin and function. They generally held a more hopeful view of human nature; they took for granted the idea of the limited state which was no great threat to the freedom of society. It is true that in the United States there has been a strong tradition of suspicion of the state and an individualistic tendency to assume that private agencies are inherently better than the state, but Americans who held such views could make no connection with the theological emphasis upon the state as primarily a remedy for and an expression of sin. They had forgotten the element of truth in the assertion in the Federalist papers that government is "the greatest of all reflections on human nature."[12] The continental theologians, for their part, lived under welfare states which embodied the posi-

[11] *Ibid.*, Bk. XIX, Chap. XXVII.

[12] From No. 51 written by Hamilton or Madison. The context is as follows: "But what is government itself, but the greatest of all reflections on human nature? If men were angels, no government would be necessary. If angels were to govern men, neither external nor internal controls on government would be necessary."

tive functions of the state and some of them belonged to state appointed theological faculties.

The Anglo-Saxon view was generally represented by the following statement of one position in the report of the conference: "Another view also derives the authority of the state from the divine moral world order. The moral obligations which are written in the conscience of all men are to be realized in the state. The state serves the divine purpose by realizing the ideals of humanity, freedom, equality and universal well-being —and by guaranteeing to all men the most favorable external conditions for their free self-development."[13]

Today this statement has a one-sided sound and it probably does not define exactly the emphasis upon the positive basis of the state as now held by many Protestants; for it represented not only a predominately liberal type of theology, but also a favorable experience of the democratic state as the instrument of widely shared social purposes.

I shall now refer to the thought of two theologians from the European continent, Emil Brunner and Karl Barth. They manage to differ from each other on this issue as much as on the more fundamental questions of theology concerning which their differences have been more publicized.

Professor Brunner, though a Calvinist in background, often expresses with great emphasis the negative view of the state. He follows the distinction between "the orders of creation" and the "orders of preservation" and he classifies the state among the latter because it is based upon the fall. He says: "In the necessity of the State we recognize the consequences of Original Sin. The fact that we need the state, and a state of this kind, constitutes a very searching call to repentance, and it is this perception which makes us humble."[14] He says that "it belongs to the essence of the State that it should have

[13] *Oxford Conference, Official Report* (Willett, Clark, 1937), p. 240.
[14] *The Divine Imperative* (the Westminster Press, 1943), p. 446.

the power to compel obedience."[15] Brunner is concerned somewhat less with the idea that the state comes into existence
as a result of sin and more with the conviction that this state,
which exists to restrain sin, becomes in an extreme way the
embodiment of sin. He says: "Every state represents human
sin on the large scale; in history, in the growth of every state
the most brutal, anti-divine forces have taken a share, to an
extent unheard of in the individual life, save in that of some
prominent criminals. In the state we human beings see our
own sin magnified a thousand times."[16]

Brunner's thinking about the state is controlled by his limited
definition of the state as the agency of compulsion and also
by a tendency to draw an absolute distinction between even
just forms of compulsion and the work of love. He quite rightly
says that the state is not "the aggregate of all human life."[17]
He is a social pluralist who desires to accent the role of the
"group forms" or associations which are other than the state.
This general trend of his thought is in principle one that will
later be supported in this book, but he carries it too far in two
ways. He seeks by a fiat that has no relation to contemporary
realities to limit the functions of the state. He says: "It is not
the duty of the state itself to engage in economic activity, or
to establish marriage or to carry on scientific work, or the work
of education."[18] He is certainly right about marriage, though
the state must regulate it. The state should support science and
provide opportunities for education while it recognizes that it
must not seek to control the inner development of either.
Though the state should not take over more responsibility for
economic activity than is socially necessary his statement on the
relation of the state to economic activity is refuted by our
contemporary experience.

[15] *Ibid.*, p. 445.
[16] *Ibid.*, p. 445.
[17] *Ibid.*, p. 458.
[18] *Ibid.*

The other difficulty in Brunner's position is that he seems to think that the coercive and non-coercive aspects of social life can be separated with only the former designated as belonging to the function of the state. As I shall attempt to show later, it is the impossibility of doing this that should prevent us from defining the state as narrowly as Brunner does.

Karl Barth's Christological doctrine of the state leads in a very different direction from Brunner's view. It is a very complex doctrine and difficult to understand except from the inside of Barth's vast theological system. It is based upon a refusal to separate the world as known through the doctrines of creation and sin from the redemptive work of Christ that has already taken place. Barth makes much of the idea that God used the state in the crucifixion of Christ and so, unknowingly, even Pilate played a part in the divine work of redemption.[19] So the very event that is the demonstration of the state's cruel and unjust use of its power is also a sign that it is not outside the sphere of redemption. Though this may seem to be a far-fetched argument it leads to conclusions which can be accepted on other grounds.

Barth makes clear that the state should not seek to become the Church, that it will never be the Kingdom of God. He also emphasizes the protecting function of the state and says that "without this political order there would be no Christian order."[20] He seems to go beyond the idea of the state's protection of human life from chaos when he speaks of "the state's effort to achieve an external, relative and provisional humanising

[19] *Church and State* (S.C.M. Press, London, 1939), Chap. I.
[20] From his essay, "The Christian Community and the Civil Community" in *Against the Stream* (Philosophical Library, 1954), p. 20. This essay is a complete refutation of those who assume that Barth is quietistic or basically negative toward all political institutions. His conclusions are usually excellent but his methodology is a forced and sometimes almost absurd attempt to derive all the necessary political guidance from revelation because of his refusal to use principles of justice that have a broader base than the Christian faith.

of man's life and the political order instituted for all . . . under which the evil are punished and the good rewarded."[21] Any quotations do injustice to the subtle and dialectical thinking of Barth in this area. He does emphasize the work of the state in dealing with sin but the whole spirit of his discussion is different from that of Protestants who see only this side of the state, and from that of Catholics who sharply divide the sphere of the state as belonging to nature from the supernatural order. He is clear about the relative and provisional character of all that the state does and often it seems that its chief function is to make possible the freedom of man to preach and respond to the Gospel. The following statement may suggest the spirit of Barth:

"It (the state) serves to protect man from the invasion of chaos and therefore to give him time: time for the preaching of the gospel; time for repentance; time for faith. Since 'according to the measure of human insight and human capacity' and 'under the threat and exercise of force' (Barmen Thesis No. 5) provision is made in the state for the establishment of human law and (in the inevitably external, relative and provisional sense) for freedom, peace and humanity, it renders a definite service to divine Providence and plan of salvation, quite apart from the judgment and desires of its members."[22]

I believe that there is in Barth's view of the state a type of Christo-centrism which in his theology as a whole is most problematic, and that there are extraordinarily arbitrary transitions as he draws analogies for the life of the state from the Kingdom of God and the Church; but Barth has helped to overcome two tendencies which have been strong in traditional Protestant theology and which have been obstacles to a relevant Christian message for the state and society today. One is the hardened Lutheran dualism between the two realms which leaves the state outside the sphere where there could be a

[21] *Ibid.*
[22] *Ibid.*, p. 21.

distinctively Christian criticism of its policies. Barth may have introduced new problems of his own but he did do a great service to the Church in overcoming this inhibiting dualism as between the two realms. Barth also by this doctrine was able to overcome conservative, backward-looking conceptions of providence based upon the "orders of creation." I do not believe that he does justice to what can be learned from the continuing historical structures which may in fact be better understood under the category of creation than under that of redemption, but it was salutary to rescue many Christians from static and legalistic interpretations of these orders of creation. To see them as under Christ's lordship made it possible to look for radical transformations of the existing structures, to look for the dynamic influence upon society, whether it is aware of it or not, of the redeeming power of God through Christ.[23]

---

[23] Dietrich Bonhoeffer held a view of the state similar to Barth's. He said such things as the following: "Government, like all created things 'consists only in Jesus Christ'; in other words, it is only in Him that it has its essence and being. If Jesus Christ did not exist, there would be no created things; all created things would be annihilated in the wrath of God." *Ethics* (Macmillan, 1955), p. 301. There are few contemporary books which have more insight and prophetic power in them than Bonhoeffer's *Ethics*, but this statement is an example of a type of passage that to me is completely opaque.

CHAPTER V

The State and the Doctrine of Man—
A Constructive Statement

In THIS chapter I shall make some suggestions toward a solution of the problem presented by the contrasting Christian positions outlined in the previous chapter.

Consider first the actual relationship between the coercive and the non-coercive aspects of the state. The one-sided emphasis upon what I have called the negative basis of the state is very closely linked with a view held in secular political theory which sees in the authority and power to coerce the essence of the state. If these theorists are right, then the theologians who stress only the negative basis of the state are right also. It is my conviction that they are wrong because their analysis does not do justice to what we know constitutes a reasonably healthy state or to the way in which coercion and consent are interwoven in the activity of the state and in the lives of citizens.

The identification of the essence of the state with coercion has been held by thinkers as different as Leo Tolstoy and Karl Marx. Tolstoy was so repelled by it that he rejected the state altogether in favor of a Christian pacifist anarchism. Marx related this view to the cynical assumption that every state was the agency by which the dominant class kept other classes in order, an idea that underlies the conception of the dictatorship of the proletariat as the successor of the more disguised dictatorship of the bourgeoisie and the conception of the withering away of the state in a classless society.

On the surface this view of the state is very plausible because the state does have and should have a monopoly of physical force with the legal right and the power to defend the nation against aggression from other nations, to prevent internal disturbances of the peace, to overcome deadlocks between conflicting interests endangering the health and welfare of the community, and to punish crime. In every nation there must be a source of final authority which can act with force in an emergency; this source of final authority is located in the state. The state has the authority and the power of life and death over its citizens. A good state, or a tolerable state, will limit itself by law in using this power. One example of such use that would be accepted by all but the most absolutistic pacifists is the use of police force to stop a riot or a lynching and this may mean shooting that results in killing in some cases.

I think that Professor Robert MacIver has provided a good formula that recognizes these facts about the state and yet permits a broader view of its essential nature and purpose. He says: "coercive power is a criterion of the state but not its essence."[1] To put this in other words, the state exists to serve many of the purposes of the national community; some of these purposes require the use of force, but for others the use of force is negligible. Moreover, a state that is not a tyranny serves these purposes, all of them, under a system of law and law limits the occasions on which force is used. The state exists to promote order and security but also justice and freedom and welfare; all of these aims are to a remarkable degree interdependent. If all of the emphasis is on coercion, there is quite sure to be a wrong preoccupation with the coercive means to the neglect of the ends which justify them. Can we not say that the healthier a nation is, the less it will have to depend upon force in serving these ends? If this is so, it can hardly be said that force is the essence of the state.

[1] *The Modern State* (Oxford University Press, 1926), p. 213.

We can move a step further if we recognize that coercion and consent are so closely interwoven in the activities of the state that it is impossible in practice to isolate the coercive functions from other functions and to see the state in terms of them alone. Take as an illustration one of the most positive and constructive of all the state's functions, its provision of educational opportunity for all citizens. Such provision for education is usually compulsory and so there is always a truant officer in the background, but it would be a mistake to emphasize that fact very much in interpreting the meaning of public education. More important, the public schools depend on taxes and the state's coercive power is always in the background when taxes are collected. The whole tax system is a perfect example of how consent and coercion are woven together. All responsible citizens believe that they should pay taxes but their consent would tend to wither away if they discovered that many other citizens were not compelled to bear their share of the burden of taxes. Also, while we may all consent to the general obligation to pay taxes, we grumble at the amount of them and many of us would not be likely to meet the deadlines for payment if there were no compulsion in the background!

Lord Lindsay illustrates this same point by referring to such a simple procedure as traffic control. He says: "We most of us think there ought to be laws regulating traffic, compelling us to light our lamps at a certain time and so on. Such rules have our consent and approval. Yet most of us, if we are honest, know that we are likely to break those laws on occasion and that we are often restrained from breaking them by the sanctions of the law. Most laws are like that. They will work and can be enforced because most people want usually to keep them; they have to be enforced to ensure that all people practically always keep them." He goes on to say, "There are rules which have little value unless everyone keeps them, and force is needed to fill up the gap between most people usually and all people always obeying."[2]

A second type of consideration is the understanding of human nature underlying our conception of the state. There is no doubt that the recent recovery of the classical Protestant doctrine of man in a modified form has been the source of much political wisdom. Neither Catholicism nor Protestant Liberalism has understood the depth or stubbornness of evil in human life. But types of theology that have been influenced by the theology of the Reformation on the European continent have been too one-sided in their pessimism. Calvinism, with its doctrine of "common grace" has been less one-sided than Lutheranism. The inspiration of Augustine with his idea of the two cities as "commingled" or entangled together in actual historical existence offers the possibility of a view that does greater justice to a balanced conception of human nature. The two cities represent tendencies in human life on a deeper level than Church and State; we can think of this intermingling within the life of both Church and State and even within the inner life of each person. Augustine's belief that there can be no wholly evil being and that, except in rare instances which he admits as possibilities, even no redeemed person overcomes all temptation—always the prayer: "forgive us our trespasses" applies to the Christian—points to a more adequate view of human nature than that of most other theologians.

There is, however, an important development in Christian thought that may enable theology to do greater justice than Augustine to the positive elements in human nature. I refer to a change in Christian thought associated with the modern criticism of the Bible and of orthodoxy which is likely to out-

[2] *The Modern Democratic State* (Oxford University Press, London, 1947), p. 206. Published on behalf of the Royal Institute of International affairs.

last Liberalism as a type of theology, to the conviction that, while the idea of the fall of man represents a universal truth about human nature, it can no longer be put in the context of temporal events. Adam and Eve are symbols of humanity with no temporal existence as individuals. I believe that, if we take this change of assumptions seriously, we may have a view of human nature which preserves the truth in the doctrine of the fall but which avoids the idea that contemporary man is to be understood chiefly as the victim of a far-off event in the lives of Adam and Eve. This provides a frame for our thought which enables us to do greater justice to both the negative and the positive aspects of human nature. Contemporary man does belong to corporate humanity and he inherits the effects of corporate sin, but when the fall is associated with a temporal event in the past, contemporary man is thought of as determined more completely by the burden of an evil inheritance than is actually the case.

To put it differently: the traditional Protestant idea of the fall meant that Adam was created in the image of God but that in his unhappy descendants the image of God was lost or almost lost or almost wholly perverted. May we not now say that all men are made in the image of God and that the idea of the fall symbolizes the continuous contradiction of that image in every man? The great contrast is not between Adam before the fall and all humanity since, but rather it is within every one of us. We may on this basis think more dynamically of the image of God and of the fall. We may give a real place to the contemporary effectiveness of the positive as well as of the negative elements in human nature. A quite different idea but one which has some of the same effects is to say, with Karl Barth, that the original image of God has been lost but that in Christ it has already been restored and, in some sense which I do not pretend to understand, that restored image is effective in the life of humanity as a whole.[3] The effectiveness of the divine image, as the positive side of human nature, cannot be separated from the direct or indirect influence of God's grace through Christ upon contemporary humanity. Taken together, they do not cancel the sinful pride and self-centeredness of contemporary man, or his inheritance of the consequences of past sins—either in the world at large or in the Church. The contradiction continues and it provides the basis for the most realistic understanding of the evil in man and for appreciation of his greatness and goodness, of his capacity for openness to the grace of God. Always, as we say these things, we must realize how far these aspects of our life are intermingled, changing one another.

The error of much theological thinking about the fall and original sin is that it begins with an *a priori* estimate of man's sinfulness which is quantitative. Actually, the fall should be the symbol for the sin that we actually find in experience rather than a doctrine that determines in advance what we shall find.

There is sufficient empirical evidence of the depth, the universality and the persistence of sin in human life, and of the corruption of our strength and virtue. Behind these manifestations of sin there is a tendency toward self-centeredness, a tendency to put ourselves or something close to ourselves in the place which belongs to God. Conventional theological language often makes this original form of sin incredible because it suggests that people are so grandiose as to try to occupy God's place objectively. It is credible if it is understood to mean that the place that should be reserved for the divine in our own lives is occupied by something human, something that

---

[3] This idea pervades the thought of Barth especially since 1940. The following references are given only as samples: *Church Dogmatics* IV, I (Scribners, 1956), pp. 79-128; *Christ and Adam* (Harper, 1957), *passim;* "The Christian Message and the New Humanism" in *Against the Stream* (Philosophical Library, 1954), pp. 183-191.

belongs to us. It may show itself as self-sufficiency. This tendency has a headstart with us before we become responsible persons. Either there are degrees of this tendency in different people or there are degrees to the extent to which it is neutralized by divine grace, common grace in Calvin's sense or grace that is known to be mediated through Christ. Sometimes the corruption of the good that remains is a kind of shadow that accompanies it and sometimes it perverts the good at the center. These comments are intended to correct the type of thinking about human nature that emphasizes original sin in *a priori*, quantitative terms as something that is total or almost total. Ideas of this kind seem in practice to be strategic,[4] designed to warn against self-righteousness rather than to provide an accurate estimate of the situation. One sign of this is that admiration for the goodness of others who are also sinful human beings seems less dangerous than the prideful admiration of our own.

There are, however, three other doctrinal convictions which are essential to Christian thinking about human nature, which are associated with the complex of traditional ideas concerning the fall and original sin.

One is the conviction that the deepest roots of sin are spiritual and have their consequences on every level of human development. Pride and self-centeredness are often most de-

[4] Professor Torrance emphasizes this strategic, or as he says "didactic," tendency in Calvin's thought: "Indeed, it is just because Calvin holds so firmly that grace completely undercuts all our claims to righteousness and wisdom, and that we do not allow grace to strike home to us until we have renounced all our righteousness and wisdom, that he employs every didactic method he can think of to deflate man's self-esteem and pride in his own integrity and achievements. . . . Unfortunately later Calvinistic theology too often turned Calvin's didactic device into dogmatic procedure, producing a doctrine of the fall of man and of human depravity apart from the context of grace, and interpreting grace as God's answer to human depravity." T. F. Torrance, *Calvin's Doctrine of Man* (Lutterworth Press, London, 1949; Wm. B. Eerdmans Publishing Co., Grand Rapids), pp. 19-20.

structive on the higher levels of our life, in our use of reason, in our idealism, in our moral self-assurance, in our social and political loyalties, and in our religious commitments which are often disguised idolatries. The idea of total depravity, a phrase which is certainly misleading and which I avoid using, is widely interpreted in these terms and so interpreted it means, not that men at any stage are totally depraved in all areas of life, but that there is no area of life that is exempt from sinful distortion.

The second doctrinal conviction to which I have referred is that a Christian should begin with his own sin, with the beam in his own eye, and not with the sins of his neighbors or of those who belong to another group or who are on the other side of some conflict. In church, at the center of Christian worship, we confess our own sin and do not bear witness to the sins of others. This is difficult enough for a Christian in his personal relations but it is vastly more difficult for the Christian as a citizen or as a member of an economic or political group. In political life we tend to be guided by black and white slogans, by ideological prejudice, by self-righteous patriotism or party spirit and yet, in spite of the difficulty in this sphere, the habit of beginning with the sin of one's own nation, with the sin of one's own "side," should be natural within the Christian community.

The third conviction is the recognition of our dependence upon the grace of God in all that we are or achieve that is good. The recognition of this undercuts the self-righteousness of the morally self-made man. There is real freedom in what we do but this itself is a gift, and the exercise of freedom is in response to what God has done in Christ. Gratitude and humility rather than pride in our own achievements or contempt for others are the characteristic marks of the Christian life. "For by grace you have been saved through faith; and this is not your own doing, it is the gift of God—not because of works, lest any man should boast." (Ephesians 2:8-9) This is a way of understanding the good that is realized in human life rather than a denial of its existence.

It is against the background of this way of thinking about human nature that I shall put my own discussion of the relation of the state to the positive and negative sides of human life.

There are three ways in which the state is related to the symptoms of human sin: (1) as the means of restraining them; (2) as, to some extent, the embodiment of them because the very power of the state is so great a temptation to those who exercise it; (3) as limited, even in its most constructive efforts, by the corporate sin of the humanity with which it must deal.

(1) Traditional Protestant theology has generally specialized on the state's responsibility to prevent disorder, to restrain the anti-social tendencies in individuals and groups within the nation, to deter and to punish crime. Its task is often more subtle than the traditional symbol of the "sword" suggests as when it helps to preserve a balance of power between elements in the economy so that they restrain one another and when it diverts the egoism of people into constructive channels by inducements more than by threats. It also has the task of providing for the security of the nation against aggression. In another chapter I shall have more to say about the state's responsibility for national defense but here I shall call attention to the dilemma, that, while provisions for the national defense do belong to the order-preserving function of the state, they arouse fear and suspicion, when a nation is powerful, in other nations and contribute to the causes of international disorder.

The traditional Christian thinking about the state as the check upon anarchy is also a reason for the emerging international institutions because the national state is a major factor in the international anarchy. But the very Christian emphasis upon the depth and persistence of sin on all levels of human development should warn us against the illusion that the concentration of power in a world state is itself a secure solution of the problems of human anarchy because the corruption of power in a world state could come near to being the final corruption.

(2) No one will question the tendency of states to become embodiments of sinful egoism. They have power, preponderant power in relation to their own citizens, and in the case of the "great powers" their policies influence the destinies of all nations. Power is morally neutral in the sense that it is a necessary condition for good as well as for evil but it is a source of special temptation. The totalitarian states have convinced most of us of the demonic possibilities in political life, both because of their treatment of their own citizens and because of their aggressiveness in dealing with other nations. The combination of tyranny and military aggression is the most destructive political evil that any of us fear except the threat of total annihilation which accompanies the danger of any large scale war.

In less spectacular ways the state tends to act in the interests of the groups which have most economic or political power within them and to do so against the interests of other groups at home and of whole nations abroad. Always state power is a temptation to those who are close to it to feather their own nests and the opportunities that it offers for profitable political corruption are endless. Fortunately, there are states in which power is so distributed within the state itself and those who exercise it are so much open to inspection and correction that these abuses are reduced to a minimum. There are nations in which public honesty has become a habit, subject to the rarest exceptions, a habit that is rooted in a combination of personal integrity and the pressures upon the individual from ready inspection of what he does and strong expectation of his good behavior by his fellow citizens.[5]

(3) It is the third relation of the state to man's sin on which there has been the most illumination from contemporary theology, especially from the work of Reinhold Niebuhr. He and all contemporary theologians who have learned from the Reformation have been clear about the need of the state to overcome disorder and they realize how far the state itself can become an embodiment of pride and imperialism in relation to other states and a tyrant in relation to its own citizens, but in his criticism of the moral idealism of much liberal theology and of much liberal politics, Dr. Niebuhr has helped us to see that even the relatively good state, in the pursuit of peace and justice, is limited not only by its own sinfulness as a center of power but also by the moral limitations of every interest group with which it deals, by the moral limitations of the people of the nation as a whole in their approach to the needs and the aspirations and the fears of other nations, by the tragic dilemmas which arise in the international sphere in which its responsibility to have the military power to defend its freedom becomes a part of the general threat to human existence in a nuclear age, and by the tendencies among ordinary men to lose incentive and to become irresponsible when the state is most effective in improving their conditions.

Some of these issues will be discussed in later chapters, but

[5] While writing this I had in mind especially the tradition of probity among British officials—I have heard most about this, but I am sure that what is said here applies to some, but all too few, other nations. In this country we always remind ourselves of the widespread municipal corruption and of the examples of corruption in our federal government which periodically receive so much emphasis. We should not forget that corruption tends to decrease in our larger political units, that there are segments of our federal government which have an excellent record, that in relation to the dollars spent corruption has been minimal in the federal government in general, that the "conflict of interests" law sets a very high standard of behavior which policy-making officials are not allowed to forget.

I shall emphasize here two insights about the limits of moral idealism which we owe in part to modern theological realism.

(a) Moral idealism in political life often takes the form of preoccupation with remedies inapplicable to the situation that exists and which become a hindrance to the effort to find the most viable policies. In the 1930's much Christian Socialism was idealism of this type for it blinded many people, including myself, to the real possibilities of achieving justice without an over-all change in the economic system. Perhaps the greater errors of moral idealism have been in the sphere of international relations. We see them in types of pacifism which do not take seriously the difficulties in changing by persuasion, or by example, opponents who live behind totalitarian walls and whose minds are encased in ideologies which for limited periods make mutual understanding impossible. Pacifists generally advocate forms of unilateral disarmament which would increase the danger of aggression. A similar misuse of moral idealism in the field of international relations is to advocate total solutions along the lines of world government, without realizing that no constitutional change in the United Nations can alter the actual location of power in the world and that so long as the real centers of power are in conflict there is not enough power beyond them to be an effective instrument of world government in relation to the most dangerous threats to peace.

(b) The second and the more destructive misuse of moral idealism is within the great historical conflicts themselves. This is true of the ideological conflict between the Communist and the non-Communist worlds. During the period of its greatest appeal Communism has been successful in mobilizing the idealism of large numbers of people, especially among the youth in many countries, behind its cause and the tragic fact is that these same idealists became the most effective agents of an expanding tyranny. Their very idealism provided rationalizations for

Communist terror and their self-righteous fanaticism made them its most willing instruments. As I write, it seems that in the western world and in Russia itself this idealism is losing its power to convince, though it will be some years before the same can be said of its influence in Asia and Africa. (The attraction of Russian technology may be greater than that of Communist "idealism.")

This distortion of idealism is not limited to one side in this conflict. Fascist movements have been less idealistic but idealism was at times one element in their fury while they lasted. And as for the more characteristic opposition to Communism in the western democracies, there have been spells of hysteria and there is often a cold self-righteousness especially in spokesmen for American policy. Fortunately, this opposition to Communism has not developed a movement of the spirit comparable to Communism in its vastness, in its centralization, and in the blinding character of its ideology. It has not lost the resources for self-criticism which in the end make the democratic world worth defending.

In the long run even more important than this illustration taken from Communism and its opponents is the recognition that modern wars, as they have become idealistic enterprises of the people, have gained in destructive fury, both in the fury of psychological weapons of which whole populations are the instruments and in the fury of bombs and missiles. These idealistic wars are difficult to bring to an end short of the total defeat of the enemy. The more a conflict is moralized, the more unconditional surrender is demanded, the more difficult a compromise settlement becomes which would give to both sides a better chance to begin again. This temptation at the heart of moral idealism has been seen, apart from theologians, by many recent observers such as Walter Lippmann and George

Kennan; it has perhaps received strongest expression in the writings of Professor Herbert Butterfield.[6]

I have said so much about the relation between the state and the symptoms of human sin that it may be difficult for the reader to realize that my desire is to give weight to the more positive side of the state's role! The state is concerned to keep order but there are many kinds of order and states often work for justice and freedom within the order. The state, as I have said, should serve a great variety of needs within the community and even corrupt or tyrannical states do this in spite of themselves. Even when they are at their worst they must win a measure of favor with the people if they are to survive. Here I am not concerned to generalize about all states but rather to stress the possibilities in a relatively just and relatively free modern state. We should not on doctrinaire grounds, theological or political, deny to the state the possibility of its being the agent of a sensitive caring for the welfare and the dignity of all of its citizens and of "the stranger who sojourns" among them. Some of its institutions are at times the instruments of a redemptive concern for the most disadvantaged people and also for offenders against society.

In other chapters I shall discuss the limits of the state, and I shall then speak of some of the true and the false warnings about the dangers of the welfare state. I realize that the more extensive the functions of the state in this field, the greater the possibilities that the state may seek to determine

---

[6] I have in mind Lippmann's *Essays in the Public Philosophy* (Little, Brown, 1955), pp. 23-24; Kennan's *Realities of American Foreign Policy* (Princeton University Press, 1954); Butterfield's *Christianity, Diplomacy and War* (Abingdon, 1954), Chap. 3. Butterfield, for example, says: "The unlimited 'war for righteousness' was known centuries ago in fact; and we can learn from its terrible results at that time that it is this theory of war—and not modern scientific invention—which gives this kind of conflict its daemonic character." He emphasizes the "wars of religion" as earlier examples of "the conflict of right and wrong" which "admitted of no relenting" (pp. 26-27).

the content of the culture and become more and more totalitarian. However, that danger cannot cancel the responsibility of the state for the external conditions for the welfare of all of the people. The state must not try to be the church and it must not seek to be the determiner of the moral and spiritual goals of the society, but it must not avoid acting as an instrument of the common conscience within society. The lines here are difficult to draw and we cannot draw them according to a pattern that is suitable for all societies, but the responsibility to draw them never ceases.

In spite of all dangers and problems the development of the state's concern for the social welfare of all segments of society and the great increase of its capacity to serve it represent an enormous moral advance. Let no emphasis upon the dangers lead to a grudging attitude toward the actual achievements. When the national community decides to use the agencies of the state to secure better opportunities for education and health for all children, it is serving justice and the sights of the community in regard to justice have been raised by love. I am impressed when I hear of the extra efforts that are made in some communities to help the most handicapped children, those who cannot even go to school. I do not know whether in practice the systems of children's allowances which have been established in Britain and in Canada are the best way of providing an economic floor below which no family is allowed to fall, for they do raise serious questions, but they are one way of demonstrating the concern of the community as a whole for all of its members. They are policies of the state in which justice and love meet. Among the other ways in which some modern states show concern for the dignity as well as for the material welfare of their people, one might mention the safeguarding of dignity that is possible when workers are able to bargain collectively and when retired people can count on annuities from Social Security which are theirs by right.

One of the most remarkable examples of the state's moving imaginatively to serve justice and welfare was the decision of the United States Supreme Court outlawing racial segregation in the schools. The implementation of this decision will produce agonizing problems in many places for a long time but what is most significant is the way in which the Court was governed by the most sensitive understanding of the harm done to children by segregation even under externally equal conditions.

We see many signs of the same sensitive concern in relation to the offenders against society. There is here a difference from the kinds of advances toward social welfare that I have mentioned. In those cases there were large segments of the population involved possessing actual or potential political strength and they were able to do a great deal to secure better conditions for themselves. This does not mean that the conscience of the community has not been at work but it works more promptly and effectively to help people who are strong enough to call attention to their needs and to organize for political action to defend their interests! In the case of the offenders against society, criminals and delinquents, no such pressure is possible and so what is accomplished for their rehabilitation has to be done against strong temptations to economize in all provisions made for them. It requires more single-minded love to accomplish much in this field.

The humanizing of punishment has gone far, sometimes farther in principle than in practice. In the past it often had to meet the opposition of a theologically doctrinaire emphasis on retribution or expiation. There was a mixture of truth and error in this emphasis. There is a retributive or expiatory element in punishment and if this is denied, the idea of the responsibility of the criminal is undercut. Degrees of responsibility are hard to measure and in cases of emotional sickness, probably much more extensive than the field covered by legally recognized insanity, there is often no responsibility. The traditional ideas were right in maintaining a degree of responsibility wherever punishment is appropriate. They were wrong in not recognizing the sharing of responsibility by society.

Professor Brunner is most helpful on this subject. He says that "legal theorists injure the idea of law when they consider criminal jurisprudence only from the utilitarian point of view of security, deterrence, and the improvement of the criminal. Regarded from this point of view, the Law loses its religious background." But he goes on to say that it is a good thing that legal theory has given up the idea of expiation in its traditional form and that "actually modern positivistic legal reformers have almost always been in the right against their 'Christian' opponents. For in practice the old idea of expiation was not only actually controlled by the spirit of primitive revenge, but it was also a fertile soil for the growth of the most hateful, harsh kind of Pharisaism."[7] Brunner follows this up with a strong, and I believe correct, indictment of capital punishment which quite obviously accents all that is wrong in the emphasis upon retribution and expiation and destroys all chance of the rehabilitation of the criminal. Though rehabilitation is not the only purpose of punishment, it is one essential purpose and what is done to serve other purposes should be consistent with it. Many modern states have moved far in their understanding of what their true attitude should be toward punishment and those who have most to do with the punishment of the criminal, judges and prison wardens, are often ahead of the public.[8]

[7] From *The Divine Imperative* by Emil Brunner. Copyright, 1947, by W. L. Jenkins, The Westminster Press. Used by permission. Also, Lutterworth Press, London.

[8] It is significant that there has been a similar change during the past century in theological conceptions of the divine penology. Today no

The state's relation to juvenile offenders brings out even more clearly what we may call its redemptive responsibility. The conscience of communities has been slow in becoming sensitive to this problem, but often those who represent the state in dealing with juvenile offenders are the very ones who have shown the greatest concern. Dean Pound in discussing the origin of juvenile courts says that they have come into being because of the initiative of "a few definitely known socially minded judges." He says that they arose "on the criminal side of the courts because of the revolt of those judges' consciences from legal rules that required trial of children over seven as criminals and sentence of children over fourteen to penalties provided for adult offenders."[9]

In recent years the public concern over the problem of juvenile delinquency has caused many local and state governments to give fresh attention to this phase of the law and of the state's redemptive role. The problem has become so vast and at times so unmanageable that we hear chiefly of difficulties rather than of solutions. The agencies of the community in dealing with it are greatly overtaxed. But there is a very general assumption that the state should not only protect society against the young offenders but also reclaim them. Only so can their number be reduced, and there is a strong redemptive concern for the young people themselves.[10]

Protestant theologian with ecumenical influence teaches a doctrine of hopeless future punishment. Theologians disagree as to the possibility of combining a belief in universal salvation with human freedom, but the sentencing of persons at death to hopeless punishment is generally rejected. Hell in some sense may be a necessary consequence of freedom but the love of God extends to whatever Hell there is, seeking to reclaim its inhabitants. The change of theological climate in this matter is quite extraordinary and is more important than particular formulations of changes in doctrine. The gospel warnings against self-righteousness extend to the contrast between Heaven and Hell.

[9] Roscoe Pound, *Interpretations of Legal History* (Macmillan, 1923), pp. 134-135.

[10] Los Angeles has had a program dealing with this problem which in a remarkable way illustrates what I have been saying about the interpenetra-

I have not attempted to estimate the degree to which the positive aspect of the state shows through even its harsher role but it does show through enough to be seen. I have sought only to remind the reader of what he knows already about the state so that it may be brought into the context of this discussion. The state is far more than a restrainer of evil or a maintainer of order. It seeks an order that is just and humane and when it restrains evil, it seeks not only to protect or rescue innocent victims, but also to reclaim the offenders.

---

tion of the punitive and the redemptive factors even in the harsher side of the work of the state. The juvenile court sends youth who have been guilty of serious crimes to "open camps" where they have constructive work to do and where the professional staff focusses on the task of changing the direction of their lives so that they may become good citizens. The penal aspects of this program are minimal and they are not imposed legalistically in proportion to the seriousness of the crime. One report of this program says that it has been remarkably successful in changing the character patterns of the boys who have had this experience: "They were hostile and sullen at first. But as individual counseling took effect, and the community about them overcame its fears of the open institution, the boys visibly changed into self-respecting young men." ("One Answer to Delinquency—Work Camps" by Gertrude Samuels in *New York Times Magazine*, Sept. 8, 1957.) One important feature of this program is that the boys know that they are trusted not to run away. A few do and they are eventually brought back, but the whole effect would be different if their environment were like a prison. This illustration shows vividly how the harsh activities of the state can be modified so that they are the mediators of a wise and sensitive concern for the young offenders as persons.

CHAPTER VI

The Continuing Controversy
over Resistance to Political Authority

THE right to resist an established political authority has been one of the open questions that have divided Christians from the beginning. There is in the New Testament a difference of emphasis which anticipates the problem that was to engage the thought of theologians and of churches in every century, not least our own. Though there are profound theological convictions underlying differences of judgment concerning resistance to political authority, convictions concerning the relation between the providence of God and the authority of the state, and convictions concerning man's own nature and the risks of sinful anarchy if he seeks to take control over his political destiny, there is a very clear interaction between these theological convictions and changing historical situations. There have been instructive changes within the traditions and sometimes the answers which are found within the churches depend upon who was persecuting whom. I believe today there is more agreement on this subject than ever before, partly because churches belonging to all traditions have shared the same experience of being subjected to hostile totalitarian rule.

The general background of thought in the New Testament had created a strong religious and theological inhibition against any kind of political resistance. While the western type of Catholicism has changed its emphasis from time to time depending on whether or not a particular regime was favorable to the Church, there has been a clearer acceptance of the right to resist a tyrannical government on what we may call the ground floor of Roman Catholic theology than is the case with Protestantism.[1] The existence of the papal authority according to which the Pope claimed the right to depose kings and emperors provided a point of reference for thinking about governments that did not exist in the case of Protestant churches which grew up within the modern nation states.

Active political resistance has been very difficult for Lutherans to accept, though in recent years there has been a change because of the experience of National Socialism in Germany and Norway. Luther was himself one of the great revolutionary spirits of all time but for him the source of spiritual oppression was the Church and not the state. In his own historical situation it was natural for him to build up the princes against the power of the emperor and the papacy. He did give permission for Protestant princes to resist the emperor, but his influence has strongly discouraged political resistance to political authority. His own violent denunciations of the peasants who revolted against the princes was in part the result of his desire to keep the Reformation from being associated with the excesses of the sectarians who claimed the support of his principles, but Luther had special abhorrence of anarchy and he was not seriously interested in problems of political justice.

It is hard for me to believe that in another situation, if he had seen a tyrannical political power as the chief enemy of Christian truth and of the Church's freedom, his own revolutionary spirit would not have been on the side of political resistance. This came to be the conviction of many Lutherans in our time as they faced the power of the Nazis. The fact that National Socialism was both a political tyranny and a form of religious idolatry made it natural for the religious re-

[1] H. A. Rommen, *The State in Catholic Thought* (Herder, 1947), pp. 474-475.

sistance which Luther approved in his own time to pass over into political resistance.

During the period of the Nazis there were all shades of conviction among Lutherans in regard to this problem of political resistance. It was easier for Norwegian Lutherans who were dealing with an obvious usurper to decide on political resistance than for German Lutherans to do so, but many of the latter were driven to the same conclusion. Some went so far as to support the attempt to assassinate Hitler and to cooperate with the underground in occupied territory; while others resisted only by a religious witness against the attempts of the Nazis to control the Church and to put the national state in place of God. But all suffered together, and the line between the two forms of resistance was in practice hard to draw. Also, religious resistance had political consequences.

The same differences have appeared in East Germany under the Communist regime. There are those who believe in spiritual resistance against the Communist ideology but draw the line at opposition to the Communist state as such, and there are those who emphasize their rejection of the political tyranny. But so far in East Germany the power of the Russian army and of the neighboring Russian state makes the idea of political resistance irrelevant.

For our purposes it is enough to emphasize the point that Lutheranism has for years been in great ferment over this issue and the result is that there is no longer a solid rejection on Lutheran soil of political resistance to a tyrannical government. One of the major theological forces in Germany itself, even among Lutherans, during the period of the Nazis was Karl Barth who comes from the Calvinist tradition which does not have the same inhibitions against political resistance. Karl Barth became in the 1930's and during the second world war the theological guide for those who were engaged in political resistance against the Nazis and from his base in neutral Switzerland he wrote strong letters to Christians in other nations urging them to fight ardently against the Nazis.[2]

John Calvin himself was very similar to Luther in his opposition to political revolution, but Calvinism became the inspirer of political revolution in many countries—in Scotland, France, Holland, England and, more indirectly, in America.

Calvin used very strong language in demanding submission to tyrants. His doctrine of divine providence ruled out any kind of active political resistance to established government. Yet he did leave a famous loophole in the last chapter of his *Institutes* for the possibility of resistance by lower political authorities to higher authorities.[3] This paralleled Luther's permission for Protestant princes to resist the emperor. Within the lifetime of Calvin, without clear encouragement from him, Calvinists took advantage of this loophole. The right of revolution was theologically supported by John Knox and others and finally we find Calvinism becoming as different as possible from Lutheranism in its encouragement of political revolution. Calvinism became open-ended toward influences from democratic Christian sects and, especially in seventeenth-century England, it developed into the very fluid Puritan movement which was the major seedbed of modern Anglo-Saxon democracy. The arguments of Calvinists in favor of revolution merged with secular doctrines of social contract and natural law which became the intellectual support of the right of the people to revolt against rulers who had broken the contract or who had defied the

---

[2] As examples of different shades of Lutheran opinion see E. Berggrav, *Man and State* (Muhlenberg Press, 1951), pp. 300-319; N. H. Søe, *Christliche Ethik* (Kaiser Verlag, Munich, 1949), pp. 355-356; Werner Elert, *The Christian Ethos* (Muhlenberg Press, 1957), pp. 122-123. Professor Elert seems to deny the right of active resistance but he allows for the following situation which provides a loophole that fitted the last stages of the Nazi regime: ". . . citizens are no longer subject to a public order which the rulers themselves have ravaged. The broken order must be replaced by a new order. *If the incumbents are unwilling to make room it becomes imperative to remove them by force.*" (Italics mine.)

[3] *Institutes of the Christian Religion*, Bk. IV, Chap. XX, par. XXXII.

natural law of justice. On this, as on many other issues, contemporary Calvinism and contemporary Lutheranism are in continuous conversation and we can expect that rapidly changing historical circumstances and mutual theological influence will overcome many of the differences between them.

Before leaving this discussion of political revolution, I want to put it in the context of the continuous warning against anarchy in the Christian tradition. A good case can be made for the position that any government is better than anarchy. It is difficult for Americans who have never had the experience to realize what it is like when there is no acceptance of any political authority and a society stumbles from tyranny through anarchy to another tyranny. A minimum of order is a precondition of life itself.[4]

Many of the activities of the most perverse government are the means of providing the necessities of life in a compli-

---

[4] There is a vivid passage by Lord Macaulay that describes the day of anarchy after James II had abandoned London and before Willam III had established his power. "Legitimate authority there was none. All those evil passions which it is the office of government to restrain, and which the best governments restrain but imperfectly, were on a sudden emancipated from control: avarice, licentiousness, revenge, the hatred of sect to sect, the hatred of nation to nation. On such occasions it will ever be found that the human vermin which, neglected by ministers of state and religion, barbarous in the midst of civilization, heathen in the midst of Christianity, burrows among all physical and moral pollution, in the cellars and garrets of great cities, will at once rise into a terrible importance. So it was now in London. When the night, the longest night, as it chanced, of the year, approached, forth came from every den of vice, from the bear garden at Hockley, and from the labyrinth of the tippling houses and brothels in the Friars, thousands of house-breakers and highwaymen, cutpurses and ringdroppers. With these were mingled thousands of idle apprentices, who wished merely for the excitement of a riot. Even men of peaceable and honest habits were impelled by religious animosity to join the lawless part of the population. For the cry of No Popery, a cry which has more than once endangered the existence of London, was the signal of outrage and rapine." *The History of England* (Dutton, Everyman's Library Edition, Vol. II, p. 131). This was long ago and London is not one of the places where it is likely to recur, but there is something universal about the three groups mentioned: the criminals, the seekers after excitement, and the normally sane citizens who hunt a scapegoat.

cated society for all citizens, the food and fuel and water, the means of communication and transportation. Because of this, so long as a tyrannical government is in power, it is possible to distinguish between its activities which still belong to the providential ordering of life and the activities which are oppressive and even demonic. This contrast was well expressed in a prayer of the Dutch churches under the occupation of the Nazis for the Queen (who was then in London) whom "God had set over them" and the occupation authorities whom "God had permitted over them."[5] This contrast does not mean that there should be no active political resistance but it helps us to see what is at stake.

The breakdown of order usually favors the effort to reestablish order, even though it may be a tyrannical regime, much more than it favors liberty. Professor Heimann says that "men cannot live, in the sense of physical existence, without order for a single day, while they can live, if need be, without freedom for a long time. That is why in a conflict between the two needs, when order and freedom appear irreconcilable, order is sure to win out and to suppress freedom."[6]

Christians with their realistic understanding of sin, of the moral anarchy that is not far below the surface of our life have often stressed the danger of disorder more than the danger of oppression and injustice and have created strong inhibitions against revolution. We can still say that it would be irresponsible for Christians to engage in a political revolt against the existing order unless there is hope of establishing another order. Both civil disobedience to a particular law or act of government with the acceptance of the consequences and non-political religious resistance to the order as such are quite different from a political revolution and may be required even though, humanly speaking, the cause is hopeless. Non-violent resistance

[5] International Church Press and Information Service, Geneva, February 1941.

[6] *Freedom and Order* (Scribners, 1947), p. 10.

is usually more prudent and more likely to be effective than violent resistance though any absolutistic judgment here depends upon the pacifist issue which will be discussed in another context.

In countries where democratic institutions provide methods of orderly change this discussion of political resistance has little relevance. There may be, as I have said, occasions for loyal civil disobedience on a concrete issue, but the democratic processes themselves are the best means of defending the rights of the people against the administrators of the state and of overcoming the more serious forms of injustice. It is certainly one of the chief advantages of democracy that it provides for its own correction by constitutional processes. Respect for these processes is itself a part of Christian responsibility, and it is one of the modern equivalents of the obedience to authorities which is enjoined in the New Testament.

CHAPTER VII

Society and the Limited State

CHRISTIAN thinking about the state must insist that it be a limited instrument of society and not in fact or in intention the all-inclusive or all-controlling social reality. Bitter experience of the totalitarian state which seeks to control all phases of society in the interests of an official ideology makes clear the need of limiting in our theory of the state the claims that it should make and the range of its activity.

The absolute state with its claim to be the source of truth, the determiner of the purposes of society, and the judge of culture is an enemy of Christ in every age. It must either deny God's existence or seek to make him over into its own image; it must either seek to destroy the Church or domesticate it for its own purposes. The modern totalitarian state differs from earlier tyrannies in part because technology has given it such efficient instruments for controlling society. There is no need here to argue against totalitarianism, but it is important to emphasize the distinction in thought between state and society for this is an essential line of defense against totalitarian thinking.

In what follows I shall use the word "society" for the most comprehensive social reality. I shall not distinguish between society and community. There are complications concerning the meaning of the words "nation" and "nationality" which could take us far afield, but for our purposes the nation will be regarded as that unit of society or community which occupies a defined territory, which is held together by a common tradition and common sense of destiny, and which is under the laws and political supervision of a particular state.

Christians have an essential clue to the fact that the state is not identical with society because the Church is a social institution and a form of community which must by its very nature distinguish itself from the state. It is quite true that historical contingencies have led to very close ties between branches of the Church and particular states but the Churches know today that such ties are unacceptable unless they are compatible with the freedom of the Church from control by the state. Freedom of the state from control by the Church is also important but it is now a major problem in only a few countries.

In addition to the distinction between the state and society, it is important to recognize that within society itself there are many social groups or institutions which have their own inner life, their own criteria, and their relationships which extend beyond the national community. Again the Church knows this to be true because it is a prime example. Some social groups or institutions may have to defend themselves against control by both the Church and the state. Freedom within the national community comes in large part because of the sheer pressure for independence of the interests and vitalities of these social groups or institutions. The freedom of the individual person comes in large part because he belongs to several groups and his commitments and loyalties are not bounded by any one of them or by the whole national community. He is no creature of the state and he is owned by no human group whatever. If he is a Christian, he knows this clearly and his membership in the Church means that he is aware that he belongs to a universal human community of which Christ is Lord. This reminds him continually that he is owned by no state.

One of the reports from the Evanston Assembly of the

World Council of Churches emphasized the existence of forms of association other than the state. It said: "Forms of association within society which have their own foundations and principles should be respected, and not controlled in their inner life by the state. Churches, families, and universities are dissimilar examples of this non-political type of association."[1]

Two books have been written on this subject within a generation by two theologians who have been Primates of state churches and who have had cause to do much thinking about the state, Archbishop William Temple and Bishop Eivind Berggrav, and both have presented much the same view of the limits of the state in relation to society. Temple during his early career had been a crusader for the freedom of the Church of England to make its own decisions as a Church without eliminating the tie with the state and Berggrav was the leader of a Church that was driven by events to resist the government of an invader and usurper. His book was actually written when he was in the custody of the police.

Temple emphasizes the role of non-political associations but even more he stresses the universal human interests—which have their associations—which lie outside the sphere of state control. He writes: "Moreover, though man is essentially social, he is not merely social; still less is he merely political. He is also a seeker after knowledge, a creator and lover of beauty, a worshipper of God. If the State forbids him to pursue knowledge or prescribes the manner of his pursuit of it— if, for example, it forbids him to seek biological truth, or orders him to seek it only in the Bible (refers to Scopes' trial) it is going beyond its true function; to refuse obedience in such a case is not only permissible, but it is a duty both to truth and to the community. Such action on the part of the State is destructive of a whole sphere of values which the community

[1] See Report of Section III of the Evanston Assembly.

should become increasingly to enjoy. It is in the same way a duty to resist any effort of the State to control aesthetic creation and appreciation." He goes on to say that "most of all is the authority of the State out of place in determining how men shall worship God."[2] He is not opposed to a close tie between the Church and the state if the state will give to the Church its essential liberty. Temple emphasizes throughout his discussion that when the State seeks to control these interests which are inherently non-political and outside its sphere, it impoverishes the "common life which it exists to preserve and to foster."[3]

Bishop Berggrav has exactly the same concern. He is inclined to move back and forth with some lack of discrimination between the relative autonomy of the units of a federal state and the interests which lie outside the sphere of the state. His whole book puts great emphasis on the principle of federalism and he is much influenced in this by American experience. He naturally is seeking a basis for criticising the totalitarian state; he is also seeking an alternative form of social authority which will have its roots in the conscience of the community which no state can create; he desires to emphasize the "vital energies" which are essential for a healthy society but which have non-political sources. He says in summary: "In all of this, however, the state can only be an external, a regulating and ministering, factor, like the ordnance department of an army. Even if the state on its part declared itself obliged to take an interest in those values which are related to the sanctity of law, freedom of conviction, and freedom of worship, for example; this would not make the state part owner, still less, the final authority, in the creative life of these vitally important, key factors."[4]

[2] *Christianity and the State* (Macmillan, London and New York, 1929), p. 125.
[3] *Ibid.*, p. 126.
[4] *Man and State* (Muhlenberg Press, 1951), p. 107.

I have quoted Professor Brunner as one who represents a one-sidedly negative view of the state, but I think that his thought is best understood in connection with his desire to limit the range of the state's authority and functions. His conception of the "orders of creation" which is open to criticism in other contexts as favoring too static a view of social institutions provides strong support for their priority to the state and their basic independence of the state. He says: "The Creator has not created the family, nor the economic order, nor culture as a member of the state. All these divine orders of creation precede the State, and have a relative independent aim, which is not primarily bound to the State."[5] He is deeply opposed not only to totalitarianism, but to the Idealistic view of the state which he regards as totalitarian in the implications of its theory and to the Aristotelian identification of the State with the *polis* in all of its life and to the tendencies toward the welfare state in western democracies.[6] He concludes his discussion of the nature of the state with the slogan: "Away from the culture State! Back to the Law State! Back to the independence of autonomous group forms."[7]

There is a close correspondence in theory between this Protestant thinking about the state and society and Roman Catholic political theory. In fact, if Protestants will read Roman Catholic political theory as political theory and forget for a moment that it seems designed to exalt the Church in relation to the state, they may learn much from it!

Roman Catholic thought has always stressed a dual conception of society. It has always seen that society is organized around two centers—Church and State, or pope and emperor, or altar and throne. It has always emphasized "the two swords" which were symbols of quite different kinds of authority and function. When this dualism was overlaid by

[5] *The Divine Imperative* (Westminster Press, 1943), p. 458.
[6] *Ibid.*
[7] *Ibid.*, p. 459.

a monistic outlook in the west, in contrast to the east, this meant a tendency for the Church or the Papacy to dominate the political as well as the religious life of society, but states have usually been able to protect themselves against this encroachment and the dualism that expressed the normative Catholic theory has reappeared.

The Catholic theory also protects the family and institutions of culture and economic life against the absolute state. Catholic theory is sometimes confused by its use of Aristotle who identified the state with the "polis." The curious phrase used of the state, "a perfect society," on the surface suggests a close identification of the state with man's social life as a whole. This phrase is intended to mean, not moral perfection, but a certain completeness and self-sufficiency in the temporal order which it is difficult to reconcile with Catholic emphasis upon the non-political associations in that order. It does safeguard the idea that the state is superior to all other secular groups or institutions as the guardian of the temporal common good.

Pope Pius XI in his encyclical "Quadragesimo Anno" emphasized the importance of respecting what he called the "smaller and lower communities." He said: "Just as it is wrong to take away from individuals what by their own ability and effort they can accomplish and commit it to the community, so it is an injury and at the same time both a serious evil and a perturbation of right order to assign to a larger and higher society what can be performed successfully by smaller and lower communities."[8] Catholic social philosophy calls this emphasis the principle of "subsidiarity." The use of such a technical word may help to preserve awareness of the reality to which it refers.

I shall discuss briefly three Roman Catholic thinkers who do not necessarily represent the universal mind of the Church,

[8] *Social Wellsprings*, (Bruce, 1942), pp. 206-7. (Ed., J. Husslein, S. J.)

but who between them have very great influence, each coming from a different national tradition: H. A. Rommen, Jacques Maritain, and John Courtney Murray.

Rommen sees the family and the state as the two "natural societies." Neither can assume the functions of the other and both are divinely ordained for the sake of their true ends. "Now the end of the family is the propagation of the human race, the mutual completion of husband and wife, the care for their children and their education."[9] The end of the state is "the common good: the enactment of an order of tranquillity, justice, and peace among the families, the persons, and their many social institutions and associations for individual and group welfare and interests."[10] There are between the family and the state various intermediate organizations and they are "in their nature self-governing." These include "economic enterprises, professional groups, institutions of learning." All of these are "partial and represent merely partial goods, not the common good."[11] It is in this context that we see the meaning of the phrase "perfect society" as applied to the state because it alone has as its end the "common good." This phrase is certainly misleading as Rommen himself uses it because the state does not exercise full authority within the family or within the intermediate associations.

The state provides a protective order under which all of the non-political associations and institutions function together. It "makes order and freedom possible for them; it strives that none of the endeavors of human social nature prevail hypertrophically over the others, but that they all grow as balanced parts of a well-organized order in unity."[12] Rommen is very clear about the need of preserving the independent inner life

[9] *The State in Catholic Thought* (Herder, 1947), p. 269. Prof. Rommen is an exile from Germany who now is a Professor at Georgetown University.
[10] *Ibid.*, p. 270.
[11] *Ibid.*, p. 269.
[12] *Ibid.*, p. 253.

of all these associations and institutions. He says that they are the source of creativity. He says that the state is not creative but that "individual persons, in their free associations and in their group life are creative."[13] He then says that "the state is a universe whose constituents, without sacrificing their individuality, achieve the common good."[14]

Rommen provides all of the materials for a view of the Church and society which emphasizes the limitation of the state and the inner independence of the non-political associations but he allows his language to blur the distinctions. This is not only true of such traditional technical phrases as "the perfect society" but also of less careful language as when he says that the state is a "universe whose constituent parts, without sacrificing their individuality, achieve the common good."[15] This suggests that the state is the whole and that all other associations are parts of it, but he clearly does not mean that.

A purely descriptive statement of the Church as one social entity among others (however much from the inside the Church has theological meaning that belongs to no other social entity) should suggest a stronger doctrine of non-political society than Rommen gives us. For him, all that is involved in this discussion is the arrangement of "natural" societies whereas the Church is a "supernatural" society. A Protestant student of society does not make the sharp distinction between the natural and the supernatural and he does not find the social structure of the Church to be as different from the social structure of so-called natural institutions as the Catholic assumes it to be. He thus finds in the Church the major example in western history of the non-political association which helps him to understand the others.

Jacques Maritain offers a much richer and more flexible

13 *Ibid.*
14 *Ibid.*
15 *Ibid.*, p. 253.

view of the pluralistic character of society. He even accepts the term, "pluralism," and associates himself with some surprise on his part with the earlier pluralistic writings of Harold Laski.[16] His analysis as a whole, with its distinctions between nation, political society, and state, is too complicated to summarize here. He uses "community" as the broadest social term for something that is naturally given. In contrast, "society" is in part the product of human freedom; it is shaped by men; it involves social relations which "proceed from a given initiative, a given idea, and the voluntary determination of human persons." "Political society" is the phrase which covers what I have meant by "society" in my previous discussion. The state is an aspect of political society. Maritain uses the phrase "perfect society" as applied to the "political society" and not to the state. The political society includes within itself "the family units" and "a multiplicity of other particular societies which proceed from the free initiative of citizens and should be as autonomous as possible."[17] I have some difficulty with this because he says that the essential rights and freedoms of the family are anterior to the political society. This use by Maritain of the term "political" for this inclusive society must be his way of retaining continuity with Aristotle, but his distinction between political society and state enables him to gain independence of the limitations of Aristotle and to do justice, not only to Christian insight but also to the actual pluralism of more complex societies than the Greek city state. Maritain emphasizes the idea that the political society depends upon the non-political interests of citizens. He says: "Family, economic, cultural, educational, religious life matter as much as does political life to the very existence and prosperity of the body politic."[18] ("The body politic" is the equivalent of "the political society.")

[16] *Man and the State* (University of Chicago Press, 1951), pp. 22-23.
[17] *Ibid.*, p. 11.
[18] *Ibid.*

The state is only a part of the political society. It is the part which "specializes in the interests of the whole." It is the part that is concerned with "the maintenance of law, the promotion of the common welfare and public order, and the administration of public affairs."[19] The most radical element in Maritain's discussion in relation to traditional European political philosophy since the sixteenth century is his insistence that the state is not even the "head" of the political society. It is an *instrument* of the political society as a whole. He combines this idea here as elsewhere in his writings with a very strongly democratic conception of the state. He opposes all absolute conceptions of the state, both those associated with the individual ruler who represents the whole and those which find in the democratic state any body, such as parliament, which in its sovereignty represents the whole. The state and all of its organs are but instruments of the whole and they are to be measured not by their power or their prestige which are sought for their own sake, but by their service to the human person, to justice in social relationships, and to the growth of freedom in the intellectual and cultural life.

It seems to me that Maritain's view of the state can become common property of Catholics and Protestants. It developed on French soil where democracy had the heritage of the French Revolution which was unfavorable to the kind of social pluralism which Maritain represents. He presents a conception of the democratic state which proves to be more consistent with Anglo-Saxon than with French experience and better able than political ideas based upon French experience to be appropriated by Christian thought, Catholic or Protestant.

Father John Courtney Murray is the very able and influential American Jesuit scholar who has made it his vocation to rethink Catholic political theory in the light of American political experience with special reference to the relations between

[19] *Ibid.*, p. 12.

Church and State. I shall discuss his thought again in that context. Father Murray holds a position which is very similar to that of Maritain but he has not developed it so systematically. His writings have taken the form of commentaries on major episodes in the development of Catholic thought and he exercises to the limit Catholic freedom to play off one tendency in the tradition against another. Much of his work has been to distinguish what is permanent from what is conditioned by late nineteenth-century European situations in the encyclicals of Pope Leo XIII. In that context he sets forth with great force the congruity between the Anglo-American political tradition in contrast to dominant Continental ideas of democracy and of the state and what he finds to be essential rather than historically relative in the political thought of Leo XIII.

He says that for us (that is for Anglo-Americans) "the state is not identically 'the perfect society,' nor the community, nor the nation, nor the people, though it touches all these things as an aspect of them. For us the state is a legal association for limited purposes." He says that the purposes of the state are defined by law and that "they are confined to such purposes as can be achieved by law. . . . It is society under the aspect of its organization for limited action under legal rules."[20]

He finds that this distinction between the state and society was strong in the Middle Ages and he sees it as especially characteristic of Anglo-American experience as contrasted with the "later absolutist Continental tradition."[21] He is referring here not only to absolute monarchs, but to democracies based upon the identification of national society with the state as a unitary sovereign power. He believes that Leo XIII was writing within the European framework, that this Anglo-American experience was "foreign to the experience of the papacy."[22] His reasons for emphasizing this conclusion is that it enables

[20] *Theological Studies*, March 1953, pp. 20-21.
[21] *Ibid.*
[22] *Ibid.*

him to show that the Papal strictures on ideas of liberalism and democracy do not apply to this conception of the limited state. Father Murray believes that the Anglo-American type of limited state with all of its emphasis upon religious freedom provides the kind of place for the Roman Catholic Church within society which is most suitable for its freedom. These aspects of Father Murray's political thinking can also become common property of Catholics and Protestants.

Where does this discussion leave us? I think that there is a remarkable agreement between all the thinkers whom I have cited, Protestant and Catholic. This agreement is in line with those types of political theory which are pluralistic in the sense that they emphasize the difference between the state and society and the importance of the various non-political associations in society, which emphasize the essential limits of the state. The state in this context of thought is regarded as having the authority and power to use force under law, but this would not generally be regarded as the essence of the state. The state is unlike all other institutions in that it makes law (the ways in which the state may also be under law will be discussed in a later chapter) and in doing so supervises the society as a whole for the sake of the common good, but it does not seek to control all aspects of society. The state is unlike other institutions in that it has jurisdiction over the whole of a particular territory and so no person or group can choose to live outside its sphere. It is becoming increasingly difficult to choose to live under another state than the one under which a person is born, and it is necessary to live under some state. This non-voluntary character of the state distinguishes it from all other social institutions.

The state's monopoly of force and the state's responsibility for the common good do mean that it must at times show itself to be the dominant factor in the national community. There are some decisions which it alone can make and they must be binding on the community as a whole, but these decisions are made for the sake of the community and they should still be limited in the areas of life which they touch. The state is as indispensable as it should be limited. The state is the instrument of the community rather than the grandiose power for which the community exists, no matter how much in times of crisis the state must call attention to its authority and power. We cannot say too often that the state exists for man and not man for the state.[23]

As an illustration of the way in which the state should be limited, I shall refer to its relationship to the university as an example of a non-political association. I shall consider first the state university which raises its peculiar problems. The state may provide the funds for the construction of university buildings and for the support of its academic program. It may decide that in one university center there be concentration on some subjects rather than others in the curriculum. It may have much to say about the external form of administration in the university. It may apply some standards of proficiency. So far it may go without destroying the inner life of the university, but it may not go much farther. It may not determine the content of the actual disciplines that are taught. It must give full academic freedom to the teacher within the area of his competence. It must not interfere with the broader intellectual freedom of the academic community, of both faculty and students. The academic community as such may make some distinctions between responsible and irresponsible use of freedom by its members, but the moment the state touches this problem it almost invariably over-reaches itself and the very threat of its doing so injures the spirit within the academic community. If individual teachers or students break laws of

[23] I think that I owe most in this discussion to the thought of Professor MacIver and Lord Lindsay, especially the former's *The Modern State* and the latter's *The Modern Democratic State*, but I have not attempted to interpret the thought of either of them.

the state that are binding on all citizens, that is another matter, but an academic community should act as a watchman for the society as a whole to warn it against laws that are intended to control the mind whether they have this general application or not.

It is desirable not only to distinguish between the academic community and the state, but also to distinguish between the particular organs of the state that affect the university and other organs of the state. In some American states the Boards of Regents have long terms which have nothing to do with the normal rhythms of politics and this enables them to develop their own ethos as related to an academic institution. The regular yearly appropriations of funds by legislatures provide an opportunity for political control that does interfere with the independence af the university. The British government which now subsidizes all British universities heavily has a procedure which protects the freedom of the universities as much as is possible in the case of any governmental device. Parliament votes its grants in a lump sum for all the universities. This money is passed, not by the Ministry of Education, but by the Chancellor of the Exchequer himself to a University Grants Committee made up entirely of academic people. All allocation of funds is the responsibility of that committee. The British have a sensitivity to the needs of institutions, that the state touches, to have their own inner freedom and vitality which no constitutional schemes can create. This is a fine example of how it is possible for the power of government to be self-limited, though such self-limitation doubtless depends in the long run partly on the alertness of the academic community in regard to everything that affects its freedom.

This discussion of state universities needs to be balanced by the recognition of the role of private universities and colleges. Their existence is of great importance in providing an independent yardstick for academic achievement and for the freedom of an academic community. They often have their own problems of freedom which come from pressures from the community, sometimes from their own alumni and from their private benefactors. But the private academic institutions which have developed traditions of independence have great influence among us and they greatly strengthen the forces working for independence in less favored private or public institutions. Pluralism within the academic community is an important protection for the academic community as a whole as against both the state and the pressures of public opinion and of private interests.

I have dealt with the university as an example of an institution that has its own standards and purposes, its own inner life which the state should not seek to control. Later I shall discuss at greater length the inner freedom of the Church. A nation that has within it free churches and free universities (with universities free from ecclesiastical control) is likely to preserve other forms of spiritual and cultural freedom.

The limited state can be seen in the context of the distinction between the state and society with its various groups and institutions, but it can also be seen in the structure of the state itself where provision is made for checks on the various centers of its power. Federal structures, the safe-guarding of the role of local government, the checks and balances within government are ways of protecting society against the all-powerful state. Federal structures enable a state to take seriously the varying needs and desires of different regions and they are also a safeguard against the abuses of extremely centralized power. Federalism remains problematic in the sense that it is difficult to preserve the reality of it when the national state inevitably gathers to itself preponderant initiative and power but its preservation is of great importance.

Both federalism and checks and balances within government at various levels take account of human realities which lie behind Christian teaching concerning the depth and pervasiveness of sin. These realities were understood by the American founders who were influenced by Calvinism. In one of the *Federalist Papers* written by James Madison[24] the general point about distributing power among many is well made:

"The genius of republican liberty seems to demand on one side, not only that all power should be derived from the people, but that those intrusted with it should be kept in dependence on the people, by a short duration of their appointments; and that even during this short period the trust should be placed not in a few, but in a number of hands."

John Calvin himself set forth this same position when he wrote:

"The vice or imperfection of men therefore renders it safer and more tolerable for the government to be in the hands of many, that they may afford each other mutual assistance and admonition, and that if any one arrogate to himself more than is right, the many may act as censors and masters to restrain his ambition."[25]

The idea of balancing power in government, which is as old as political theory as a self-conscious activity, has been elaborately embodied in the government of the United States under the influence of Montesquieu and it can hardly be said that the results have been wholly favorable. The conflicts between the executive and the legislative branches make for stalemates and weak government and some re-organization of the American scheme of government at that point might be an advantage, but this is not likely to occur in the foreseeable future. I was interested in the comment of a very sympathetic observer of American institutions, William Temple, who wrote of Montesquieu's "celebrated mistake about the British Constitution by which he imposed upon the United States the

[24] No. 37.
[25] *Institutes*, Bk. IV, Chap. XX, Par. VIII.

disastrous exclusion of Executive Ministers from Congress."[26] We have various substitutes for this such as the long hours which the members of the Cabinet spend with Congressional committees and also the press conferences which enable the executive branch to be put on the spot in public. But it seems quite clear that the precise balancing of power in the American system is not to be universally recommended.

Far more significant than the separation of the executive and the legislative branches of government is the independent judiciary. Professor McIlwain distinguishes sharply between the separation of powers and the legal limitation of government which depends upon the independence of the judges from immediate political control. He warns that "never in recorded history has the individual been in greater danger from government than now" and he emphasizes that the law is the essential protection against this danger. He says: "And the one institution above all others essential to the preservation of the law has always been and still is an honest, able, learned, independent judiciary."[27] The judiciary is a check on both of the other branches of government in the American system. Judicial review of legislation is dependent upon a written constitution and is not essential to the preservation of law as British experience proves, but I do not see how a written constitution could be preserved without it. In any case, the absence of any judicial check on a legislature presupposes great maturity and restraint on the part of the legislature.

Justice Benjamin Cardozo makes the point that the value of judicial review is "not to be measured by counting the occasions of its exercise." He says that "by conscious or subconscious influence, the presence of this restraining power, aloof in the background, but none the less always in reserve, tends to stabilize

[26] *Op. cit.*, p. 77.
[27] *Constitutionalism: Ancient and Modern* (Cornell University Press, 1940), pp. 140-141.

and rationalize the legislative judgment, to infuse it with the glow of principle, to hold the standard aloft for those who must run the race and keep the faith."[28]

Judicial check upon the executive branch and especially on all law enforcement agencies is necessary to all free government. In the early 1950's the American people lived through a period of public hysteria to which both Congress and the Executive were too responsive. The courts have proved again and again that they could rise above the hysteria and they have protected individuals frequently against rulings of executive departments, against over-eager prosecutors, against Congressional committees and often in resounding statements they have helped to maintain the best in the constitutional tradition.

Courts also can produce stalemates and their independence should not be absolute in relation to legislation. The saying that the Supreme Court follows the election returns puts in an extreme and undignified way an important truth. If the Supreme Court had not changed its direction in regard to economic legislation in the mid-thirties under the leadership of Chief Justice Hughes, even before there was a change of personnel on the Court, it is difficult to imagine the catastrophes that might have come because of the inability of the government to act effectively in dealing with the problems of the depression. A majority of the Court had been guided by a doctrinaire individualism which they read into constitutional law. The dissenting opinions of Holmes and Brandeis and others had prepared the way for the change. Years before, in 1905, Justice Holmes had in his famous dissent in *Lochner v. New York* accused the majority of the Court of reading Herbert Spencer's individualism expressed in his *Social Statics* into the Fourteenth Amendment because they had ruled against a law of the State of New York which provided for a ten-hour day and a sixty-hour

[28] *The Nature of the Judicial Process* (Yale University Press, 1921), pp. 92-93.

week for bakery workers. The change of the Court was very gradual and yet there was the decisive moment in the 1930's when the minority became the majority and the legislation associated with the New Deal became possible. The principle of giving the benefit of the doubt to the legislature enables the Court to avoid the kind of obstructionism that can make the government too weak to deal with grave national problems.

Another protection against the centralization of power in the state is the emphasis upon the special functions and the relative independence of local and regional units. Technological unification of the national community makes it difficult to defend the relative independence of units of government other than the national government, but that is all the more reason for emphasizing the importance of doing so. The line of least resistance is to leave things to the unit of government with most resources and with the broadest jurisdiction.

In this country we usually state this problem in terms of "states' rights." It is unfortunate that as a slogan this is used most often among us to prevent the most effective unit of government from doing something that should be done. It was used to seal off parts of the country against interference with slavery. It is used now to hamper interference with racial segregation. It has been used for generations to prevent the enactment of social legislation that would be effective anywhere and to forestall it entirely in the states where the less privileged social groups are not well organized politically to improve their conditions of life. This unfortunate use of "states' rights" as a shield for narrow and often reactionary interests should not obscure the value of encouraging the initiative and the limited independence of the states. It has often been said that it is a great advantage to have forty-eight laboratories in which social and governmental experiments can be tried. There are obvious advantages in having so many people participating in government on many levels. There is a better chance to relate governmental decisions to the varying needs of each region. Above all, the distribution of power as between the federal government and the states is a form of limitation upon each center of political power and as such it deserves strong defence. The resolution to defend it should be combined with much openness and discrimination as we approach the many difficult issues of competing jurisdictions.

NOTE

ON THE LOCATION OF "SOVEREIGNTY"

One of the major problems of political theory related to this chapter is the location of sovereignty as the source of final decision in society. The idea of an absolute unitary sovereign—whether it be a monarch or a body of men—has been taken for granted in much political thinking since the sixteenth century and was expressed in somewhat different ways in the thought of Thomas Hobbes, Jean Bodin, and John Austin. In democratic societies the idea of an absolute distinction between sovereign and subjects, between those who command and those who are commanded, no longer holds. The federal structure of the state does not fit this idea of absolute unitary sovereignty. There must be a source of final decision, but this is not always located in the same place. Different agencies of government make the final decision about different problems. In the United States the issue of sovereignty is especially complicated because the constitution interpreted by the Supreme Court limits the sovereignty of Congress. In a sense, the sovereignty is in the people as a whole, but the people are under a constitution which they can amend only with difficulty. The people organized to choose their representatives for the amending process are likely to get quite different results than when organized for other purposes. Moreover, different results can be expected because of timing or because of electoral procedure in the choice of the President, the House of Representatives, and the Senate. The Supreme Court which often in practice does have the last word is chosen by a still different method and the timing again is different. By these means, Leviathan is indeed much curbed and the result would be complete stalemate and confusion if those chosen by the people by whatever process and at whatever time did not respond to the same events and take note of the most recent election returns.

CHAPTER VIII

The Law of the State and the State Under Law

IT IS more than usually precarious for one who is not trained in
the law to write about it even briefly. However, theology and
law have this in common: both are always mixing in everyone's
business and not least in each others. In earlier societies religion
and law were one. In most of the history of "Christendom" the
lawmakers and the theologians had the same general outlook
concerning the ultimate criteria of the law and concerning the
relation between law and ethics and between law and theology.
The Church inherited and enriched the classical conceptions
of natural law and shared with jurists the responsibility to interpret their meaning for the positive law of the state.

The Reformation did not change the Church's assumption
that the law of the state should give expression to the law of
God. Luther and Calvin were as sure as their predecessors as to
what the law of God was and as to the conviction that it was
binding on the state. Luther separated more than Calvin did
the law of God for the state from the more distinctively Christian law or the law that was influenced by the Gospel, but it
would not have occurred to him to allow the law of the state
to become a secular positive law uncontrolled by the divine law.
The whole modern period has been a period of the loosening
of the relationship between the law of the state and the law of
God. The development has not been uniform and the natural
law which originally was regarded as the divine law often maintained itself without necessary reference to its divine sanction,

and theorists who did most to secularize the law and the state often continued to do lip service to God, to the Christian tradition and to the Church.

It is significant that the United States was founded on the basis of a higher law above the law of the state and this higher law was equated with the law of God, vaguely so under Deistic influence and more clearly so in the context of Revelation where the Puritan influence remained strong. Much American legal thinking has lost both this reference to the higher law of God and even to the higher law tradition itself, but these remain in the national consciousness and in the minds of legislators and jurists even when legal theory has sought to free the law from them. The higher law is embodied in American Constitutional law to an important extent and thus its influence remains strong regardless of changes in theory.

Catholic teaching emphasizes the natural law as the criterion of all positive law and as being itself the law of God, known to the reason and confirmed by revelation. Catholic theologians and legal thinkers do differ among themselves on the question as to how much the natural law should be enacted into positive law. One may know what the natural law is and yet hesitate to ask the state to enforce all of its precepts. The relating of the natural law to the actual legislation of states should be governed by "'prudence" and since the practice of this virtue is open to both Catholics and non-Catholics there is often considerable agreement in practice between Catholics and their fellow citizens even though they may differ profoundly in their premises concerning the relationship between God, the natural law and the postive law. Also, the positive law, enacted by a legitimate political authority, has very great practical authority with Catholics and even differences between such enactments and the natural law do not interfere with the duty to obey the law except in extreme cases. Not obedience or disobedience to positive law is as much involved in the Catholic emphasis upon the Church's knowledge of law as the conscience of citizen, legislator and jurist in the making of the law.

Protestant thinking about the law and about its relation to the law of God, to the natural law or to standards of justice above the positive law is confused or non-existent. Protestants, unlike Catholics, have no common tradition about the natural law which might be relevant to the discussion. They are no more moral relativists in their ultimate outlook than Catholics and they take for granted that there is a difference between just and unjust laws, that in some sense the law of the state is under the divine judgment. But it is difficult for Protestants to find a structure of thought into which all of these convictions can be fitted.

Protestants have been troubled by the conception of the natural law for two reasons which strengthen each other. The first is that they do not have the rationalistic confidence that the natural law is universally known without such knowledge being seriously distorted by human sin and finiteness. The law of God is objectively real and it is made clear by revelation, but man's natural knowledge of it is, to say the least, problematic. There are endless variations among Protestants as to how significant the natural knowledge of the law is and how far it needs correction or clarification by revelation.

The second reason for the Protestant difficulty with natural law is the tendency to rigidity in the way it is applied. It does not make room for the endless variation in human situations, for the dynamic nature of history. In the context of Roman Catholic thought this rigidity is seen in its most extreme form in Catholic teaching about birth control and about medical ethics. But there is also a tendency to absolutize the type of mediaeval society in which the Church was most at home. In quite another context ideas of natural law became frozen in the western legal tradition in terms of a one-sided individualism. This was a very great handicap to the American courts as they dealt with the problems of industrial society.

The modern experience of totalitarianism has made it more urgent to emphasize criteria of justice above the law of the state. Professor Brunner is certainly right when he says: "But if there is no sacred, eternal, divine, absolute law, there is no possibility of denouncing any form of law or polity or national act as unjust. If the positivistic theory of law is right, there is no possibility of waging war against the totalitarian state as a monster of injustice."[1] The adjectives "sacred," "eternal," "absolute" are all suitable words so long as they are not applied too easily to the content of the law! Professor Brunner shares the Protestant sense of difficulty about the natural law and indeed is doubtful about the use of the phrase, but his whole book is an effort to give a more adequate substance to the ultimate criteria of justice that ideas about natural law have been intended to express. There is a delicate balance in this book by Professor Brunner between the strong affirmation of the ultimate law against the kind of moral and legal relativism that has prepared the way for totalitarianism, an affirmation which tends toward the moral rigidity against which that relativism has been at times a justified protest on the one hand, and, on the other, the recognition of the dynamic and variable elements in all applications of the law to human life.

Legal thinking since the eighteenth century has moved far away from the earlier confidence in natural law. It has been preoccupied much of the time with the history of law and has attempted to find the sanction for and the content of law in the developing custom of the various nations. This has often been related, especially in Germany, to a Romantic tendency to magnify the uniqueness of different historical configurations, and to play down the universal structures which are supported by universal rational convictions.

More significant for American legal thinking has been the work of the "analytical" jurists who have emphasized the positive law which gets its sanction because it was promulgated or

[1] *Justice and the Social Order* (Harper, 1945), p. 8.

enacted by the sovereign, the final authority in the state. They have been concerned about the inner consistency of the law, about its formal characteristics as law rather than with its correspondence with a moral law above the law. They have separated law from morality, not necessarily because they were indifferent to morality, but because when law is identified with morality there is a blurring of some real issues. Roscoe Pound, whose writings emphasize the role of morality in relation to law, has this to say about what is true in the desire to make the distinction between law and morality:

"When we have found a moral principle we cannot stop at that. We have more to do than to formulate it into a legal rule. We must ask how far it has to do with things that may be governed by legal rules. We must ask how far legal machinery of rule and remedy are adapted to the claims which it recognizes and would secure. We must ask how far, if we formulate a precept in terms of our moral principle, it may be made effective in action. Even more we must consider how far it is possible to give the moral principle legal recognition and efficacy by juridical action or juristic reasoning, on the basis of the received legal materials and with the received legal techniques, without impairing the general security by unsettling the legal system as a whole."[2]

It is the work of the analytical jurists that arouses the strongest criticism of Professor Brunner and many others on the ground that quite without intention their work, by undermining the belief in any objective justice above the state, prepared the way for the totalitarian state.[3]

Legal positivism when it is combined with a thoroughgoing moral relativism does have the effect that Professor Brunner attributes to it. It is not necessary for a legal positivist to be a moral relativist and he may recognize that the legislator and the judge who fashion the positive law should themselves be gov-

[2] *Law and Morals* (University of North Carolina Press, 1924), pp. 66-67.

[3] Professor John H. Hallowell develops this view of the trend in German legal philosophy in his *The Decline of Liberalism as an Ideology* (University of California Press, 1943).

erned by morality. John Austin, who was the major British representative of this type of thought, made it very clear that the positive laws should be in harmony with the "law of God."[4] He identified that law with the principle of "utility" and that is a narrow and secularized distortion of the divine law, but it makes clear that the law is not self-sufficient and that it is under a moral judgment. Austin's chief concern was to say that it is not the morality of the law that makes it binding but the fact that the "sovereign" willed and enacted the law. Austin objects to the contention of Blackstone that a law that is not in harmony with the law of God is not "legally binding."[5] His idea of the "sovereign" is open to criticism but what he is saying is not different from what Brunner himself says when he admits that the law of the state cannot "tolerate a competition" presented by "a second legal system" or by the law of nature. Brunner says: "The laws of the state actually obtaining must possess a monopoly of binding legal force; the law of nature must claim no binding force for itself if the legal security of the state is to remain unshaken.[6] Brunner goes on to say that at this point the Reformers diverged most widely from the view of mediaeval Catholicism.

Just as Protestant theologians have criticized the idea of natural law, so have many jurists and for quite similar reasons. One reason is to make clear that as law the positive law of the state is not superseded by the natural law. (This is not to deny that an extra-legal revolt against the law on the basis of a higher law may not at times be justified.) They reflect the same scepticism about universal knowledge of the natural law, though they would not emphasize the role of sin in the distortions of man's mind. Justice Holmes states the problem when he says: "The jurists who believe in natural law seem to me to be in the naïve state of

[4] *The Austinian Theory of Law* (Ed., W. Jethro Brown, J. Murray, London, 1920), p. 71.
[5] *Ibid.*, p. 72.
[6] *Op. cit.*, p. 93.

mind that accepts what has been familiar and accepted by them and their neighbors as something that must be accepted by all men everywhere."[7] Many of them, including Justice Holmes, have criticized the individualistic formulations of natural law to which I have referred. They have a clear sense of the need for flexibility when general principles are related to the concrete case and for the law to be restated to meet changing social needs. When the law maker—legislator or jurist—who shares these ideas about the limitation of natural law concepts is also a complete moral relativist without any convictions as to whether laws are more or less just, we may well expect the worst. But there is no necessary connection between these two things.

I have mentioned Justice Holmes in this connection and, since it is sometimes said that this man who is so much of an American sage and hero, and whose work is such an important landmark in the history of American constitutional law was really the kind of legal positivist and moral relativist whose theories in another situation might lead to the totalitarianism which he would himself have loathed, I shall consider him at greater length. No one doubts that Holmes himself was brought up to have the right moral likes and dislikes. This kind of criticism is directed against the trend of his theory.

Holmes rejected all forms of historical religion. He did so in a spirit of indifference rather than in one of hostility. He, therefore, had neither a Christian nor a theistic basis for his thinking. He is a refutation of the kind of Christian apologetics that assumes that if a man lives long enough some weakness in his armor will appear and he will either choose the faith or at least feel betrayed by his secular world view! He was an evolutionist with fewer optimistic illusions than most and his evolutionism made him cautious about universal and final claims for moral ideals. He also had a sense of the mystery of things which re-

---

[7] Essay on "Natural Law" in *The Mind and Faith of Justice Holmes* (Ed., Max Lerner. Little, Brown, 1943), p. 396.

sulted in a kind of natural piety and which kept him from claiming to know much about ultimates. He was a pragmatist who shared the pragmatic preference for experience as against logic. He liked to speak in a rather hard-boiled fashion eschewing idealistic or humanitarian sentiments. As I have said, he rejected the idea of natural law with a measure of contempt. He felt it very important to distinguish between the law and morality and he liked to shock people who claimed to have more profound ideas about the nature of the law by saying that the law is what the courts say it is. Yet he also said that "law is the witness and external deposit of moral life."[8]

This sceptical and very open view of the law was not a careless or cynical attitude, but it was closely connected with a desire to free the legislature from the veto of the courts. Holmes had a strong sense of changing social needs. He also saw how rigid the courts often were in interpreting the unchanging natural law and his concern was to give a reasonable legislative act the benefit of the doubt. He did not try to impose his own idea on the law if he believed that a reasonable man might take another view. His work in preparing the Supreme Court for a more flexible attitude to social legislation has been of great importance even though he always retained a measure of aristocratic scepticism about the effects of economic reforms. So his whole theory and method were on the side of a much needed legal flexibility and this was itself a principle with him.

But there was something more in Holmes' philosophy and it would have prevented its use for totalitarian purposes. In the very passage in which he criticizes the naïve jurists who believe in natural law, he admits that there are some arrangements that seem to be necessary in any civilized society. He says that all of these are "at the bottom of all, some protection for the person."[9] Here we have something for which he says that he cannot

---

[8] "The Path of the Law," Lerner, *op. cit.*, p. 73.
[9] *Ibid.*, p. 396.

provide an "ought," for it requires a "transcendental basis in the sense that its foundation is arbitrary."[10] That is not satisfactory as an ultimate grounding of a moral judgment, but this statement at least does not cover over the roots of the problem. Holmes' moral conviction was not unsure because he admitted that it rested upon an ultimate value judgment. At least twice in letters nineteen years apart he refers to human "can't helps" which are beliefs that are stable for him though he does not know whether they have cosmic support.[11] This belief in the protection of the person underlay his civil liberties dissents which are comparable in importance with those which asked that Congress be permitted to enact social legislation. In his dissent in *U. S. v. Schwimmer* he wrote the famous words: ". . . if there is any principle of the Constitution that more imperatively calls for attachment than any other it is the principle of free thought—not free thought for those who agree with us but freedom for the thought that we hate."[12] This was a principle which for Holmes transcended moral scepticism, but it was also a principle supported by a degree of scepticism about most other principles.

Professor Gabriel says of Holmes in this connection that "in spite of his disclaimer, a philosophy of the fundamental law was implicit in his concept of liberty and in his behavior as he defended it." In discussing Holmes' famous dissent in *Abrams v. the U. S.* (a free-speech case) Gabriel says that Holmes did not on this occasion "turn to the majority to discover the 'truth' about freedom of thought and expression. He saw in it a universal."[13]

I think that Professor Gabriel in this judgment is much fairer than Professor Hallowell, who says: "But recognition that

[10] *Ibid.*

[11] *Ibid.*, pp. 415 and 431.

[12] *Ibid.*, pp. 361-362.

[13] Ralph H. Gabriel, *The Course of American Democratic Thought* (Ronald Press, 1940), p. 394.

Holmes was a gentleman and an ardent champion of freedom of speech and of press must not obscure the recognition that his underlying philosophy was potentially dangerous to the foundations of the democracy he thought he was defending."[14] I recognize that Holmes' underlying philosophy completely lacked ultimate Christian convictions and that if his type of scepticism became general, it would be a threat to freedom not because of the scepticism itself, but because it would leave a spiritual vacuum that would almost certainly be filled by an idolatrous faith in time of crisis. At such times only a true absolutism can check a false one and the sceptic is left on the side lines if he is not swept along by the idolatry. On most occasions, however, the representatives of the true absolutism[15] need to have a few such honest and clear-minded sceptics as critics.

Also, Professor Hallowell fails to do justice to Holmes' acknowledgement of stubborn value judgments about the protection of the person to which I have referred. Even though his account of their basis or derivation is inadequate, this does not destroy their claim upon him. Can we not distinguish between the problem created when ideas have within them the germ of tyranny and the problem created when ideas favorable to freedom are so rootless that they are likely to give way under pressure in a new situation? The latter problem rather than the former is involved in Holmes' ideas about freedom. It is only fair in this connection to say that the sad distortion of the natural law in terms of pure individualism in American jurisprudence was enough to make Holmes strike out against the

[14] John H. Hallowell, *Main Currents in Modern Political Thought* (Henry Holt, 1950), p. 363.

[15] When I speak of "true absolutism" I should explain that Christian faith is an unusual kind of absolute; it might be called an "open absolute." Every formulation of Christian truth, every embodiment of it, every application of it, all human grasp of it, must be open to a transcendent judgment. There is revelation of that judgment in Christ, but this is the kind of judgment that calls in question all other judgments that appear in history and it defies all final human systematization or interpretation or codification.

kind of moral confidence that was embodied in the whole tradition of natural law. Christian thinkers should be grateful for a purging element in Holmes' scepticism and move beyond it to a position which is the better because of it. In what follows I shall suggest some ways in which this can be done.

Law has a built-in tendency that is favorable to justice and, unless there is a deliberate perversion of law by political power, this is the first point of contact between law and morality. Professor Corwin summarizes this character of the law succinctly in the sentence: "Law must be general; it must afford equal protection to all; it may not validly operate retroactively; it must be enforced through courts."[16] One of the greatest of the Analytical legal theorists who has sought to distinguish most clearly between morality and law, Hans Kelsen, makes the distinction between "justice under the law" and "justice above the law." "Justice under the law" refers to the aspect of the law which I am now discussing. "Justice above the law" refers to the many difficult problems that are associated with the concept of natural law or of a transcendent morality. Kelsen says that "justice under the law" is "the maintenance of a positive order by the conscientious application of it."[17] As I have said, this can be destroyed by the lawless fiat of those who have political power and, of course, there are many ways of corrupting it through the corruption of the courts. Also, justice for the poor is often frustrated by the cost of litigation. But the law in this sense is one of the highest human achievements and one of the most precious gifts of "common grace." As the meaning of the "all" to whom equal protection is afforded comes to be securely *all* human beings of all races and of all social backgrounds and not merely a limited group of "citizens," and as the statute law comes to devise truly effective protections for the weak, "justice under the law" gains in its moral meaning.

[16] The "Higher Law," Background of American Constitutional Law (Great Seal Books, 1955), p. 68.

[17] In Interpretations of Modern Legal Philosophies (Ed., Paul Sayre. Oxford, 1947), p. 398.

One decisive development is when it is clearly recognized that the law applies to "rulers" themselves, that they are under the laws which they proclaim. To make this stick in the case of an absolute monarchy or a dictatorship is impossible for long because there must be not only independent courts to proclaim what the laws are and apply them, but there must also be power behind the courts based upon something more than the will of the king or dictator. In a democracy it is an important protection that all law makers must obey the laws which they enact; they must pay the taxes which they prescribe for their fellow citizens and there are legal processes by which they can be removed from office. The immunities surrounding the speech of members of Congress, which have been known to be abused, do not apply outside the legislative chambers themselves.

The law *is* an amazing process of self-correction—again, when there is no deliberate interference. It includes the following elements: the procedures in the court, the limited roles of the various participants, the rules of evidence, the publicity, the carefully kept records, the appeals to higher courts, the establishment of precedents which become guides for the future but which later experience can overturn, the emphasis in all of this on "due process" so that actions can be invalidated if this process of self-correction is not faithfully observed. Back of all that happens in the courts of one nation is a great legal tradition which has its history in many nations and its ancient sources. The super-national character of the legal tradition as it is applied within the courts of this country is itself a significant protection against provincial distortions.

Even in Russia, after the death of Stalin, there has been a process of quiet self-criticism under the influence of widely accepted ideas of due process and the Russian courts claim to be abandoning some of the most grievously unjust procedures which were characteristic of the great purges, but so long as the political power is concentrated in the present oligarchy or dictator any judicial reforms are precarious. Yet the continuous discussion of them is a sign that even Russian law cannot be law and isolate itself from the broad legal tradition.

"Justice under the law" is not enough and the more important question is how the content of the law can be kept under a conception of justice that transcends the law. Procedural justice that is inherent in the law can develop its own flaws and should be kept under the criticism of a higher justice. Much of what adherents of the idea of "natural law" call for is needed. Christians see even the best positive law under the law of God.

Law may be brought under the judgment of God by those in the community who are engaged in making and applying law and by all who form public opinion who know themselves to be under divine judgment. The overlapping moral and religious convictions within the community which are expressed by churches and synagogues, by many voluntary groups that are dedicated to particular social objectives, by the consciences of individual citizens press upon the law and help to mould it. Even legal theorists who have gone furthest in separating law from morality emphasized the role of morality in legislation. As Dean Pound summarizes their view: "Law was for the courts morals for legislators."[18] That distinction cannot hold because the courts make law and they also are guided by the moral convictions of the judges and the interpretation by the judges of the conscience of the community. But be that as it may, it is important to see that the whole range of legislation is under moral judgment as it is expressed through the overlapping moral convictions in the community, moral convictions also that stand up under publicity and much open criticism, which are sometimes lower and sometimes higher than the private convictions of the citizens. The conscience of the community that is expressed in the ways that I have suggested should not seek to enact into law everything that may seem right to it, and the churches should not press to have every sin made into

18 *Law and Morals*, p. 47.

a crime under the law. This is the wisdom in Dean Pound's quotation from a fifteenth-century Year Book: "Some things are for the law of the land, and some things are for the chancellor, and some things are between a man and his confessor."[19]

Judges as well as legislators make law in their interpretation of law as is now very generally admitted in this country. They are limited by the existing law when the statutes are clear, but few statutes prescribe their application to all future contingencies and American judges have to interpret the constitutional law which is much more general than statutes.

Justice Cardozo, one of the most respected judges of the U. S. Supreme Court in this century, has written down what he has found to be the relation between the judicial function and the justice or morality which is above the law in his extraordinarily illuminating book, *The Nature of the Judicial Process*, from which I have quoted. He describes how the judge may be faced with two alternative paths to which the logic of the law may lead and that in his choice of one the judge is governed by his conviction that it will lead to justice. After describing the dilemma in one difficult case he says: "In the end, the principle that was thought to be most fundamental, to represent the larger and deeper social interests, put its competitors to flight."[20] The judge must be guided by considerations of the public good and often this is a matter of "mere expediency or prudence" but there are times when the demands which the judge must heed are "those of religion or of ethics or of the social sense of justice, whether formulated in creed or system, or immanent in the common mind."[21] In criticizing those legal theorists who put great emphasis on the distinction between law and morals, he says that this is often a matter of "nomenclature" and that the concern may be only to avoid confusion between moral pre-

[19] Quoted in *Law and Morals*, pp. 66-67.
[20] Yale University Press, 1921, p. 42.
[21] *Ibid.*, p. 72.

cepts before they have become law and the law itself. However, Justice Cardozo makes a very strong statement about the danger of this emphasis. He says: "What really matters is this, that the judge is under a duty, within the limits of his power of innovation, to maintain a relation between law and morals, between the precepts of jurisprudence and those of reason and good conscience. I suppose it is true in a certain sense that this duty was never doubted. One feels at times, however, that it was obscured by the analytical jurists, who, in stressing verbal niceties of definition, made a corresponding sacrifice of emphasis upon the deeper and finer realities of ends and aims and functions. The constant insistence that morality and justice are not law has tended to breed distrust and contempt of law as something to which morality and justice are not merely alien, but hostile."[22]

Justice Cardozo raises the question as to whether the judge should be guided by his own private sense of justice or by the convictions which he believes to be more characteristic of the community. He preserves a fine balance here. He points out that it would be judicial tyranny if the judge imposed his own private moral convictions as against what he knew to be the "accepted standards of the community." And yet he says that this does not mean that "a judge is powerless to raise the level of prevailing conduct." He has the responsibility to appeal from sentiments and standards that may have great momentary influence to "what the considerate judgment of the community condemns." He also distinguishes between some relationships in which nothing but "customary morality" should be enforced and relationships which impose "a duty to act in accordance with the highest standards which a man of the most delicate conscience and the nicest sense of honor might impose upon himself." He refers as examples to obligations involved in the role

[22] *Ibid.*, p. 134.

of a trustee, and he says that in such cases the judge should enforce adherence to those high standards.[23]

Professor Edmond Cahn in his *The Moral Decision*[24] makes use of a decision by Justice Cardozo which illustrates in a remarkable way the law's reflection of the best conscience of the community. The case involved a man who had been injured while trying to save another who had accidentally been thrown off a railroad car in a violent lurch. Cardozo, for a unanimous Court of Appeals in New York State, ruled that this man who had been injured in his endeavor to help another was entitled to damages from the railroad. He said: "Danger invites rescue. The cry of distress is the summons to relief. The law does not ignore these reactions of the mind in tracing conduct to its consequences. It recognizes them as normal. It places their effects within the range of the natural and the probable. The wrong that imperils life is a wrong to the imperilled victim; it is a wrong also to his rescuer." He went on to say: "The law does not discriminate between the rescuer oblivious of peril and the one who counts the cost. It is enough that the act, whether impulsive or deliberate, is the child of the occasion."[25] Professor Cahn's own comments on this decision are as remarkable as the decision itself, coming as they do from a Professor of Law. He emphasizes the "duty to provide assistance." He says that "the person in need stands for the whole human species, unlimited and unqualified by personal attributes of identification." He warns against "quixotic or officious interferences" and against the danger of being trapped by fraudulent appeals for help and then he says: "The desert of the victim is not material; the genuineness of his plight certainly is." Attempts at rescue may fail and "the only guarantee that we have —the only one we are entitled to—is that attempts of this kind glorify our existences which without them would be like grass

[23] *Ibid.*, pp. 109-110.
[24] Indiana University Press, 1955.
[25] *Ibid.*, p. 184.

and like dust."[26] The law in the hands of Justice Cardozo and Professor Cahn is certainly stretched by something more than the *average* conscience of the community.

Justice Cardozo has fine things to say about the importance of judicial self-criticism which should go far beyond the application of ordinary standards of honesty which exclude what he calls "the power of favor or prejudice in any sordid or vulgar or evil sense." He says of that type of dishonesty that he has found among the judges whom he has known "no trace, not even the faintest." But he does call attention to the danger of the influences which come from "the spirit of the group in which the accidents of birth or education or occupation or fellowship have given us a place."[27] He realizes that "no effort or revolution of the mind will overthrow utterly and at all times the empire of these subconscious loyalties." He shows here real insight into the realities on which theological teaching about human nature has thrown much light. He takes comfort here in one of the self-correcting elements in the legal structure when he says that "the eccentricities of judges balance one another."[28] Plainly it is partly in the self-discipline of a judge, aided by what is best in the law itself as well as by all that has formed his own conscience, that we find one of the links between law and morality.

Citizens who vote and who are the moulders and bearers of the opinion and the conscience of the community, legislators and judges—all make law and all stand under the judgment of whatever they believe to be ultimate. They can never cease from questioning and criticizing the law in the light of that judgment. They know that there is a difference between just and unjust laws.

The acid test which may not often have to be applied is whether or not in the background of their own minds there is the recognition that there may be occasions when it is their

[26] *Ibid.*, pp. 195-196.
[27] *Ibid.*, pp. 174-175.
[28] *Ibid.*, p. 177

moral duty to disobey a law. The state cannot treat such a law as having no binding force as law, and civil disobedience cannot be ignored by the law-enforcement agencies. It is the part of wisdom for lawmakers to limit as far as possible the occasions for conscientious civil disobedience, to include in the law, as in the case of military conscription laws alternative forms of obedience for those who sincerely oppose the law's primary purpose. But there can come a point at which law and the conscience of an individual or a group collide.

That this is a sign of the transcendence of the standards of right which control the conscience should be admitted by the community and even by the custodians of the law. Chief Justice Hughes as such a custodian expressed this when he said in his dissenting opinion in the Macintosh case: "When one's belief collides with the power of the state, the latter is supreme within its sphere and submission to punishment follows. But, in the forum of conscience, duty to a moral power higher than the state has always been maintained."[29] There are loose ends here that cannot be tied together completely. To say that the law ceases to be law under such conditions and is superseded as law by a kind of super-constitution made up of "natural law" will not do. Those who represent both sides should recognize the conflict and respect each other's roles. And the law, while not annulled by the conflict, remains open and may be changed as a result of the conflict.[30]

Christians find the clearest understanding of the transcendence of law in the witness of the Old Testament prophets to the sovereignty of God and his righteousness over every human power. Israel as a state was a theocracy and even the fact of

[29] Quoted in Anson Phelps Stokes, Church and State in the United States (Harper, 1950), Vol. III, p. 272.

[30] Actually Justice Hughes' position became that of the Court's majority in Girouard v. U. S. in 1946, which declared "that the Schwimmer, Macintosh and Bland cases do not state the correct rule of law." See: Stokes, Church and State in the United States, Vol. III, pp. 742-743.

human kingship was originally an embarrassment in that it obscured the divine kingship. The theocratic institutions of the Old Testament do not constitute a model for modern political life for when such institutions are created by men, even in a spirit of sincere obedience to God, the human powers always in practice are given a false sanctity. Distinction between state and Church (whether this should be "separation" in the American sense will be discussed later) is essential to preserve the state from this false sanctity that can be a cover for the deepest corruption of power, and to preserve the freedom of the prophetic witness and with it the freedom of man's spirit in general.

In the political structure of the Old Testament period in which there was an independent state and a strong prophetic voice we do find some of the elements which are essential to the Christian understanding of the law that is above the state. These are graphically portrayed in such episodes as the confrontation of Nathan and David, and of Elijah and Ahab. In both cases human rights that belonged to the divine justice were at stake. When the prophet said "Thou art the man" to the King, he revealed the transcendent judgment of God that limited the king's right to do what he willed with a man, in this case a man who was actually a foreigner in origin. The king was brought to repentance and this indicated that he shared the prophet's understanding of the divine sovereignty. The right of Uriah to his wife and to his life and the right of the poor man in Nathan's parable to his lamb were in the eyes of both prophet and king guaranteed by God.

When Ahab coveted Naboth's vineyard, we find a similar disclosure of God's protection of the rights of a man, the right to life and to property in the vineyard. The story is in some details very modern with the execution of Naboth on false charges of blasphemy and sedition so that the king could have his way. Elijah represented the justice of God and Ahab "went about dejectedly" less from the contrition that David expressed than from the fear of punishment, but he, also, recognized that he had sinned against God.

In these stories we have, as I have said, most of the elements that Christians see to be necessary for the ultimate frame within which our state and its laws are set. The righteousness of God is above the state. That righteousness is on the side of elemental human rights. The prophet takes freedom to challenge the king and his lawless use of power. The king recognizes that he is under God, that his power and his will are not ultimate.

In the modern state the human sovereign is usually, in some sense, the people rather than a king, and in a religiously pluralistic society all the people do not recognize the transcendent sovereignty of God or, if they do, they do not mean the same thing by it. This fact underlies the problems discussed in the second part of this book. Those citizens who do see that the law of the state stands under the righteousness of God have a responsibility to bear witness to this faith. This is the task of the churches. But today we have to make sure that those who perform this task accept and preserve the freedom of expression for those who deny that the law of the state is under the law of God or who give contrasting interpretations of that law.

CHAPTER IX

The Extension of the State's Role in Economic Life
—The Conflict of Economic Systems

THE debate over the extension of state activities in economic life has stimulated more thought and stirred more feeling in recent decades than any other issue concerning the functions of the state. There has been a tendency for thought to polarize as between "liberals" and "conservatives" on this subject. The location of the issues and the alignment of participants in the debate change from decade to decade as a result of events, of social necessities, of many a *fait accompli*, of the appearance of a new generation. The dogmatic individualism which dominated American thinking and which had its last line of defence in the courts has finally given way and it now represents a small minority. Both major political parties have accepted the main results of the economic revolution of the 1930's. We now have in this country and in other western democracies an economy in which both social controls and individual initiative have essential roles.

Not only has the older dogmatic individualism given way, but also the dogmatic socialism of many intellectuals and religious leaders has been abandoned. Dogmatic socialism has had a similar fate in other democratic countries where its influence has been strong in political life. I believe that in the United States the break-through of the 1930's in the New Deal which did establish the state's responsibility to preserve economic stability and in many ways to do what private initiative neither would nor could do to promote the welfare of all the people has created a situation in which the debate about the exact limits of the activity of the state can continue fruitfully.

We must not drift into the control of an all-embracing state. Those who fear the overwhelming of private initiative by government power represent vital concerns. But what they say has relevance only after they accept the break-through, as many of them have. Moreover, those who easily accept any extension of state functions should be helped to see that because a change may be needed and would be good, we should not assume that an indefinite extension of it would be better. Now that it has become clear that there are no absolute solutions in this area, we can expect to live in the midst of an experimental process which will be less exciting than the advocacy of total systems and final goals, but it may more effectively meet particular needs and avoid the more ghastly errors.

I have been dogmatic about what I have called the essential break-through which I identify not so much with particular legislation but with the change of mind that accepts the responsibility of the national state to act to prevent large scale unemployment and other national economic disasters, and to cooperate with the states in meeting many social needs such as the provision for social security and public housing. I need not enumerate the many other ways in which the state should regulate the activities of private economic institutions in the public interest. Such forms of regulations have had to fight their way against serious odds and often the regulatory agencies have been captured by those who have sought to make them ineffective, but this type of regulation in principle was accepted long before the 1930's. I shall not enlarge on these matters but I do want to say several things about the moral necessity of the break-through.

(1) The most obvious reason for the need of state action in the economic sphere is that the national state is the only agency

in the national community that can deal effectively with problems which affect the welfare of the whole nation. Its central position, its administrative capacities and its authority and power to use coercion when that is needed to get universal compliance or almost universal compliance are found nowhere else. As Lord Lindsay said in a sentence that I have quoted, there are some things that must be done by everyone involved if they are to be done at all. The great depression of the 1930's proved to all but the most blind individualists that a *laissez-faire* economy cannot of itself, through its own self-regulating processes, produce either order or justice in society. It requires the guidance and supplementation of the kind that only government can provide. If a completely free economy might over the long term right itself, the process would be too costly in human values to be permitted. It is both morally and politically impossible for a democratic nation to sit back and watch such a process work itself out to the bitter end.

(2) As I have said in an earlier chapter, there are areas of life and inner problems of non-political institutions such as the family, the church, and the university which the state must not touch, but this is not true of economic institutions to the same degree. There are good reasons for avoiding a general union of political and economic power. There are many situations in which private organizations can do things better than the state, but there is no inherent moral or social principle which makes it wrong for the state to have a part in producing or distributing electric power or in building houses. Whether it should have a part in such matters, or how large a part it should have, can only be settled in concrete terms after weighing a variety of considerations; but for the state to determine what the content of worship should be in a church, or what a professor of political science should teach in a university, is out of bounds in principle.

(3) It is often assumed by the extreme individualists that

the state is the one enemy of freedom against which people should be on their guard. The cause of economic individualism of the rigid type is often presented as the cause of human freedom in the broadest sense. It is said that freedom is indivisible. The truth in that statement can best be expressed by saying that the major forms of freedom are in some degree interdependent but not that they are so indivisible that we cannot limit freedom in one area without its involving an equal limitation of freedom in another area. It is better that there be many centers of economic initiative, but it is not necessarily better that they have untrammelled freedom. Private property is a very important protection of the freedom of the individual, but that argument really favors a wide distribution of property so that as many persons as possible can have the benefit of this freedom.

Instead of looking upon the state only as an enemy of freedom, it is more accurate to see the state as in many situations the best protection of freedom, especially the freedom of the economically weak. I think that this has been said with all the necessary qualifications in the report of the Section on Social Problems of the Evanston Assembly. The report says: "While the state is sometimes the enemy of freedom, under many circumstances the state is the only instrument which can make freedom possible for large sections of the population." The report balances this statement with the equally true statement: "Therefore we must warn against the danger that the union of political and economic power may result in an all-controlling state."[1]

[1] It may be useful to present the context of these quotations from the Evanston report. There is first a reference to a statement of the Oxford Conference that the state is not "the lord but the servant of justice." Then there is the following paragraph:

"The Oxford statement applies in the following way to the function of the state with regard to social justice in economic life. While the state is sometimes the enemy of freedom, under many circumstances the state is the only instrument which can make freedom possible for large sectors of

The state is an instrument of freedom for those who are the victims of circumstance, of the impersonal economic forces that may throw them out of work, of the power of employers unless their right to collective bargaining is protected, of all kinds of injury incidental to employment unless the law of the state provides some means of redress. The abstract individualism of the market combined with the abstract individualism of the law turned out in practice to favor the rights and the welfare of the strong and it was the state alone that could change that tendency. It did so by changing the law, first through the action of legislatures and then through the decisions of judges who came to see the unjust effect of the laws that granted freedom to all parties in the abstract but which meant in practice that the freedom of the economically defenseless might be the freedom to work twelve hours a day or starve. As Chief Justice Stone said: "There is a grim irony in speaking of the freedom of contract of those who, because of their economic necessities, give their services for less than is needful to keep body and soul together."[2] Dean Pound who had much to do with the adaptation of the law to the human realities in our type of economy

---

the population. The state is not the source of social justice, but it must be its guardian, ready if necessary to accept responsibility to counteract depression or inflation and to relieve the impact of unemployment, industrial injury, low wages, and unfavorable working conditions, sickness and old age. But in doing so the state remains the servant not the lord of social justice. Therefore we must warn against the danger that the union of economic and political power may result in an all-controlling state. In contra-distinction to actions of the state it is the task of the non-governmental sectors in economic life to be the guardian of responsible private action in society. But within the private sector, both employers and employees in all their varied organizations in their turn are the servant, and not the lord, of freedom and welfare. When necessary in the public interest, the state must intervene to prevent any centre of economic or social power which represents partial interest from becoming stronger than itself, for the state alone has the power and the authority under God to act as trustee for society as a whole." (Report of Section III: "Social Problems—The Responsible Society in a World Perspective.")

[2] Quoted in The Mind and Faith of Justice Holmes (Ed., Max Lerner. Little, Brown, 1943), pp. 175-176.

writes that "down to the end of the last century, lawyers took seriously the existence of theoretical remedies which in practice were unavailable and regarded the abstract justice of abstract rules as quite enough, be the concrete results what they may."[3] Indeed, in this country it was not until a third of this century was over that there was a fully reliable change in this respect in our highest court.

One of the most decisive events in American history in this connection was the action of the U. S. Supreme Court in upholding the Wagner Act. Chief Justice Hughes, in speaking for the Court, said that "union was essential to give laborers opportunity to deal on an equality with their employer." Professor E. S. Corwin in commenting on this decision says: "This 'liberty' is recognized as something that may be infringed by other forces as well as by government; indeed, something that may require *the positive intervention of government against these other forces.*"[4] In quite a different context Professor Corwin is saying exactly what the Evanston Assembly said as quoted above.

(4) It is sometimes said that the state should not act in the economic sphere because morally it is better for people to do voluntarily what they ought to do. In terms of motive this is true and also, as I emphasized in my discussion of consent and coercion, unless there is a large element of willing acceptance legal coercion is likely to fail. But it is morally better to decide that what is required to meet the needs of people be effectively done even though this may involve coercion of oneself as well as others, than it is to oppose such legal action so that one may have the experience of feeling more moral. The willing acceptance of law as applied to oneself is a true form of voluntarism when the situation demands it. This is involved in all willingness to be taxed when taxation is necessary for a

[3] *The Spirit of the Common Law* (Marshall Jones, 1921), p. 212.
[4] *Constitutional Revolution Ltd.* (Claremont Colleges, 1941), p. 67.

purpose in which one believes. There are all degrees of this voluntary acceptance of law and often this acceptance comes after the law has been in force for some time. Law is necessary in part because of man's sin, because of his tendency to be unwilling to do enough voluntarily. We cannot leave to a system of voluntary compliance the regulations which may be necessary to preserve basic economic stability, nor can we leave to an optimistic voluntarism the livelihood of the unemployed in a time of recession, the building of schools for the whole community at any time, the rationing of food in days of scarcity, the protection of tenants against the criminal negligence of landlords, the insurance of workers against injuries, and the many other essential human needs which these suggest.[5]

(5) A fifth consideration is that the greatest danger of totalitarianism comes not from the gradual extension of the role of government but rather from the breakdown of a society partly because the government has been too weak to deal with its problems. I do not deny that there is danger from the more gradual process, but in recent history totalitarian societies have come from a failure on the part of government to cope with economic and political and cultural crises. When there is no longer a dependable order or when national unity has been destroyed, totalitarian movements win support because they promise a new order and a new unity.

I have indicated some of the reasons why we should accept what I have called the "break-through" which has substituted for an earlier dogmatic individualism an acceptance of the gen-

[5] Nicholai Berdyaev, in spite of his powerful protest against a legalistic view of life, makes clear that the freedom of human personality "is not always protected through grace, but frequently has to be protected by law." He says that we must not make "man's freedom dependent upon the gracious regeneration of other men. . . . Human freedom cannot be made to depend entirely on the spiritual condition of other men, society and its rulers. . . . A society that chose to be based solely upon grace and declined to have any law would be a despotic society." *The Destiny of Man* (Geoffrey Bles, London, 1937), pp. 100-101.

eral responsibility of the state for the economic and social welfare of the people. There has emerged in the ecumenical
discussions of recent years a way of thinking about the whole
problem of economic systems which involves a rejection of the
stereotypes and labels and clichés connected with both Capitalism and Socialism, a rejection of the ideologies that make for
rigid thinking on this issue. A doctrinaire socialism based upon
Marxism as a philosophy of history has lost its hold on the
socialistic movements in western Europe and it never has had
significant influence in this country. A doctrinaire capitalistic
philosophy has lost its viability even in this country which is
the stronghold of capitalism, though some of its slogans are
still used.

The deepest impulse behind the socialist movements was a
drive toward social justice under the pull of the idea of equality,
and this has gained great strength among people who reject
socialism as a system. Without the concentration and dedication of socialists to this goal it is doubtful if this could be said
today. We owe much to this influence and this is especially
true of the churches in which the Christian conscience has been
stimulated and inspired by "Christian Socialism" in its many
varieties.[6]

Capitalism in most of the world is a bad symbol, especially in
Asia where it is associated with imperialism. Capitalism as a

[6] The importance of the socialistic impulse in the thought of the churches
can be seen from the fact that the three most influential figures in Anglo-
Saxon Protestantism in this century in the area of Christian social concern
—Walter Rauschenbusch, Archbishop William Temple, and Reinhold
Niebuhr—have all been "Christian Socialists." Neither Rauschenbusch nor
Temple were directly influenced much by Marxism, but they believed in
the goals of a moderate democratic socialism. Reinhold Niebuhr was more
influenced by the Marxist view of history and of economic life until the
middle 1930's. Since then he has become one of the most profound critics
of Marxist thought. However, while no longer a believer in an over-all
socialistic system, he still shares much of what I have called the socialistic
impulse and his emphasis upon economic justice separates him in spirit and
in political convictions from the modern conservatives who share his en-
thusiasm for Edmund Burke and hail his criticisms of Marxist illusions.

doctrinaire philosophy which assumes, as was said in a very controversial sentence in one of the reports of the Amsterdam Assembly, that "justice will follow as a by-product of free enterprise"[7] is false. But capitalism as a flexible pattern of institutions and behavior includes elements which are important for any society. The emphasis upon them does and should vary from country to country and especially the new nations which must in a few years make real progress in the solution of overwhelming problems will give a greater place to the initiative and direction of the state than is necessary or desirable in the United States. There are at least three things about capitalistic institutions which should be preserved among us and recommended to other nations.

First, capitalism preserves many centers of power and initiative in society. When it becomes so monopolistic that this ceases to be true of it, the case for it disappears. It is not desirable to have a complete union of political and economic power in society, but this is likely to take place in the most anti-social fashion if there ceases to be a distribution of power among the capitalistic institutions themselves. Competition between industries is a check upon the power of each of them which gives the consuming public a chance to exercise power over all of them.

The continuous bargaining between management and labor also represents a desirable division of power and this can be threatened when either party can dominate the other or when both parties can combine against the interests of the public. State action that regulates but does not destroy the bargaining flexibilities is necessary. Support by the state of the rights of members of labor unions as against their leaders when the latter become intrenched dictators is also needed. The preservation of a pluralistic and flexible system that is not dominated by the state or by any one powerful segment of the economy or by

[7] Report of Section III, 1948.

leaders of management and labor in collusion with each other is a never-ending struggle and it will require enormous patience and skill on the part of policy makers, awareness of issues among the people, and on all sides both integrity and belief in the values of a society which distributes power in this way.

One illustration which shows how difficult it is to find a blueprint for the exact distribution of power that will be good for all occasions is the problem raised by strikes in essential industries or public services. Any rigid procedure that denies the right to strike may be grossly unfair to labor and play into the hands of employers. Neither management nor labor favors compulsory arbitration because this threatens the freedom of both and as an established system it would give the state the preponderant power in the economy. Yet the state as the trustee for the public welfare cannot permit a situation that is injurious to the public to continue indefinitely. It must do everything short of the exercise of its full power to coerce first, and there will have to be a good deal of playing by ear in the light of quite clear objectives and of quite clear warnings concerning the effects of what might be done or left undone. To establish a system that settled in advance the way the power of the state should be used would either cripple it in dealing with real emergencies or threaten forms of freedom and flexibility that are normally desirable. A socialist state that acts too easily to prevent strikes by using state power will destroy the freedom of the workers and, in so doing, it will arouse resentment among the very groups which have given socialism the greatest moral support.

A second element in capitalism that has permanent value is that it takes seriously the problem of incentive. Traditional capitalism was too dogmatic about exclusive reliance on the selfish monetary incentives. Dogmatic socialism has been too trustful of the social incentives. Christians who have been socialists chiefly because of moral rejection of the "profit motive," or more broadly the motive of economic advantage which applies to wages and salaries as much as to profits, have not learned from Christian theology about the place of self-interest in human nature.

We have to walk warily here because the very vulnerability of human nature which Christian teaching has emphasized should warn us against accepting an economy that not only uses the self-centered motives to get work done but also greatly over-exercises them, encouraging greed and creating a climate in which the highest place is given to money-making and prosperous display. The moral dangers that we have on both sides should keep us from giving simple answers.

Financial rewards undoubtedly do stimulate a desirable economic initiative and creativity and risk-taking which, in spite of all the dangers involved, should not be rejected. Actually, those rewards as sources of motive are not to be separated from other motives such as the love of creativity and adventure and the desire for prestige and power. The last two may be satisfied through wealth, but they do not depend entirely upon wealth for satisfaction. The more social motives may also be present, but they may not be the original stimulus when we are thinking of this type of economic enterprise. But the economic incentives are needed for efficiency and productivity throughout the economy. The relation between these incentives and Christian vocation is more complicated than is generally realized by Christian idealists or by cynics. There are few people who are not helped in organizing themselves and in working steadily when they do not enjoy their work by the necessity of making a living for themselves and their families. Most of the work of the world is not intrinsically of sufficient interest to enable it to depend upon non-economic incentives even among people of integrity and good will. Semi-socialist societies have discovered this to be true and in Communist societies the economic incentives play a great role.

If I were writing about Christian vocation in economic life,

I should have much to say about the place that it has both as a motive for faithful and efficient work and also as the source of concern to improve the conditions and the relationships accompanying work. But we cannot base the economic institutions of a mixed society on Christian vocation alone though they should be greatly influenced by it and I do not believe that Christians themselves, even "true Christians," can dispense at all stages of their lives with the spur that economic incentives provide. These incentives have to do with family loyalty more than with a narrow personal acquisitiveness. If there were a guaranteed economic security of a kind that was reasonably satisfactory for all, there would undoubtedly be a great let-down among most.[8]

The third element in capitalism that should find a place in whatever mixed economy may develop is the regulating of large segments of the economy by the market. This needs to take place within a framework that safeguards important social values, but it is certainly far better to make place for this kind of regulation than it is to try to plan all economic activity in a few centers. This is most obviously desirable in the retail trades in giving consumers freedom of choice and their choice, of course, gives direction to the production of goods. There is no need to deny the consumer this freedom except in times of emergency. Also, in many other respects we see that there can be no all-wise centers of planning that can take account of all

[8] I have learned a great deal from some years of collaboration with economists in the National Council of Churches' study of Ethics and Economics in Society. The Study Committee has published a series of twelve books on that subject. The most important thing that I have learned from the economists was that students of theology and ethics were strong on justice in distribution but weak in their realization of the importance of productivity. I came to recognize more clearly that no amount of justice can make up for the lack of goods to distribute. The economists stand guard over the productivity and flexibility of the economy and they have a keen sense for the by-products of economic policies in relation to freedom. See especially *Christian Values and Economic Life*, Bennett, Bowen, Brown and Oxnam (Harper, 1954); and *Goals of Economic Life* (Ed., Dudley Ward. Harper, 1953).

local needs and of the many contingent factors that determine what products will be most useful.

I have written these things about capitalism as one who takes for granted the validity of the socialistic criticism of the exploitative features of nineteenth-century capitalism generally and of the economic disorder and the human misery that have come with capitalistic depressions. American capitalism has been changed beyond recognition in recent decades and only because of such changes is it morally tolerable. I understand that most experts in this field believe that it is technically possible to prevent the most destructive swings of depression and inflation, but no one can be sure that there will be both the wisdom and the self-discipline either in government or in the various sectors of the economy to do what will be required to prevent these disasters. We have learned much from past mistakes and there is a general awareness that a serious depression would probably bring even this modified capitalism as we know it to an end.

It is important for the churches to avoid baptizing a Christian capitalism as it is important for them to avoid the identification of Christianity and socialism. American Christians who believe in the desirability of the type of free economy which I have defended in this chapter should realize that many Christians in other countries, both Britain and India for example, find socialism a more fitting symbol than capitalism.[9]

[9] There was a conference of Indian Christian leaders in Bombay in 1956 which took as its theme "A Socialistic Pattern of Society." The conception of socialism that was assumed certainly had a larger element of social ownership and planning than would be thought desirable in this country, but the conception was as flexible, starting from its end as contemporary ideas, and even more practices, in this country are, starting at the other end. Dr. John Matthai, a leading Christian layman who had been in the national cabinet, in his inaugural address at the conference defined socialism as involving two ideas. "One is the idea of freedom and the other is the idea of equality. To what extent they form part of socialism and in what form they are expressed in policy are a different matter; but through every form of socialism you get these two fundamental ideas, freedom and

After I have said these things, I still urge that the three elements in capitalism which I have emphasized be regarded as desirable ingredients in any mixture of economic institutions and practices. They represent an important limitation on the state. They do not, of themeslves, insure justice, and the freedom that they favor may easily become too much the freedom of the strong. All this discussion goes to show that there are no final systems though there are criteria and values by which all systems should be judged. While these criteria and values are not exclusively Christian, the Christian faith does help to give them vitality and to keep them within a context which illumines the total human good.

---

equality. If I may venture a broad suggestion, what differentiates socialism from communism, is that the idea of freedom is much more part of the socialist philosophy than of the communist philosophy. I would not define socialism as anything more than this. It is not a definite creed, nor a definite type of organization; it is a way of life, an attitude to society which aims at the widest practicable diffusion of social justice by methods which may be regarded as appropriate to a free, that is a democratic community." (Report of the Conference published by National Christian Council of India and the Christian Institute for the Study of Society.) I am sure that people will find themselves doing many of the same things under the different symbols of "democratic socialism" and "the new capitalism."

CHAPTER X

From Christian Freedom to Civil Liberties

CHRISTIAN freedom and the constitutional protection of man's freedom of expression in society belong to different dimensions and the road from one to the other has not generally been clear. There is such a road and today most Christians find themselves travelling it, but they have to admit that most of their predecessors, Catholic or Protestant, had not discovered it before the year 1700. There were pioneers before that year —such men as Roger Williams, Castellio, John Milton, the Quakers—and after that year it took another century and a half before religious disabilities for minorities were generally overcome in Protestant territory; even today minorities continue to struggle for freedom in Catholic territory and the Catholic Church is divided in its own mind about the very principle of freedom for those in "error." Today the impulse to restrict freedom of conscience and of expression comes chiefly from political systems and from states rather than from churches.

Today the practical problems of civil liberties raise issues which are more difficult than they were to thinkers in the periods of greatest confidence in reason. So long as it was possible to believe that truth would always triumph over error because of its power universally to persuade the minds of men, the risks of freedom were not much considered. Today we may still say that in the long run errors will tend to cancel each other out, that truth has great power in itself and will make its way *if the channels of communication remain open*. But the problem today is what to do about the freedom of those who first by propaganda and then by conspiracy seek to gain the political power by which they can control the channels of communication in the interests of their own conception of truth. We have also had the experience of seeing large communities of men seemingly changed in their understanding of the world by politically controlled indoctrination, some of them brainwashed so that they became mouthpieces of the official propaganda.

We have seen these things and yet I doubt if the first impression that they made upon many of us, including myself, was correct. There is striking evidence that large groups of people do not long remain brainwashed, that even when a generation has been subjected to many years of propaganda and indoctrination, it remains only partly convinced and a change in the external situation will soon reveal that minds do right themselves when they are exposed to a more objective view of the situation. Moreover, such changes in the external situation do come even for the most carefully planned totalitarian societies.

Rationalistic libertarians were too optimistic because they never guessed the full risks of freedom; they did not realize into what blind alleys of destructive error whole nations could for a time be led. And yet they were partly right in believing that there were limits to the extent to which such large communities of men could be deceived on matters concerning which there is much available evidence. There is comfort in this but not enough comfort to make us indifferent to the risks of freedom. The power of political tyranny to control the culture and the channels of communication, to indoctrinate masses of men and to confuse as many more remains a grave threat to man's spirit.

The constricting of the channels of communication may come without any totalitarianism or tyranny in the state. The fact that in a modern technological society the control of the press and the other mass media is in the hands of a relatively few persons represents another major threat to freedom. The need of large capital resources to establish or maintain a newspaper or a broadcasting system limits enormously the opportunity for free expression and gives great emphasis to the need of self-discipline and also regulation by government in the interests of free expression. The tension between the various media as commercial enterprises and their responsibility as servants of the public's need for channels of free expression is always with us but it seems to be an inevitable difficulty which accompanies the chief alternative to government-sponsored channels of information.[1]

Paul was the apostle of Christian freedom. This always meant for him two things: freedom from quite definite forms of bondage, especially bondage to sin, and freedom to become a slave of Christ. "For freedom Christ has set us free." (Galatians 5:1) "Do you not know that if you yield yourselves to any one as obedient slaves, you are slaves of the one whom you obey, either of sin, which leads to death, or of obedience, which leads to righteousness." (Romans 6:16) The free man from Paul's point of view has exchanged one form of bondage for

[1] These problems are discussed with great competence and fairness in Professor Wilbur Schramm's *Responsibility in Mass Communication* (Harper, 1957). I agree with one criticism in Professor Reinhold Niebuhr's introduction that Professor Schramm fails to do justice to the possibilities of public corporations initiated by government but not under immediate government control which might supplement the private systems of communication. I do not see why it is not natural to have public broadcasting agencies side by side with private agencies. This would add to the community's freedom because it would increase the opportunities for programs which commercial sponsors find unprofitable and it would provide occasional relief from the sponsors' own contributions of verse and song. A system of communications dominated primarily by the government would be disastrous. But we have not explored enough the possibilities of the kind of agency that has independence of the immediate political pressures comparable to that of the higher courts and the best state universities as supplementary media.

another. This freedom Paul thought of as quite independent of external circumstances. Of himself he could say, "in any and all circumstances I have learned the secret of facing plenty and hunger, abundance and want. I can do all things in him who strengthens me." (Philippians 4:12-13) And in his letter to Philemon he speaks of the external form of slavery as a matter of indifference. In his first letter to the Corinthians he writes: "Were you a slave when called? Never mind. But if you can gain your freedom, avail yourself of the opportunity. For he who was called in the Lord as a slave is a freedman of the Lord. Likewise he who was free when called is a slave of Christ." (I Corinthians 7:21-22)

The idea that Christian freedom can be independent of all external circumstances is a vital one, but it can be misleading even on its own terms. It may often be true of mature Christians who are called to face imprisonment or death because of their loyalty to Christ. The reader of Dietrich Bonhoeffer's *Prisoner for God* certainly senses this Christian freedom. Bonhoeffer writes: "You really must not worry about me, for I'm getting on uncommonly well, and you would be astonished if you came to see me."[2] He astonishes those who know what it is to be bored even outside of prison when he writes: "Another month gone! Do you find times flies as I do here?"[3] But this freedom is only possible for persons who are already strong in faith and in convictions; and, there are combinations of physical and psychological torture and drugs which may be too much even for the strong. This emphasis does not meet the need for freedom in the case of most Christians who are at a lower level of maturity and strength and those who have enough strength themselves cannot be indifferent to the needs of others. So it is always necessary to struggle for the freedom of the Church, for the Church's right to preach the Gospel, to

[2] Macmillan, 1954, p. 121.
[3] *Ibid.*

teach its youth, to maintain pastoral relations with its people. The inner freedom of the Christian saint cannot take the place of the external freedom of the Church. Even on this level of Christian freedom we see the beginning of the road to civil freedom.

I shall now deal with the Christian grounds for the institutions of civil freedom.[4]

(1) The first link between Christian freedom and civil freedom is implied in Christian obedience itself. Those who are under this obedience are sure to take freedom to "obey God rather than men." They will often be forced to struggle for the freedom of the Church which I have already emphasized and in doing so they will find themselves resisting—sometimes passively, sometimes through positive spiritual force and sometimes through political action—the existing political powers.

Paul himself in his own career took for granted the real opportunities afforded by the degree of civil freedom which existed in the Roman Empire of the first century. His world was one in which he could go about and preach the Gospel and organize churches and maintain communication with them. He had trouble from ship-wreck and from false brethren, but he did get around and that is more than he would be able to do across many national boundaries today. Christian freedom at its center is not the same thing as civil freedom, but from Paul's day to our own it has led men to cut their way through many obstacles, to snatch for themselves freedom to witness and to act.

In the history of all forms of freedom or liberty in the Anglo-

---

[4] I have not attempted to make any distinction between liberty and freedom as the words are so often used interchangeably, I realize that this distinction is sometimes made. "Liberty" is reserved for the absence of external impediments to action; whereas, "freedom" refers to "freedom for" commitments and positive forms of expression. In common usage each word is used with both references; but the distinction between the two ideas is very important. There is a helpful discussion of these concepts in Dorothy Fosdick's *What is Liberty?* (Harper, 1939).

Saxon countries the struggle for religious freedom has been basic. Our ancestors did not usually believe in freedom in the abstract, but they brooked no hindrance to their own freedom to speak the truth of God as they saw it. It is doubtful if freedom of expression will mean much to people who have nothing important to express, and it was the importance of expressing religious truth that created the moral pressure behind the demand for freedom in much of western history. When Christians struggle for this freedom against the political or ecclesiastical authorities who would hinder them, they open the door for freedom for others whether they intend to do so or not. When we trace the history of the development of this broader freedom, we find that many non-religious factors are involved. The mere fact of a variety of strong religious movements in conflict with each other creates a situation in which a general policy of toleration becomes expedient for social peace and for economic enterprise.

The first link between Christian freedom and civil freedom may seem very problematic in spite of its unintended by-products of external freedom for society in general. Christians, both Catholic and Protestant, until recent centuries were concerned about their own freedom and they were inclined to deny freedom to others. There was a widespread assumption that religious uniformity was essential to national unity. So while secular forces finally came to support freedom, it was the secular interest in such religious uniformity which made common cause with religious fanaticism in penalizing religious dissent for many centuries. But it remains true that there has been an explosive factor in Christianity which has threatened closed political or cultural or ideological systems. This has not been inconsistent with the effort to establish a Christian closed system but this explosive factor remains and Christian systems do not generally remain closed. This explosive factor is faith in God who transcends and judges every human system, and obedience to God leads men, in spite of themselves, on paths which they often do not choose to take and which bring them into opposition to the "powers that be" in Church and State.

(2) A second link between Christian freedom and civil liberties leads directly to the acceptance of the right of others to differ from what one may regard as essential truth. It is a corollary of Christian love based upon our understanding of the way the minds and spirits of persons grow. Christians took a long time to see that it is a sin against love for those in power to bring pressure on any human souls to cause them to assent to that which they do not believe with inner sincerity. To intimidate with threats of persecution or to bribe with promises of reward is to tempt people to hypocrisy. It is also the surest way in which to destroy the the sparks of creativity of mind or spirit that there may be in a people. There are many evil and repellent aspects of modern totalitarian societies, but by far the worst is the use of terror to break the spirits of men so that they will betray their cause and their associates against their own consciences. This is to turn a person into a subhuman creature to be manipulated by those who have the power. Democratic societies have their equivalents of this kind of treatment of people though the methods used are not so brutal. There are non-violent forms of intimidation, the suggestion that a person's economic security, his job, his promotion, his chance to secure customers or clients depend on his not saying anything that will be disapproved.

No one has stated more effectively this truth about the relation between honest convictions and freedom than Martin Luther. He wrote:

"For the proverb is true, 'thoughts are free.' Why then would they constrain people to believe from the heart, when they see that it is impossible? In this way they compel weak consciences to lie, to deny, and to say what they do not believe in their hearts, and they load themselves down with dreadful alien sins. For all the lies and false confessions which such weak consciences utter fall back upon him who compels them. It were far better, if their subjects erred, simply to let them err, than that they should constrain them to lie and to say what is not in their hearts: neither is it right to defend evil with what is worse."[5]

Luther was not always consistent in his attitude toward those who differed from him, but those words reveal a clear understanding of the true situation and they express one of his reasons for desiring to keep distinct the "two realms" so that the sword of the prince or the police power of the state would not interfere with the realm where only the persuasion of the Word of God could be effective. This conviction of Luther's became a commonplace of all who were pioneers in the struggle for religious tolerance or religious liberty. To refer to only one who was wholly different from Luther in temper, John Locke wrote: "No way whatsoever that I shall walk in against the dictates of my conscience will ever bring me to the mansions of the blessed. . . . Faith only and inward sincerity are the things that procure acceptance with God."[6]

We cannot separate inner freedom of thought from freedom of expression. At least there must be the possibility of not complying with those who can bring the pressure, there must be the possibility of saying "no." External freedom of expression, protected by law and by the habits of a community, is essential if there is to be the air in which minds and spirits can grow. This freedom depends in large part on the existence of institutions which live by it—such institutions as churches, colleges and universities, and the press.

(3) A third link between Christian freedom and civil freedom is the recognition of the limits of human wisdom and insight. This limitation comes both from our finiteness and from the sinful distortion of our minds by vested interests, by pride

---

[5] "On Secular Authority," *The Works of Martin Luther* (A. J. Holman, 1930), Vol. II, p. 254.
[6] *First Letter of Toleration* (Library of Liberal Arts, 1955), p. 34.

of opinion, and by plain inertia. This limitation is present in all areas of life and makes it necessary to be open to criticism and correction from whatever source it may come. And it may come from very unlikely sources.

A large part of the secular case for civil freedom in matters of opinion comes from scepticism concerning the adequacy of our present grasp of truth. I have already referred to Justice Holmes' scepticism and this underlay his strong championing of the right of free speech. As I suggested in my discussion of him, the secular sceptic can help to keep the society open though I doubt if it will stay open long unless there is spiritual health in it that depends on more than scepticism. The churches with dogmatic convictions did vastly more than sceptics in resisting National Socialism.

This emphasis on the limits of our knowledge of the truth is more natural on Protestant soil than on Catholic soil but there are Protestant groups which have little doubt of their own infallibility and there is in the Catholic Church, as a universal community, surprising diversity. Protestants who are sure that in Christ they find the true and central revelation of God and his purpose may accept the fact that their formulations and institutionalizations and applications of the truth given in Christ are defective and in need of correction. The opportunity for this is limited in Catholicism, but it is wide open in Protestantism. One of the most important insights which is now very widely accepted by Protestant theologians of many confessions and of many schools of thought is that what is given as revelation in Christ is not to be identified with the Bible as a book or with any creed or system of doctrine or with any conceptual formulations whatever. This means that every human way of expressing Christian truth remains under both the inspiration and judgment of Christ. There is continuity in faith and in purpose in the Christian Church, and the many attempts to express this faith and this purpose in creeds and systems are not wasted effort. They do carry Christian truth, but they are not final and they will be modified by restatement and reinterpretation.

I am always helped by words on this subject by Karl Barth who is not noted for a lack of confidence in his own theology. He writes: "Christian dogmatics will always be a thinking, an investigation and an exposition which are relative and liable to error. Even dogmatics with the best knowledge and conscience can do no more than question after the better, never forget that we are succeeded by other, later men; and he who is faithful in this task will hope that those other, later men may think and say better and more profoundly what we were endeavoring to think and say."[7]

Reinhold Niebuhr has put the matter very well in saying that "truth oftens comes on the back of error."[8] He uses as an illustration the fact that emphasis on the rights of women which was true often came with a rationalistic feminism which was false. This abstract and mistaken feminism was a radical protest against the male imperialism of the ages. This has obviously been a man's world in both state and Church though women have not always failed to get their way.

We see illustrations of the same relationship between truth and error in the Marxist protest against the injustices of early, unreconstructed capitalism, in the rationalistic criticism of many forms of superstition and intolerance, in the atheistic rejection of false *conceptions* of God.

We never know from what direction the criticism may happen to come which at a given moment may be most needed. It will surely be mixed with much error, but if we make rules censoring the error we shall lose the needed, if partial, truth. The correction often comes from those who are not respectable in the eyes of society for the respectable are so well adjusted

[7] *Dogmatics in Outline* (Philosophical Library, 1949), p. 11.
[8] *The Children of Light and the Children of Darkness* (Scribners, 1944), pp. 75-76.

to the *status quo* that they are likely to be blind to many of its shortcomings. So the new insight is often brought to us by the very rebels against whom society is only too eager to protect itself and we may not be able to tell in the early stages when rebels are real destroyers, when they are foolish cranks, or when they are prophets or constructive critics. Laws and practices which inhibit one of these kinds of rebels will discourage all and society will lose sources of its own renewal.

(4) Christian understanding of sin should help us to realize the special temptations of those who assume the function of investigating and censoring others. Usually they over-reach themselves. They easily identify as subversive anything that threatens their power. They become specialists concerning the stereotyped forms of error which accompany the truth that may be needed and they have eyes only for the error. They become single-track in their judgments, careless about the wounds that they inflict on the institutions of freedom even when they claim to be their defenders. I do not say that there should be no investigating or curbing of subversion or of obscenity, but these tasks bring with them their own temptations and they need to be carried on in such a way that those who specialize on them do not make policy, and all that follows from their findings should be held within a frame that is controlled by society's broader interests in due process of law and in spiritual and cultural freedom.

During the period of intensive investigations of subversion in this country which is associated with the name of Senator McCarthy things went wrong partly because all was done in an atmosphere of hysteria fanned by the investigators themselves. If we had ransacked the nation to discover persons to carry on those widely publicized investigations who were least fitted for the task we could not have produced any less fitted than some of the men who were actually put in charge of them. Overeagerness, callousness, and the desire for publicity, polit-

ical partisanship, and unwillingness to discriminate between dis-
loyalty and innocent mistakes seemed to be the chief quailfica-
tions. One prime qualification for this task should be reluctance
to engage in it!

I began this chapter by saying that there is a real danger
that the channels of communication may be closed by those
who capture political power in the interests of a totalitarian
ideology. That is a factor that no generalizations about freedom should obscure. It is possible to use freedom to destroy the
very institutions of freedom themselves—for a time. It is difficult to say anything useful about this problem when situations
change as rapidly as they do; but in addition to the care in
choosing the personnel to deal with this problem, which I
have emphasized, I offer these suggestions:

The first is an underlining of Professor Sidney Hook's familiar
distinction between heresy and conspiracy. Where the fact of
conspiracy exists, it is important to deal with it efficiently
for the sake of freedom. It can best be handled by experts
trained for such intelligence work rather than in public by
congressional committees.

Second, very careful attention should be given to the date
at which any person in this country has been involved in Communist activities. If to some extent Communist activity or
even the proclaiming of Communist ideas above-ground is an
indication of the existence of conspiracy underground, such
activities or such proclaiming may be used as sources of evidence. But when we are confronted by things said or done
during three decades, it makes all of the difference in the world
in which decade we place them. In the 1930's it was possible
for many Americans to become involved in Communist activities because at that time they were convinced that Communism
offered the one way out of a morass of capitalistic disintegration and the strongest alternative to a threatening Fascism.
There was no cold war with Russia. Russia was not to any

degree an international danger; the international danger was Hitler's Germany. These factors made many people into Communists or Communist sympathizers without in any way corrupting their basic loyalty to America. Most of them came to be disillusioned about Communism until by 1950 the number of such Communists or fellow-travellers became very small. This kind of rapid turnover coupled with disillusionment has been very common in the Communist movements in many western countries. One of the chief errors during the period of Senator McCarthy's influence was a failure to take seriously the reality of this turnover, of these changes from decade to decade. It was a terrible injustice to ferret out in the 1950's what many men did in the 1930's or even in the early 1940's and smear them publicly as though what they did then had the same moral meaning that it would have had if they had done it during the period of the cold war when there has been much less excuse for illusions about Communism.

In the third place, there should be great discrimination in the way in which those responsible for policies in this area deal with *ideas* which suggest Communism. Here the difference between heresy and conspiracy is involved but also something much broader. It is not only a question of distinguishing between those who teach Communism as a system of ideas and those who are engaged in conspiracy. It is also a question of distinguishing between Communism as a context for ideas and similar ideas in a different context. There is much overlapping in ideas between Communism and democratic socialism, between Communism and many criticisms of capitalism which are widely accepted; but the meaning of these ideas is essentially different in the Communist context from what it is in other contexts. In the Communist context they are part of a total ideological scheme which is an instrument of a particular power movement. They are not necessarily wrong as ideas in the abstract or when they are combined with quite different political purposes. Much of the persecution of people for their allegedly Communist ideas has really been a persecution of them for differing on matters of economic organization or of foreign policy from those who did the persecuting. Guilt by association may be based on nothing more than the association of ideas taken out of their most significant contexts. Any economic proposal that is opposed is called "creeping socialism" and then Communism is called "socialism in a hurry" and so the smearing easily follows.

This is a book about the state and not about all aspects of society. It is only fair to the state to call attention to the fact that the state is not the only threat to civil freedom. In the chapter on economic institutions I emphasized the way in which the freedom of men is threatened or destroyed by forms of economic power. Here it is important to emphasize the power of public opinion, the climate that can become quite stifling that is created by the majority. No constitutional safeguards of freedom can shield individuals and minority groups against all the pressures that come from an intolerant majority. When the powers of the state make common cause with this intolerance, the result may be a truly terrible spiritual tyranny, but the powers of the state may not be so allied with this intolerance of the majority and it still may be severely oppressive.

Edmund Burke eloquently expressed this when he was observing the results of the tyranny of the majority in revolutionary France. While he referred to a situation under state control his perception of the pervasiveness of the pressure of a majority has a wider application. He wrote:

"Of this I am certain, that in a democracy, the majority of citizens is capable of exercising the most cruel oppression upon the minority, whenever strong divisions prevail in that kind of polity as they often must; and that oppression of the minority will extend to far greater numbers, and will be carried on with much greater fury, than can almost ever be apprehended from the dominion of a single sceptre. In such a popular persecution, individual sufferers are in a much more deplorable condition than in any other. Under a cruel prince they have the balmy compassion of mankind to assuage the smart of their wounds . . . but those who are subjected to wrong under multitudes, are deprived of all external consolation. They seem deserted by mankind, overpowered by a conspiracy of the whole species."[9]

Burke identified this tendency with democracy, but we see it in its extreme form in the chief contemporary alternative to democracy, an ideological dictatorship with a mass base. This has often been called "totalitarian democracy" and Burke was right about it. Today the contrast is not between democracy and Burke's "single sceptre" or "cruel prince" in a more or less traditional society with some natural protections of freedom but between democracy which is dedicated to the safeguarding of minorities and of the individual conscience and "totalitarian democracies."

Alexis de Toqueville is very sobering because he saw in the 1830's a milder form of the same thing in America that Burke saw in France. He wrote: "I know of no country in which there is so little independence of mind and real freedom of discussion as in America." Then he compares America with European monarchy and says that the individual "who raises his voice in the cause of truth if he is unfortunate enough to live under an absolute government" will find the people often on his side; "if he inhabits a free country, he can, if necessary find a shelter behind the throne. The aristocratic part of society supports him in some countries, and the democracy in others. But in a nation where democratic institutions exist, organized like those in the United States, there is but one authority, one element of strength and success, with nothing beyond it. . . . In

[9] *Reflections on the French Revolution* (Everyman's Library Edition), p. 122.

America the majority raises formidable barriers around liberty of opinion. . . ."[10]

As I have said, the state need not be an instrument of this intolerance. In the United States the courts have often safe-guarded the individual, and the dissenter is likely to have some strong defenders in public life. But the pluralism of society which is a factor which limits the state, is also important as a source of freedom from the worst effects of this pressure from the majority. The academic freedom of educational insti-tutions is one line of defense. Also, the churches can help in local communities where this kind of pressure is likely to be most oppressive. The Church by its very nature is under no local authority and it brings to the community a Gospel and a judgment which are strange to its prejudices.[11] When the community captures the Church and makes it an instrument of its intolerance, as sometimes happens, the results are dark indeed. "If then the light in you is darkness, how great is the darkness!" But this real possibility should not hide the re-source for freedom in the Church. There is some help in the divisions within the Church and all discussions of Church union should take account of the need of avoiding the conformism that can smother spiritual freedom in the Church as well as in the world.

[10] *Democracy in America* (Ed., Phillips Bradley. Knopf, 1948), Vol. I, pp. 263-264.

[11] Many people in Georgia must have noticed this contrast when they read a statement by eighty Protestant ministers in Atlanta on Nov. 3, 1957, calling for first-class citizenship for Negroes and emphasizing obedience to the law, the preservation of the public school system, and freedom of speech in the context of the controversy over desegregation. *New York Times*, Nov. 11, 1957, p. 99. (Published in full in *The Christian Century*, Nov. 20, 1957.)

CHAPTER XI

The Affinity Between Christianity and Democracy

CHRISTIANS are rightly reluctant to identify their faith with any particular social or political structure or economic system. Much Christian thinking has been vitiated by the natural tendency to regard familiar institutions as the inevitable Christian institutions. Does this mean that there are no criteria for political institutions which we find support for in Christian faith? Does it mean that there is no affinity between Christianity and any direction of political development?

Historically it is certainly true that Christianity has been closely linked with most of the types of political structure which are possible. There have been states claiming to be Christian which have been despotic and in which there has often been little or no sense of conflict between the Christian faith and that form of government. Christians generally have felt more affinity with constitutional aristocracies than with despotisms or democracies. A Christian despotism is likely to feel the effect of the explosive element in Christianity to which I have referred. In the Christian west the tension between Church and Empire or national rulers always made trouble for a closed political system. The Church made its own the classical natural law tradition which in itself provided no means of enforcement and yet which kept alive sources of criticism upon power. The extremely loose structure of mediaeval feudalism gave limited powers to many rulers under the rather distant lordship of emperor and pope. It is of special interest that both Thomas Aquinas and John Calvin, two of the great Christian thinkers who had most interest in political questions, were both believers in Aristotle's mixed polity which was a constitutional aristocracy.

Professor James Hastings Nichols in his provocative book, *Democracy and the Churches*,[1] makes a strong case for the view that most forms of the Christian tradition have been unfavorable to democracy and that modern democracy is dependent chiefly on two types of Christianity, the Calvinistic or Reformed tradition and the left-wing sectarian tradition which has had enormous political influence in the Anglo-Saxon countries. These two traditions he labels "Puritan Protestantism." The other Christian traditions, Roman, Eastern Orthodox, Lutheran and Anglican, have not on the whole been favorable to the rise of democracy. He admits that some democratic ideas have many sources, including the Greek political thinkers, Catholic natural law, the secular thinkers of the enlightenment. But what he is concerned about is the spiritual roots of the working democratic institutions which are with us now and which have had a considerable history. If we limit what is considered here in this way to the effective spiritual influences which have been favorable to democratic living as distinguished from the sources of democratic ideas, I think that Professor Nichols' contention is difficult to refute. Even if we may decide that it requires some qualifications it does underline the point that I am making that historically there has been no general affinity between Christianity and democracy. Lutheranism, in Scandinavian countries especially, Anglicanism and, in some countries, Roman Catholicism have adjusted themselves to democracy and, after they have made the adjustment, they have released spiritual influences which have been favorable to democratic life though the relationship between Roman Catholicism and democracy even in such cases remains problematic.

[1] Westminster Press, 1951, Chap. I.

Anglo-Saxon democracy owes most to the sectarian tradition which flowered in the seventeenth century and which was the seed-bed of many influences favoring human rights, especially the "rights of Englishmen," the structures of free government, religious liberty and the free Church. The extraordinary debates in Cromwell's army expressed most of the convictions on which democratic institutions are based with elemental power behind which we see both a very human struggle for justice and freedom and a devout religious faith. Reinhold Niebuhr points out that while the French Revolution is usually given credit for shattering the "mold of an organic aristocratic civilization," the Cromwellian revolution, more than a century earlier, was the source of the impulses and convictions of democracy in a much wiser form than the French "abstract liberalism." He suggests that the apparent failure of the Cromwellian revolution because of the restoration of the Stuarts has obscured the real continuity between the influence of that revolution and later British democratic achievements. Even Americans are more aware of the French Revolution than they are of the Cromwellian revolution though the latter was so closely related to the Puritan sources of the American tradition.[2]

Archbishop William Temple pays a very significant tribute to the sectarian source of democracy in England when he says that the English people learned democracy in the "dissenting congregations."[3] Temple himself embodied the kind of Anglican support for both political and economic democracy which has been important for the greater part of a century. Anglicanism as the dominant tradition had greater difficulty than the free

[2] Niebuhr's article, "Liberty and Equality" in *The Yale Review*, Autumn, 1957, p. 9. Also Chap. V in *Pious and Secular America* (Scribners, 1958). Niebuhr recognizes also the influence of the mediaeval tradition on John Locke by way of Hooker. This shows how varied are the Christian sources of convictions which enter into democratic thought.

[3] *Christianity and Social Order* (Penguin), p. 51.

churches in becoming convinced about the claims of democracy. We may say the same about the Puritan established churches of New England in contrast with the Baptists and the Quakers. The democratic impulse does come initially from below the established authorities of Church or state. But, when it wins its way, it may gain the support of those established authorities or their successors.

So far I have emphasized the fact that historically there has been no general support for democracy in the Church, that the spiritual impulse that has made democratic life possible is dependent upon a quite limited range of tradition in Christian history, though some democratic ideas have had their antecedents in other Christian sources. Yet, Christians in most traditions today claim that there is a special affinity between Christianity and democracy. This is true of almost all Protestant confessions and it is true of Catholics in many countries. Catholics rightly contend that Pope Pius XII has given less ambiguous support to democracy than any of his predecessors.[4]

The Ecumenical Assemblies have not generally used the word "democracy" in their pronouncements but under the name "Responsible Society" the World Council of Churches has given strong support to the substance of democracy as it will be understood in this chapter. This concept of "The Responsible Society" was developed at the Amsterdam Assembly

[4] Pius XII's Christmas letter of 1944.

Also, Karl Barth, who is associated with the warning against identification of Christianity with human systems, says: "It must be admitted that the word and the concept 'democracy' ('the rule of the people') is powerless to describe even approximately the kind of State which, in the Christian view, most nearly corresponds to the divine ordinance. This is no reason, however, why it should be overlooked or denied that Christian choices and purposes in politics tend on the whole toward the form of State, which, if it is not actually realized in the so-called 'democracies,' is at any rate more or less clearly intended and desired. Taking everything into account, it must be said that the Christian view shows a stronger trend in this direction than in any other. There certainly is an affinity between the Christian community and the civil communities of free peoples." *Against the Stream* (Philosophical Library, 1954), p. 44.

in 1954. Here is no accidental pronouncement of a Church assembly but a development of a position over a period of years with very strong support in two Assemblies of the World Council and with widespread acceptance by the churches. I shall quote two key passages from the report of the Third Section of the Amsterdam Assembly. The first was reaffirmed in so many words at Evanston and the substance of the second was repeated there in an abbreviated form.

The Responsible Society as a concept was defined at Amsterdam as "a society where freedom is the freedom of men who acknowledge responsibility to justice and public order, and where those who hold political authority or economic power are responsible for its exercise to God and the people whose welfare is affected by it." This is explained in more definitely political terms in the statement that for "a society to be responsible under modern conditions it is required that the people have freedom to control, to criticize and to change their governments, that power be made responsible by law and tradition, and be distributed as widely as possible through the whole community." Much of the latter statement is said more briefly but with an important addition in regard to the actual institutions of democracy by the Third Section of the Evanston Assembly: "Channels of political action must be developed by which the people can without recourse to violence change their governments." Again, I should say the word "democracy" is not used in these documents and I doubt if "democracy" as such should be used ecumenically at the present time. It is too ambiguous a word because of the difference between Anglo-Saxon assumptions about democracy and those of the French Revolution, and because there is a similar contrast between democracy as used in the non-Communist world and democracy as it enters into the idea of "peoples' democracies" in Communist countries.[5]

[5] Cf. C. H. Carr, *Soviet Impact on the Western World* (Macmillan, 1947), Chap. I. (Also see footnote p. 151.)

When I use the word "democracy," I refer to a type of political structure that is characterized by two things: (1) government based upon the consent and participation of all elements in the population; (2) constitutional safeguards of freedom of expression for all persons and of the right of minorities to organize politically in order to become majorities.

This right of all elements of the population to participate in government means that there should be no part of the population that is governed by the rest of the population without its consent. It does not mean that there should be no qualificaions for voting that are applied to the individual, but these qualifications should not be so designed that they disenfranchise any continuing racial or social group in the nation. The reason why universal suffrage in this sense is desirable is that any group that does not have a share in the political power will be neglected or exploited by other groups. In the southern states of this country we have had a kind of laboratory in which the disabilities which accompany the absence of political rights in the case of the Negro minority (sometimes even the majority) could be readily observed. In recent years great advances have been made in assuring the Negroes their rights, but where they have not been able to vote, they have had no defense against the white man's laws, no defense even against the police.

In other periods there has been a widespread assumption that the right to vote should depend upon the possession of a certain amount of property. This was supposed to guarantee that

---

It is well to realize that the word "democracy" has not been used in this country as the non-controversial word for our form of government until this century. It was often said that we were a Republic but not a democracy. Charles A. Beard finds the change to have come at the time of Woodrow Wilson. [See *The Republic* (Viking Press, 1943), pp. 32-33] Lord Percy's *The Heresy of Democracy* (Eyre and Spottiswoode, London, 1954) is an illuminating historical account of the contrast between "Totalism" and "Dualism." The first he identifies with democracy and rejects. The second is in line with Anglo-Saxon institutions, but they are always threatened by modern pressures toward Totalism.

the voter would be responsible, that he would have a stake in the stability of social institutions. This case was well put by Ireton, one of Cromwell's generals, in the famous army debates at Putney. He was arguing against the idea that every man by the law of nature should have the vote whether he had any property or not and he said that if he had no property, "possibly I may not have so real a regard to the peace of the kingdom as that man who hath a permanent interest in it. He that is here today, and gone tomorrow, I do not see that he hath a permanent interest."[6] There is a case here, but if this means the disenfranchisement of a portion of the population, those people will be the victims of the others. One of the remarkable developments in modern political history is that the logic of democracy has forced the classes which had the advantage of limited suffrage to yield that advantage so that today universal suffrage is the rule in democratic countries. The older democracies have long since established universal suffrage (though the men of Switzerland go to the polls every few years to deny the vote to the other half of the population), and such new nations as India and Pakistan moved to universal suffrage immediately in spite of the high percentage of illiteracy among their people.

Ireton had much prudence on his side, but the argument has finally been won by those who opposed him and who said, as Col. Rainbourough did in that debate: "For I really think that the poorest he that is in England hath a life to live, as the greatest he; and therefore truly, sir, I think it's clear, that every man that is to live under a government ought first by his own consent to put himself under that government. . . ."[7] The extreme voluntarism of the last part of that statement is unrealistic but this great stress on the need of keeping government in close touch with the life of all who are affected by it through

[6] *Puritanism and Liberty* (Ed., A. S. P. Woodhouse. J. M. Dent, London, 1938), p. 58.
[7] *Ibid.*, p. 53.

universal suffrage is right. Otherwise, important elements in the national experience will not be taken seriously by those who have the power to make decisions.

The other element in democracy, the constitutional protection of minorities, is equally important. Indeed, at the present time it should have priority. It is easily lost and, if it goes, popular sovereignty with universal suffrage may soon lose its value. Today a society can vote itself into a tyranny with a mass base. The leaders of a majority, even if it is an honest majority at one stage, can so entrench themselves that they cannot be put out of power when they have lost the real support of most of the people. The right and power of a minority to win through to majority status is itself the essential safeguard of majority rule in the long run. Quite apart from that important reason for insisting on the rights of minorities it is only in a society which has such protections that there can be spiritual and cultural freedom. The threat of what Professor Talmon[8] and others have called "totalitarian democracy" always hangs over popular government in these days of rapid change, of mass movements controlled by fanatical ideologies, of the weakening of the sense of objective norms of any kind, of the easy manipulation of opinion by those who control the power of government.

It is these two elements in democracy and not the special institutions of any one democratic community which should be emphasized when we think of the relation between the claims of democracy and Christianity. They are in line with the conception of "the responsible society."

The historic connection of democracy with an optimistic or perfectionist conception of man must be abandoned. Not only is that conception false; it is no harmless error for it lends itself to emphasis upon expansive utopian programs which

[8] J. L. Talmon, *The Origins of Totalitarian Democracy* (The Beacon Press, 1952).

do not fit the real needs of society and may lead to totalitarianism. If a political movement is convinced that it has the final solution of humanity's problem and that, if given power, it can put that solution into effect it has a rationalization for any ruthless and tyrannical shortcuts in order to gain power. This very optimism about its social scheme goes with a blindness to its own temptations as a movement to misuse power and to the realities of its own corruption. This is the tragedy of Communism. Social optimism of an extreme sort need not have these results; instead of becoming ruthless it may be only confusing and irrelevant.

Reinhold Niebuhr has done more than any other thinker in the Church (perhaps also more than any thinker outside the Church) to make clear the dangers of "utopian" democracy and he has shown that the institutions of political democracy have a better foundation in Christian realism about human nature than in the optimism of the Enlightenment. He has summarized his thought in the epigram that is now famous: "Man's capacity for justice makes democracy possible; but man's inclination to injustice makes democracy necessary."[9] In this emphasis he is building upon one of the traditions which have nourished Anglo-Saxon democracy, a tradition that owes more to Calvinism than to the Enlightenment, which was expressed within the spiritual and political ferment in the Cromwellian period in England and in the realism of some of the American founding fathers. Dr. Niebuhr makes clear that a cynical or one-sidedly pessimistic view of the human situation is incompatible with democracy. Those who share such a view—either a Luther or a Thomas Hobbes—are so much afraid of disorder that they will clamp down on the people; they will guard any existing system of order no matter how unjust because of their fear that any change may bring anarchy. So, the basis for

[9] *The Children of Light and the Children of Darkness* (Scribners, 1944), p. xi.

democracy should not be either a one-sided pessimism or a one-sided optimism. Democracy is necessary because no group can be trusted with power over those who have no chance to criticize it and to participate in its control. The balancing of power in society is, from this point of view, the surest way of maintaining an approximate justice.

Why should Christians now be concerned to support or to extend democracy when, as I have said, most of Christian history has been on the side of other forms of political organization? The answer is that from the beginning there have been essential elements of Christian teaching which had democratic implications but that only in the modern period have events so shaped the political alternatives that these implications are clearly seen. Also, I believe that these elements of Christian teaching which I have in mind can be easily distorted unless all of them are emphasized together.

I refer to three essentials of Christian faith. The first is the belief in the sovereignty of God as transcending all of the authorities and powers of the world. The second is God's love for all persons regardless of their status in society. The third is the doctrine of sin which warns us against a political system which allows anyone to have arbitrary, unchecked power over others.

The sovereignty of God, whether recognized or not, is the ultimate basis for the right and duty of the person to claim for himself and his neighbors the kind of freedom which a democratic constitution protects. If there is no love or compassion which continually seeks to raise up the poor and defenseless and the disadvantaged to a position where they can develop their capacities and maintain their just rights, and if there is no stress upon the sin which accompanies the most respectable forms of power, faith in God's sovereignty may not be democratic in its effects at all. It may give divine sanction to a small group who claim to be the beneficiaries of God's providence or who convince themselves that they have inside knowledge of God's will. The combination of the understanding of God's love as known in Christ which knows no favored class—unless it be those who have been lost or who have been neglected—and the application of the doctrine of sin to the privileged and the powerful correct any such misuse of the Christian faith in the divine sovereignty.

Even Christian love without the self-criticism that applies this idea of sin to one's own self-understanding can lead to a paternalism that does much good for others but which never raises the question of the distribution of power. This paternalism has often seemed to Christians who have had the power and privilege to be a substitute for democracy.

As I have said, the doctrine of sin, taken by itself, can easily lead to a Christian pessimism that sees no alternative to a type of order which keeps the people from having an opportunity to create disorder.

These three elements in Christian faith not only provide the basis for democracy for our thought, but they also are the surest source of the motives among the citizens on which the working of democratic institutions depends. There need not always be awareness of the relation of these motives to Christian faith but unless such motives have strength among many citizens democracy can hardly maintain itself. The direct and indirect influence of the Christian community, in so far as these elements of Christian faith are living realities in the lives of its members, upon the larger community at this level of motive is its greatest contribution to political life.

So far I have tried to show that there is a real affinity between Christianity and democracy; now I shall deal with several serious difficulties in this position. First, we should not allow the truth about this affinity to result in a kind of legalistic absolute according to which it is assumed that in all situations it is the duty of Christians to work directly for the establishment of democratic institutions. Democracy is a very precarious system of government. Paper democratic constitutions may be of no value unless there are conditions within the national community which are favorable to democratic behavior. To move too rapidly toward popular government may indeed in some situations result in disorder of which those who favor a totalitarian system can take advantage. Christians who live under relatively stable authoritarian governments which have preserved a measure of acceptance among the people should not necessarily assume that it is their responsibility to work directly for the establishment of democratic institutions tomorrow. Guglielmo Ferrero, the Italian historian, has made a point of great importance in his discussion of "legitimacy" as attached to a government. This quality of legitimacy may be attached to any kind of political system—democratic or otherwise—but it depends upon a measure of acceptance among the people. When it is gone, the government is controlled by fear of its own subjects as is the case with our modern dictatorships which never become "legitimate" in this sense. Ferrero says: "Without legitimacy a government fears its subjects and this is the cause of the worst crimes of government. . . . Arbitrary and violent despotism is always the result of illegitimacy."[10]

I confess that I never realized the importance of this consideration until I read Ferrero. In so far as it is true, it means that there can be a reckless impatience with an existing order that is not democratic which may lead not to democracy but to arbitrary despotism. To go around the world with a blue-print of democracy and to insist that Christians everywhere should identify their faith with that blue-print would be destructive folly. Legitimacy depends upon acceptance and such acceptance does easily dissolve where a government goes too far in abusing its power, where the shepherds too obviously are chiefly concerned to feed themselves, where great social problems go too

[10] *Principles of Power* (G. P. Putnam, 1942), p. 41.

long neglected. I think that legitimacy that does not have a democratic basis is likely to give way under the pressure of these unsolved problems, but, where possible, some continuity should be preserved so that some of the majesty of an old tradition can give its sanctiort to new and more democratic institutions.

The extraordinary achievement of the British in adapting their monarchy and much else in their tradition to a modern semi-socialist democracy took so many centuries that nations which have to make rapid transitions today may not be much helped by their example, but their experience does illustrate the role of political legitimacy. The American liberals, who for a time at the end of the Second World War advocated the deposing of the Emperor of Japan, had no understanding of this principle and we can be thankful that they were over-ruled by wiser counsels.

This warning against an absolutizing of the duty to establish democratic institutions in the name of Christianity can be sharpened if we realize that political democracy, if it is to work, depends on favorable non-political conditions among the people of a nation. It depends upon attitudes which can never be taken for granted and which cannot be created by law or by political fiat. It depends upon the existence of common purposes among the people, upon respect for and patience with political opponents, which are deeper than campaign hostilities, upon the willingness to accept changes when once they have been legally established which go against self-interest, upon integrity among public servants and a general interest in honest elections, upon a willingness to participate in political life, upon a considerable public understanding of the issues at stake in political controversies. The non-political institutions need to be favorable to the development of habits of democratic behavior. I do not believe that such institutions as the family or the school or the Church need be democratic in the same way in which this is appropriate for political society, but families and schools can be so authoritarian that they do not train children to take responsibility and a Church with an authoritarian polity does create difficulties for democracy, though the Church's right to its own type of polity should be safeguarded by a democratic constitution. The existence of democratic habits in innumerable voluntary organizations is one of the most favorable nonpolitical supports for democracy.

Economic institutions especially need to be favorable to democracy. Those who control the means of livelihood usually have more effective power over people than the state. A plutocracy can pervert to its own ends the most perfect democratic constitution. If democracy is not to be undercut by economic institutions, wealth must be widely distributed, there must be many centers of economic power which can keep one another in balance, there must be real opportunity for the people of all classes to develop their capacities, and there must be a fluid class-structure. These need only be trends rather than total achievements, but if the trends are in the opposite direction, democratic political institutions can hardly grow.[11]

In recent years there have been warning voices from some responsible conservatives who echo in large part the thought of Edmund Burke and de Toqueville about the limitations of democracy. These conservatives are to be distinguished from the reckless rightists who are willing to destroy precious traditions of freedom in their anti-Communist zeal. Also they should be distinguished from the type of conservative who seeks to restore the capitalistic institutions of a half-century or more ago. We may often learn more from English conservatives, such as Lord Percy, who are not tempted to confuse conservatism with

[11] In my book, *The Christian as Citizen*, I have dealt with the question as to what the real alternatives to democracy are today and I have said more about the responsibility of Christians in countries which have had no democratic experience. In this book I have chosen to emphasize the responsibility of Christians in countries which have both a strong Christian tradition and considerable democratic experience.

the restoration of untrammelled economic individualism than we do from American conservatives who are generally confused on this issue.[12]

Many of these conservative warnings I have already suggested in what I have said about "totalitarian democracy," about the tyranny of the majority even in a politically free society, about the deadly effect of rationalistic illusions concerning a future society, about the importance of taking seriously the principle of legitimacy. I shall here call attention to two concerns which come more from conservative than from liberal minds and which are in some conflict with the democratic impulse, the general validity of which I have stressed.

The first of these concerns is that liberty may not be sacrificed to equality. The democratic impulse, for which we may thank God because it has given most of the human race new possibilities of life which were unheard of when the conservatives of the past had their callous way, needs some supplementation and correction, so long as it is not prevented from doing its work. If we drive ahead with only the concern for equality we shall lose quality. We shall lose the liberty to be different. This is not primarily a matter of politics, and political democracy need not destroy quality; it is more a matter of the many cultural institutions in a mass society. Yet, political decisions can favor a tendency to undermine quality. This is perhaps most evident in the field of education. Already American education tends to be so contemporaneous and utilitarian that it often fails to include the disciplines which enable gifted minds to discover their capacities. Equal opportunity should mean the opportunity for children and young people to develop not only the abilities which they share in common with others, but their own unusual gifts. The private agencies of mass communication may be just as responsible as the schools for the levelling down of intellectual interests and attainments.

[12] Professor Clinton Rossiter's *Conservatism in America* (Knopf, 1955), is discriminating at this point and differs from the writings of Russell Kirk who does not escape from an uncritical economic individualism.

The trend toward greater economic equality is in the interests of justice and fraternity. This trend should continue, but a single-track doctrinaire pressure for economic equality would reduce incentive; it would involve much regimentation in order to enforce equality; and it would make extremely difficult the existence of independent cultural enterprises which are favorable to freedom and excellence. We may well be worried about the difficulty of the individual in standing up against the majority in the community unless there are centers of power and influence which have their own private economic base. Traditional aristocracies, as de Toqueville says, may perform this function. Such aristocracies, where they do not exist, cannot be artificially created and even though they have advantages over oligarchies that depend on wealth alone, no nation that does not have them is likely to want them and their snobbery. But the problem remains that some equivalent is needed for the traditional centers of power and influence which can be a break on the tyranny of dictators, of economic over-lords, and of the pressure to conform to the will of the majority.

The second warning that I shall link with my discussion of democracy is the warning that the levelling down process encouraged by democracy makes strong political leadership difficult. Leadership that has the capacity to make lonely and difficult decisions and that is able to impress the people with its competence and its integrity and which has that plus quality that brings the best out of a nation and instills into it courage to face trials and suffering is rare, but unless it appears from time to time democracies may falter and be destroyed. No democratic system can insure that it will be available, and democracies can be misled by false glamour or by clever political manipulators. The American system of checks and balances as between the legislature and the executive may frustrate any leaders at critical times. But without such leadership part of the time and without at other times at least the competence and

authority that can decide and organize and act, the best dem
ocratic instituions will work badly or not at all.

After we have done our balancing of equality and liberty and
after we have heard the warnings of conservatives, we should
still allow the democratic impulse to have the last word. Conservatism cannot provide the support for the economic and
social changes which most of the world still needs; it lacks compassion, and it is generally blind to the real effects of institutions
upon people who do not benefit from them. Priorities differ
from country to country and in those parts of the world where
most people still suffer from poverty and hunger, their needs
must have priority. Conservative warnings in such situations are
no answer to "totalitarian democracy"; the only answer is a
discriminating but still revolutionary program. There is a Christian bias which we cannot escape in favor of the people who are
victims, who are neglected by the comfortable. The love of God
known to us in Christ goes out to all men and seeks to raise
them up. It constrains us to defend those who are least able to
defend themselves. Karl Barth is true to an essential aspect of
the Gospel when he writes: "The Church is witness of the fact
that the Son of man came to seek and to save the lost. And this
implies that—casting all false impartiality aside—the Church
must concentrate first on the lower and lowest levels of society.
The poor, the socially and economically weak and threatened,
will always be the object of its primary and particular concern,
and it will always insist on the State's special responsibility for
these weaker members of society."[13]

Yes, and the Church should help the weaker members of
society as they become stronger to understand that this new-
found strength brings temptations of the kind that were so
conspicuous in the strong at whose hands they once suffered.

[13] *Aganst the Stream*, p. 36. This is elaborated with Barth's characteristic
force in *Church Dogmatics*, Vol. IV, Pt. I (Scribners, 1956), pp. 188-192.

CHAPTER XII

Christian Ethics and the Dilemmas of Foreign Policy

It is in the sphere of foreign policy that the moral dilemmas confronting the state are most perplexing and fateful. Christians as citizens live with these dilemmas in the nuclear age with very little direct traditional guidance. Protestant political theory has much to say about the state and about its responsibility under God to maintain order, but it is the conflicts between states which create the most destructive disorder. The major Christian traditions since the time of St. Augustine have taken for granted that there are just wars which are rightly waged as a last resort for the sake of a just cause and with moderation; but this idea of the "just war" reflects a situation in which wars were technologically and morally limited.[1]

There has generally been a minority pacifist voice which has claimed the support of the teachings of Jesus and this voice has had great influence in the Church since the First World War. The state as itself the embodiment of a prideful and egoistic will to power has been widely recognized as a fact, but until this century there has been little Protestant theological interest in

[1] The concept of the just war has, in one important respect, fallen apart. It has traditionally referred both to the justice of the objective of the war, or the cause that was at stake, and to the justice of the means used, with emphasis upon moderation and upon the effect of such means upon the health of post-war institutions and relationships. A just war in the first sense is still a possibility, but it is impossible to imagine a just war in the second sense on a world scale. The kind of limited war that was waged in Korea can fit the criteria of the just war in both senses.

the problem of taming that will for the sake of international order. The Roman Catholic system preserves in the Papacy a unifying spiritual center among the nations, but Catholics, like Protestants, have been strongly identified with their separate nations, and Papal influence has had little effect on modern international politics.

In recent decades Christians have been forced to face international problems with a sense of terrible urgency. Human existence on earth is at stake. Also at stake is the freedom of many nations from at least temporary totalitarian domination. Is there any reality harder to live with than the fact that at the very time when the weapons of war threaten mutual annihilation, the moral and spiritual split within humanity has become deepest? Because of this split, it is difficult to arrive at any accord that might make possible reduction and control of armaments and the development of a United Nations strong enough to restrain any recalcitrant great power.

The present split is the more baffling because, while it is the Communist world that is dominated by anti-religious ideology, by arbitrary political power, by ingenious distortions of the very moral concepts which have given some unity to the west, the Communist rulers win wide support because of past and present moral failures of the "Christian" white west. What they mean by justice and freedom seems so often to be a perversion of what we mean by the same words, and yet they make much headway because of our failures to live up to our own understanding of justice and freedom. This is especially true of the influence of Communism on the uncommitted peoples who have recently won their freedom from western imperial powers. This confusing situation makes a direct approach by western Christians as Christians to the problem of the moral and spiritual split almost as difficult as the approach of western statesmen to the political conflict. It also means that when these two approaches are combined into a pretentiously moralistic political policy, it is usually self-defeating.[2]

A. Pacifism vs. Non-Pacifism

I cannot go further in discussing the relation between Christian ethics and foreign policy without first dealing with one approach to the problem—or, more accurately, one group of approaches—the Christian pacifist position. Our attitude toward the pacifist type of solution will determine our attitude toward the most perplexing dilemmas associated with foreign policy.

I have said that Christian pacifism has been a minority voice during most of Christian history. And yet it does express the imperative of Christian love in a way which at least on the surface would seem to give it a first claim on the attention of Christians. While in the great Churches in the past pacifism was a kind of heresy, in our time there has come a reversal that puts the burden of proof on the non-pacifist.[3] This is more true of liberal Protestantism and especially of Ango-Saxon liberal Protestantism than it is of other segments of the Chuch, but pacifist convictions have been very pervasive since the First World War. Pacifism remains a heresy in Roman Catholicism, but the Catholic idea of a just war has great difficulty in maintaining itself in days of total war and there is a pragmatic pacifism among Roman Catholics based upon the view that modern wars cannot be expected to be just. Historical events have favored a kind of Christian pacifism in two nations where a short time ago it was almost unheard of: Germany and Japan.

One of the landmarks in Protestant, or more broadly non-

[2] I have sometimes allowed myself to use "west" to mean the non-Communist world, but I do so with apologies to the part of the non-Communist world not in the geographical west. I have avoided the identification of Communism with the east, but I use west in order to avoid having to repeat "non-Communist" so often.

[3] John Knox has said this very persuasively in his chapter in *Religion and the Present Crisis* (University of Chicago Press, 1942), p. 34.

Roman Catholic, thinking on this subject was the report of the Oxford Conference in 1937. That Conference was held on the eve of the Second World War. It discussed the problem of war with full awareness of traditional Christian thinking on the subject and with a realistic understanding of what the immediate threat of war meant for those who were present at the conference. It did two things which are important for our thought today. It set forth a view of war in general as a problem for the Christian conscience which remains sound as far as it goes, though it requires now the addition of a judgment concerning the degree to which a large-scale nuclear war would defeat the purposes for which it might be fought. The second thing that the Conference did was to decide that there is no one Christian position on the problem of war, that, in fact, there are three positions all of which should be respected within the Christian Church.

(1) One of these positions was Christian pacifism. It was summarized as the view that war is "always a denial of the nature of God as love, of the redemptive way of the cross, and of the community of the Holy Spirit; that war is always ultimately destructive in its effects, and ends in futility by corrupting even the noblest purpose for which it is waged; and that the Church will become a creative, regenerative and reconciling instrument for the healing of the nations only as it renounces war absolutely." Those who hold this view "are therefore constrained to refuse to take part in war themselves, to plead among their fellows for a similar repudiation of war in favor of a better way, and to replace military force by methods of active peacemaking."[4]

(2) Another position was the acceptance of the possibility of "just wars" and of the duty of Christians to take up arms when they believe that a war is just, if all other means have

[4] *Oxford Conference: Official Report* (Willett, Clark, 1937), p. 163.

failed. This view puts the burden on the individual conscience to determine when a war is just.

(3) The other view puts the emphasis on obedience to the state. "This means that normally a Christian must take up arms for his country. Only when he is absolutely certain that his country is fighting for a wrong cause—for example, in the case of an unjustifiable war of aggression—has the ordinary citizen a right to refuse military service."[5]

It is significant that this third position was presented with qualifications which provided a basis for conscientious objection and many Christians in Germany who would have found the third position most acceptable were forced to oppose their own country in a war. At about the same time, one such German, Dietrich Bonhoeffer, was writing that "a Christian is neither obliged nor able to examine the rightfulness of the demand of government in each particular case. His duty of obedience is binding on him until government directly compels him to offend against the divine commandment, that is to say, until government openly denies its divine commission and thereby forfeits its claim."[6] I believe that the experiences of the past two decades have really caused the second and the third positions at Oxford to merge into one, allowing, of course, for many different emphases in the way it is held.[7]

In discussing the Christian pacifist position, there are two types of pacifism that should be distinguished. There are, in the first place, pacifists who emphasize the conflict of Christian faith and love with the deeds which war requires and who seek to witness against war and the whole military aspect of national life and to preserve in the world resources of healing and recon-

[5] *Ibid.*, p. 165.
[6] *Ethics* (Macmillan, 1955), p. 307.
[7] There is confirmation of this judgment in the fact that when the Amsterdam Assembly faced the same problems in 1948, while it also outlined three possible positions in regard to war, the two non-pacifist ones were not mutually exclusive.

ciliation, but who do not claim that there is always an alternative policy that they can recommend to governments by which to deal with the threat of aggression. These pacifists may or may not be ultimately pessimistic about the political order. They may or may not renounce the use of all force short of that which is involved in military action. All must withdraw to some extent from public affairs, but there are many degrees of this withdrawal. In this context these differences are not very important. The significant thing about this type of pacifism is that it is an absolute religious witness that does not involve a pacifistic political strategy. It is a matter of personal vocation or of the vocation of limited and disciplined groups. There are difficulties even in such a selective withdrawal from political responsibility though as a matter of vocational concentration on other responsibilities, it remains defensible. The vocational pacifist who is himself convinced that the population as a whole should fight even if he refuses to have any part in the fighting is open to the charge of being dependent on the sins of others. But this again may be defensible as a matter of vocation if the pacifist does not claim to escape guilt.

The second type of pacifist does offer a political alternative to a policy based upon military preparations. He may do this because he is an absolutist who holds that the use of force on any scale is always incompatible with the will of a loving God. Or, he may be no perfectionist or absolutist in his pacifism, but one who is convinced that modern war is so destructive that it is always the greatest conceivable evil. This is a pragmatic judgment, based upon the view that any large-scale use of force by a nation, under present conditions, is inevitably self-defeating, that the evils which it is sure to let loose are greater than any that it may prevent. Those who hold this view may believe that the use of force by an international body is morally different from its use by a nation because the former is comparable to police action and it has some chance of being limited, whereas the latter can be expected to get completely out of bounds in an anarchical world. The development of nuclear weapons adds to the force of this argument but makes more difficult an alternative pacifist political strategy.

It is important to recognize that this type of pacifism need not be perfectionist. It may depend more upon the desire to avoid the worst possible evil than upon the hope of achieving an absolute good. It need not be accompanied by any illusion that it provides a guarantee against sharing the common guilt. It may be controlled by the judgment that, since it is so difficult to draw the line this side of the most horrible and destructive methods of warfare, the only tolerable course is to renounce all warfare.

This second type of pacifist usually makes two mistakes. He usually fails to take account of the special responsibilities of government as a trustee for a nation which is not pacifist in convictions and which is therefore incapable of following a pacifist strategy consistently. (The first type of pacifist may recognize this fully.) Also, he tends to take a too optimistic view of the possibility of persuading by example those on the other side of a conflict who may represent tyranny or aggression. It is especially difficult to communicate with the people who live behind walls of censorship and whose opinions about the outside world are formed by propaganda from within. If persuasion is to be effective there must be real spiritual continuity between those who persuade and those who are persuaded. The obvious example of this is the effect of Gandhi's strategy upon the British; he had an ally in the conscience of Britain. There is nothing comparable to this in the appeal that western pacifists might make at present to the rulers of Russia or China. There certainly was nothing comparable to it in dealing with the Nazis. This second type of pacifism does not take seriously enough either the tragic character of some human conflicts or the depth and stubbornness of some forms of corporate evil.

Concentration upon the human costs of war has often made them less sensitive to the human costs of oppression.

In the period before the Second World War many churchmen, including myself, who had been inclined toward the type of pragmatic pacifism that I have described became convinced that they were confronting an unexpected evil which they had left out of their calculations when they saw a totalitarian tyranny extending its power through military aggression. They came to believe that Christians should not urge policies on their governments which would leave them no alternative except surrender to such a power. Here the Christian distrust of unlimited power which has often become the basis for the support of revolution after the power has been established could be a basis for using the only possible means for preventing the spread of tyranny.

The pattern of events in the 1930's which made a pacifist political strategy unconvincing to many who would have liked to believe in it has been repeated in part in the 1950's but with two differences. One difference is that military force is not as important a factor in the strategy of Communism as it was in that of National Socialism. Communism relies more on propaganda and conspiracy, on stimulating revolution in countries that are especially vulnerable. The other difference is that in the 1950's the continuous development of nuclear weapons has made a general war an unimaginable horror that could be expected to destroy all that both sides would be fighting for; that might even mean the end of the human race. It is highly doubtful if victory by the free nations would leave a world in which the institutions of freedom could survive.

The aspect of the nuclear problem that morally is most agonizing is that we seem committed to the position that if nuclear war should ever start, there will be no moral limits. The deliberate launching of a preventive war we regard as out of bounds, but if general war starts through some accident or if we are deliberately attacked, it seems that we shall be the agents as well as the victims of all degrees of destruction. Everything will be permitted. It is hard to imagine the spiritual effect upon nations and Churches of living for decades with the assumption that at any moment one's own nation may be destroyed while it lets loose the forces of destruction on another nation. What will this do to the faith and the consciences of men, to their sense of the providence of God and to their moral sensitivity? I do not know the answers to those questions, but it is hard to believe that they can be favorable to our humanity.

This situation is in one way favorable to the pacifist argument and yet there remains an objection to the argument that seems to me to be conclusive. Let us suppose that the effective military power were only in the Communist world, that non-Communist countries, because of moral scruples, refused to develop nuclear weapons. In such a hypothetical situation, the whole free world would be subject to Communist pressure of a black-mailing kind. There would not need to be overt aggression. This steady pressure would enable Communism to extend its power into the politically weaker countries and gradually the free world might so shrink that it would be unable to maintain itself. If we have the power to prevent such a thing from happening and if there is a reasonable hope of doing this without provoking a general war, we should not be justified in unilaterally abandoning that power. Moreover, it is politically impossible for the United States to adopt pacifism as a national creed and so many pacifists admit that they could not themselves take responsibility for foreign policy. This means that they must recognize the role of a second-best foreign policy which is politically possible. Most Christian citizens will have to define their responsibility for a foreign policy fashioned in the light of possible political alternatives. Pacifists who are fully aware of the dilemmas and who do not assume that they can occupy a morally secure position that enables them to escape from all involvement in corporate guilt may help to remind the non-pacifist of much that the pressures of the immediate situation may cause him to neglect.

The real situation in which we live presupposes the existence of nuclear military power on both sides of the iron curtain. There is the moral split that I have mentioned which makes it difficult to communicate between the two worlds and which prevents any real mutual trust. No government of the United States could decide to expose its people to nuclear attack without having, as a deterrent, the power to retaliate. The existence of a military balance does protect the freedom of non-Communist countries including neutral countries. Also military strength in the free world is important if negotiations with the Communist world are to be successful. And yet, while it is essential to insist on the effort to maintain this military balance I am much less confident than I was before the arms race became a race to develop intercontinental missiles that the military balance will prevent war in the long run. These missiles put a terrible premium on being the first to strike and there is a great danger that, with perpetual mobilization of the decisive striking power on both sides, one nation may strike first in the fear that its opponent is about to attack. Indeed sober interpreters are coming to place considerable emphasis on the danger that this may happen as a result of error. No longer can we accept the missiles race with a grim complacency based upon the idea that there is real security in a "balance of terror." There will be even less security in it when more nations have nuclear weapons.

Those who follow this policy of military balance must be reminded emphatically that by itself it can accomplish nothing constructive. It is a necessary holding operation to gain time. It would be folly to neglect the non-military means to strengthen the free world against Communist non-military penetration. It would also be folly to lose any opportunity to scale down armaments by agreement or to reach other accords with the Communist countries that would be favorable to peaceful coexistence. One of the most hopeful approaches is to take advantage of every chance to promote understanding on a human basis in spite of the moral and spiritual split that I have emphasized. Communism as an ideology is wearing thin and though this may not soon weaken the power of Communist nations in the international sphere, it may help to restore human communications. Communists are people who change and nothing is more important than a willingness on the part of the free nations to be open to any changes in their outlook. Changes may be only in priorities and emphases and not in formal renunciations of their creed or announced objectives. American rigidity based upon the assumptions that Communists are Communists and can never change may at times be as great a danger to the world as Communist intransigence.

What have all of these calculations to do with Christianity? What place does such a secular political analysis have in a book that is supposed to be about Christian faith and ethics? The initial answer to that question is that Christianity offers us no escape from even the most tragic dilemmas. We have to act in the world as it is and not as we should like it to be. There is no specifically Christian analysis of the actual historical situation. Christians must use their minds to understand the conditions under which they make their decisions. There is no "Christian" way around such conditions.

Christians should be controlled by obedience to God which is the same as love for their neighbors, for all neighbors. If their minds come to the conclusion that a military balance in the world is necessary to protect freedom and to prevent war, they can only express this obedience and love by seeking to find policies which take this judgment into account. The commandment "love your enemies" is never repealed in peace or war. Nothing that I have said suggests anything other than concern for the welfare and the dignity of the people in Communist countries. They should be allowed to choose their own social system. When they are used by their rulers to fasten their system on other nations who do not choose it, Christians in the free world need to be concerned about their victims as well as about them.

The second thing to say about how these calculations are related to Christianity is that we do need to keep the calculations themselves under a continuous Christian judgment. The fact that they are in line with many American prejudices makes it very important to keep checking them by comparing them with what Christians see and judge in other situations. As I write, these calculations may be in the main correct, but new factors may enter the picture very soon which would change the emphasis. The American churches with their ecumenical relations should be sensitive to the judgments of Christians in other nations on our policies and should help our people to preserve a spirit of openness to new possibilities. They should be especially on their guard against the development of a hard, self-righteous American anti-Communism that is unable to recognize changing realities.

I have presented a non-pacifist interpretation of foreign policy. Let me say again that this is only one Christian interpretation and that Christian pacifism has full rights within the Christian community. The interaction between pacifism and non-pacifism has its value if it helps the non-pacifist to keep his position under continuous judgment and if it helps the pacifist to realize that, whatever may be said for or against his strategy, it has its own moral risks and those who recommend it cannot escape from the common guilt. They have a special responsibility for evil which they may have done nothing to prevent or which they may have unintentionally encouraged.

Christian non-pacifists should defend the rights of conscientious objectors to military service to make their witness. Though I cannot see that what we might call "nuclear pacifism" can provide an adequate strategy, we should all be humbled before the immensity of the dilemma that is involved and honor the consciences of those whose judgment about the dilemma differs from our own. Even though I believe that there is an element of escape in the position, I cannot fail to have sympathy with those who cut through the dilemma by saying that, while they are not sure about all these calculations, they are sure that nuclear weapons are so evil that they will have no part in them.

It is worth remembering that in the Second World War there emerged a type of Christian non-pacifism which was different from the views prevailing in the Churches in the First World War. It was a correction of the self-righteous crusading spirit which is so natural for modern nations to develop in time of war. I shall briefly summarize some of the elements in this outlook.

(1) It was controlled by the recognition that the War was itself the result of an historical situation to which all the great powers had contributed. While there was no doubt about the malign purpose and cruel methods of National Socialism, it was itself in part the consequence of the failure of the former allied nations in the First World War to deal creatively with defeated Germany. When they did make concessions to Germany, these concessions were timed to strengthen Hitler. There was for this and other reasons a considerable sense of the common guilt that lay behind the war. The idea of a "holy war" was given little or no sanction in the Churches.

(2) There was much discussion in the Churches about the possibility of loving enemies in the midst of war. There was the natural feeling that it was hypocritical to speak of loving enemies while one was trying to destroy them. And yet there was also a sense that soldiers and civilians on both sides were caught in a tragic situation in which hatred was not appropriate either. I think that post-war developments show that hatred did not go very deep, that there was a kind of battle frenzy that soon wore off, but not an implacable feeling of hatred. The contrast between the slogans about the Japanese during the war and the relations between American soldiers and the Japa-

nese people immediately after the war indicates this. The bitterness against Nazis as Nazis continued, but that was not only
because they were national enemies, but also it was because of
crimes that they had committed against millions of Jews and
against many other Germans. Even the feelings against the
Nazis from this distance was more an amazed horror at their
deeds than hatred. The people who perpetrated them seemed
almost too incredible to hate. There was little hatred of Germans
as Germans.

(3) There was a sense that membership in the world Christian community to which Germans and Japanese also belonged
was a reality in the midst of war. The World Council of
Churches, which was at the time "in process of formation," had
a great influence on the attitudes of the Churches and there was
no time during the War that Christians in Germany were iso-
lated from Christians in other countries. This was, of course, in
part because they were also opposed to Hitler. Contact with
Japanese Christians was lost, but the rapidity with which ties
between American and Japanese churches were re-established
indicated that the sense of this common membership in the
Church of Christ was never lost.

(4) There was within the Church considerable alertness to
the moral issues raised by the conduct of the war. This was certainly much more in evidence than was the case during the
First World War. Churchmen frequently criticized the policies
of total war.[8] There was criticism of the dropping of the atomic
bombs in Japan. This was a perfect example of how helpless
civilians are in time of war in relation to the most fateful decisions of government.[9] Perhaps the most significant case of criticism of government by Churches in time of war was the

---

[8] See Report of the Commission of the Federal Council of Churches in
"The Church and the War in the Light of the Christian Faith" (*Social
Action*, Dec. 1944), pp. 67-68.
[9] See the Second Report of the Commission mentioned above dealing
with the Atomic problem, "Atomic Warfare and the Christian Faith"

attitude of Churches toward the evacuation of the Japanese Americans from their homes on the West Coast. The record of the Churches on the coast in dealing with the problems raised by this policy was one of the bright spots in the Churches' dealing with social issues in recent years.

(5) There was a general desire to keep the symbols of the faith and the Church's worship as free as possible from the military symbols and from the spirit generated by the war. Since the people at war were the members of the Church and since many of their problems with which the Church had to deal pastorally were related to the war it was impossible to separate the Church from the war. The role of chaplains in the armed forces was magnified and their distinctively religious functions, even their independence as representatives of the Church, were emphasized by the government. Throughout there was a strong effort to prevent the development of a militarized Christianity. Even prayers for victory were widely criticized.[10]

(6) There was a far more ungrudging acceptance of the role of conscientious objectors in the Second World War than in the First. Churches recognized that their convictions had generally been formed by Christian teaching. They strongly supported the laws which provided for non-military service for the objectors and raised funds for their maintenance in the camps

---

(Federal Council of Churches, 1946). Criticism of the use of the atomic bomb on Japan was sometimes based on the assumption that it could have been used first as a demonstration in an uninhabited area. Sometimes the criticism was directed against the use of the second bomb. There was wide recognition of the dilemma facing those who made the decision for they believed that the shortening of the war would in the end save more lives than the bombs destroyed. They did not realize the intangible effect on all future efforts to limit the use of nuclear bombs from the fact that the United States set the example of using the bomb *first*.

[10] See Archbishop Temple's *Thoughts in War-Time* (Macmillan, London, 1940), p. 43. This attitude in an Archbishop of Canterbury with his special responsibility for the nation may seem remarkable. Actually Archbishop Randall Davidson in the First World War anticipated this position. Cf. G.K.A. Bell, *Randall Davidson* (Oxford University Press, 1952), Chap. LI and pp. 736-738.

to which they were assigned, though the main financial burden fell upon the denominations which have made a specialty of pacifist teachings (the Friends, the Mennonites, and the Church of the Brethren).

(7) During the War there was within the Churches great emphasis on the conviction that the war could only stop aggression and defeat a tyrannical government, causing its overthrow, but that it could not of itself produce a positive result. The work of the American Churches in planning for post-war developments was guided by the Commission on a Just and Durable Peace of the Federal Council of Churches. Mr. John Foster Dulles was the Chairman of this Commission and it helped to mobilize Christian opinion in support of America's acceptance of international responsibility after the War. The Churches had much to do with the prevention of a reversion to isolationism, with the support of the United Nations, and with the development of imaginative policies for post-war reconstruction.

I believe that these seven characteristics of the outlook of American Churches during the Second World War, when taken together, do represent a type of Christian non-pacifism which needs to be remembered today. Similar attitudes would be present today in the case of a limited war; they were present at the time of the Korean War. What the attitude of Churches would be during a general nuclear war it is impossible to imagine. The horror of such a war might well create a sense of an overwhelming common tragedy more than it would stimulate feelings of hate toward the enemy, and retaliatory actions, even if they were the *only* form of self-defense, would bring a sense of guilt. Such a war would certainly be no crusade and there could be no satisfaction in victory. It would belong to an apocalyptic dimension and the churches would be occupied in healing the victims and in mediating the divine mercy and forgiveness.

In the context of the decisions that are related to war and

peace we may see most clearly the relevance for political life of Christian teaching about justification by grace through faith. This teaching has often been forgotten when men were convinced that they could make ideal choices if only they tried hard enough. That is an illusion in most of our life, but it is most obviously so in international relations. The best we can find to do there is full of moral risk. It may be our duty to do that which morally repels us. This is true of the whole process of building up nuclear armaments to preserve the necessary balance of which I have spoken. Professor Brunner says that "we never see the real meaning of 'original sin,' we never perceive the depth and the universality of evil, or what evil really means in the depths common to us all, until we are obliged to do something which, in itself, is evil."[11] For this reason Brunner has based his book on Christian Ethics on the doctrine of justification.

Justification here means the divine forgiveness. We do not win it by finding the perfectly good act. It is a gift of God that comes to us in our need, that comes to us at the very point at which we may be most tempted to despair over the moral alternatives which we face. It may deliver us from irresoluteness when we must act for the sake of our duty in ways which disturb our consciences.

This gospel of justification or forgiveness is completely distorted if it makes us less sensitive to the evil in our choices, if it provides a kind of moral escape. Actually, when it is kept integrally related to the whole of Christian truth it should enable us to be more realistic about the evil in which we become involved because it removes the necessity of self-deception as a means of spiritual security. The man who understands this dimension of forgiveness should be enabled to live in the world as it is without either self-deception or despair.

There is one aspect of this teaching about justification that seems to me to require clarification. There is a tendency, in the

<hr>

[11] *The Divine Imperative* (Westminster Press, 1943), p. 227.

proclaiming of the gospel of justification in relation to a particular moral predicament, to make no distinction, on the one hand, between the man who, faced with a choice of evils, does the best that he can find to do and who with great integrity and sensitivity of spirit does make the hard decisions which he believes to be commanded and, on the other, the man who selfishly follows the line of least resistance without conscientious and sensitive efforts to find the best choice, or who may even share responsibility for the conditions which limit the choice. The first man needs divine healing and comfort for the evil into which his faithfulness leads him. The other man needs to be brought to repentance and to be forgiven. There is a difference between forgiveness for guilt and healing for the hurt that accompanies the best that one can find to do. St. Augustine makes the distinction here between guilt and what he calls "the misery of these necessities."[12] As a matter of emphasis, this distinction has validity but it should not be so developed that the man whose experience does not involve guilt in a particular relationship gains a false moral self-sufficiency and develops around himself a protective hardness from confidence in his righteousness. He, too, is vulnerable and the good in him is a gift. He, too, in his life as a whole needs to repent and to be forgiven.

B. The Claims and Limits of National Interest

One of the basic issues in the discussion of the relation of Christian faith and ethics to foreign policy is the assessment of the place of national interest. There is great confusion about this matter with a tendency for Christian idealists to regard considerations of national interest as unworthy of having a place in our ethical judgments and with a tendency among political theorists to write in a hard-boiled way about national interest as the only determinant of foreign policy when they themselves are actually concerned about broad human interests. Part of the confusion, of course, has to do with the conception that one has of the range of national interest.

[12] The City of God, Bk. XIX, Chap. VI.

I shall mention some reasons for giving great weight to national interest in our thinking.

(1) Those who are responsible for foreign policy are trustees for the national interest. This is true of statesmen, diplomats and legislators. They have no right to pursue a policy based primarily on their private idealisms in disregard of the national security and welfare and they would not be allowed to do so for long. Those who are the leaders of government can and should use their influence to extend the peoples' conception of the range of national interest, to lead them to see what is in the long term interest of the nation in contrast to what may be dictated by short-term expediency, but the responsibility of trusteeship remains.

Also, it should be recognized that the real welfare of a particular nation is the real welfare of people, of 160,000,000 people in the case of the United States; and there is a division of labor which makes it right for those who have the special responsibility to do so to concentrate on the interests of these people. This should not be a narrow and truculent nationalism under any circumstances, but it may be a Christian vocation to devote oneself to the real interests of one's own nation. No Christian can absolutize these interests, but they have their significant place.

(2) A second and quite different reason for stressing national interest as a guide to policy is given special emphasis in the writings of George Kennan. It is the appeal to national interest as a limiting concept. The United States especially has been inclined to identify its policies with ideals to be promoted everywhere in the world. There is generally among our people a great deal of pressure for policies that are guided by an abstract idea of right regardless of the consequences. This might lead to a war to liberate people at a distance or to unify a divided country even though the effect might be so destructive that those liberated or united would probably be destroyed. National crusading for principles can be unlimited; policies that are kept in

close relation to real national interest will be guided by a prudent sense of national limitations. Even though prudence does not seem to be a very high virtue, in the field of foreign policy it may save a nation from a blunder backed by moral intentions but too costly in terms of real human values. This type of American moralism is also a special cause of resentment abroad.

(3) A frank recognition of national interest is often better in its effects than emphasis upon generous intentions that also may enter into a policy. This is true, for example, of foreign economic aid. If much is made of generosity in this connection and if gratitude is tacitly expected, it is more likely to be resented or to be regarded as evidence of self-deception and hypocrisy. As a matter of fact, all the foreign aid that would be useful to "under-developed countries" can be given on the basis of genuine mutuality of interest. It can be defended before Congress on the ground that it is in the national interest, but it can also be defended because it is in the interest of the receiving country. It can be based upon a wide range of mixed motives and if it is given, not to procure some definite *quid pro quo* but because the economic health and political stability of another nation are in its interest and in our own, it will make for the best relations between the countries involved. Both generosity, when it is emphasized, and manipulation are resented. As Dr. Kenneth Thompson has said in connection with aid of this kind to India: "If we would avoid the stigma of hypocrisy, we should not conceal the fact that the imperatives of our national existence command us to lend what assistance we can to this pivotal Asian member of the British Commonwealth. If we are less forthright, we shall only invite resentment, disdain and rebuke of the Indians, who will point to the dross of self-interest that joins inextricably to the gold of moral purpose in every foreign policy. . . . Indeed the highest moral standard for nations may be the mutuality of their national interests and purposes."[13]

The heart of this problem of the place of national interest is one's interpretation of its range. The difference between a narrow, unimaginative view of national interest and one that is wise and farsighted is enormous. Christian statesmen should do all that they can to educate the public so that it shares the broader view. It is easy at the present time to show that the real national interest of the United States is served by everything that is done to bring stability and justice and peace to any part of the world. It is to our interest to improve the social and economic health of other nations, to help them to find alternatives to totalitarianism. We have special problems of economic competition with particular nations, but we have a stake in the general economic well-being of those very nations —Japan, for instance. As I have said, the true basis of economic aid to other nations is the very real area of mutual interest which unites us to them.

I do not assume that in all situations there is always this harmony between the real interests of nations except for a common interest in preventing total war. Nations that have more limited economies which are dependent upon the export of a few commodities may find themselves facing deeper conflicts of interest with their neighbors than is the case with the United States. Also, nations that have depended upon colonial possessions may face similar conflicts. In the latter case it is in the long-term interest of a nation to adjust itself to changes that are just and inevitable, but they may be very costly changes. Nations which feel that their national interests are tied to very tight immigration policies may have serious moral conflicts in relating their interests to policies that take account of the needs of other countries. This is to some extent our problem and it will call for continuous re-adjustments on our part.

Now I shall suggest ways in which Churches and Christian citizens should break through the limits of national interest. It

[18] "Prophets and Politics" in *Christianity and Crisis*, May 16, 1955.

is obvious that they can never regard national interest as ultimate. The Church in one nation is part of a universal Christian community and when it does not live as a loyal part of the whole, it ceases to be a Christian Church. Christians should be more concerned about the solidarity of men in Christ than they are about their relationship to a nation even though loyal and responsible citizenship within a particular nation is one essential expression of this solidarity. To care about neighbors in general and not about the particular neighbors who are within reach and whose welfare is most influenced by one's loyal citizenship is to sacrifice an important part of the substance of our Christian responsibility. Love of country in this context and not in the context of a narrow nationalism is one of the most precious unifying factors which overcome selfish interests and factionalism and enable the kind of free institutions, which have been so much emphasized in previous chapters, to function. Yet these considerations can never justify the tendency to make national interest the ultimate point of reference or to assume that God cares more about the interests of one's own nation than for those of other nations.

It may be helpful to distinguish between enlightened national interest as at times the indicator of policy rather than as the only motive among the people. Unless there are many citizens who really care about the welfare of other nations and about the larger issues of justice and freedom and peace for their own sake, it is doubtful if a nation will ever rise to an enlightened view of national interest. I realize the danger of self-deception in this emphasis, but that danger does not annul its importance.

Christian citizens and others who share this wider concern have to work in part through government and in doing so, they must recognize the limitations of governmental action, but their wider concern will help to raise the sights of government. It will enable government to put greater emphasis on the very wide area of mutual interest which exists and which is a sign of human solidarity. At least at the present time and as far as we can see ahead, the most important contribution of Christian citizens and of Christian statesmen in the United States will be to emphasize these areas of mutual interest so that many more people will support policies from a combination of motives, a combination in which neither the wider concern nor the national concern is hidden and in which neither is allowed to distort the other. I put this in ideal terms but an approach to this kind of relationship between the national interest and the wider interest is involved in every-day Christian citizenship.

Those who implement programs of technical assistance and other forms of economic aid abroad need to have a genuine interest in the people among whom they work. Many of those who vote for the policy may be concerned only about American interest but those who do the actual work in a foreign country will do it better if they have a real sense of solidarity with the people among whom they work. The work will serve the national interest better if this is the case, but the concern for the welfare of the other country should not be simulated that it may have this effect! The problem is more complicated in the case of diplomatic representatives. If they were to become so identified with the country to which they are sent that their reports to their own government are distorted by a bias in favor of that country, their value as diplomats would be destroyed. But the empathy of a Chester Bowles and a John Sherman Cooper enhanced their value as diplomats and it surely came from an outgoing concern for India as well as for America and not from an exceptionally artful form of diplomatic calculation!

The place I have given to national interest does not mean that Christian citizens or statesmen should ever put that interest above costly faithfulness to obligations that have been accepted. George Kennan, who has done so much to call Americans from a naïvely moralistic or idealistic foreign policy to a sober regard for national interests, says that "we should conduct ourselves at all times in such a way as to satisfy our own ideas of morality. But let us do this as a matter of obligation to ourselves, and not as a matter of obligation to others."[14] I am not sure that I understand all that is meant by those words. If they are a warning against our always assuming that we know what is good for others, this belongs to the national self-limitation that is a part of wisdom. But this distinction between our obligation to ourselves and our obligation to others cannot finally stand. It does, however, suggest to me one element of national interest that really transcends national interest: a people which has developed a conscience needs to be able to live with its conscience. Carelessness about the pledged word, lack of consideration for the dignity and the real needs of other nations, callousness toward human suffering at a distance or on our national doorstep are offenses against our own national conscience as well as against others. Christian influence on a national conscience should make it more sensitive on such matters.

There are times when on the basis of a very wide national consensus a government is right in taking steps that are heedless in their generosity. Government policy cannot long be based upon such heedlessness, but emergencies do arise when it is morally demanded. One example of this that has been impressive was the policy of the Austrian government in dealing with Hungarian refugees at the time of the Hungarian revolution in 1956. This problem was indeed on its doorstep and so could not be evaded as a human problem. But there was a willingness to assume a financial burden that was indeterminate and, even more important, there was a willingness to risk the effects of Russian disapproval with Russian power so dangerously near.

I shall conclude this discussion of national interest by pointing out that the relations with people in other countries often have nothing to do with national interest. The mutual affection

[14] *Realities of American Foreign Policy* (Princeton University Press, 1954), p. 47.

and loyalty of friendship know no national boundaries. There is also a dedication to international objectives, to the development of international institutions without any thought of their relation to the interest of one's own country. If the United Nations and similar organizations in their civil service or international personnel could not often command such dedication, they would not be able to serve their purposes. Many of the non-political interests—professional, scientific, artistic—develop their own international communities which help to correct nationalistic distortions of the mind and spirit.

I have often referred to the ecumenical Christian community. It is still divided by denominations which often coincide with nations, but I believe that it has been more effective in overcoming purely national barriers than any other. There are cultural barriers that are more difficult, and the current Communist-non-Communist split greatly limits contacts between Christians who are geographically if not spiritually on both sides and this split greatly confuses the ecclesiastical contacts that are possible. But this is not primarily a matter of national differences. There are differences of outlook between the churches in so-called under-developed continents with a heritage of resentment against imperial powers and the older Churches of Europe and America, but these are not primarily national differences and they are partly corrected by a very great deal of contact between Churches.

The missionary movement is one of the most astonishing examples of the capacity of Christians to identify themselves with people in other nations. Missionaries have been much criticized for bringing their national culture with them and for allowing themselves to be used as instruments of western imperialism. But after we have made full allowance for the truth in such criticisms, there has been a vast amount of real identification with people of another nation in the service of Christ rather than of any western values or interests. Very often today the missionaries are so identified with the nations to which they go that they represent them to the nations from which they come. They become most effective defenders of the interests and the aspirations of the peoples with whom they have identified themselves against both the national selfishness and the moral pretensions of western peoples.

The ecumenical Christian community can encourage many non-governmental projects which embody the outgoing concern of people in one country for those in another with less ambiguity than any projects of governments. Here also there is danger of the patronising corruptions of generosity but generosity can be more readily accepted within the Christian community than as an aspect of political relationships because in that community it is more believable, for givers and receivers know that response to the love of Christ makes it natural and in that context it is no cause for pride. In the future there will be more emphasis on mutuality of contributions as between one part of the Church and another, though as far as we can see ahead this will not alter the fact that some will be in greater need of personnel and material resources than others.

C. Two Areas of Decision

I shall not attempt in this book to deal with the many particular problems of foreign policy. These require special technical competence, and they are discussed in innumerable places. It will be sufficient to call attention to two major areas of decision.

The first is our dual responsibility to do all that we can to prevent the extension of the area of totalitarian power and to prevent a third world war. The prevention of the war should have priority because a nuclear war has greater finality as a threat to humanity than Communism. Communism is not eternal and as a world phenomenon may be modified or be succeeded by other systems more favorable to freedom. Yet the practical situation is that so long as there is a reasonable chance of preventing both the extension of Communist tyranny and the world war, governments of free nations have a responsibility to try to prevent both. The United States, more than any other country, is the one that is able to defend the free world and it does this for the sake of its own freedom, for the sake of having a free world in which to breathe, and out of loyalty to other nations which have similar values. Policy decisions would be easier to make if we might cease to trouble ourselves about both of these objectives at the same time and concentrate on one. They might be disastrous decisions, but there would be much less moral and intellectual perplexity about them!

I have already said that the power of Communism is not primarily military power and so the prevention of its spread will involve a many-sided program within which military preparations have an indispensable and yet subordinate part. This combination of the indispensability and yet subordinate role of military preparations is a difficult thing to keep in mind because they are so very costly to us who have major responsibility for them. It is important for the Church to remind the nation of those things which it is most tempted to forget and it will have to keep reminding this nation of the limits of military power. The fact that the Church has a strong pacifist element within it and cannot speak with the same clarity about the indispensability of military power is a source of some confusion, but there is no way of avoiding that. The Church has a special responsibility to help the nation to understand the needs and aspirations of other nations and to realize the contradictions in our own national life which often hide from other peoples what is true in our purposes. Understanding of the great uncommitted world of new nations which feel in the bodies and souls of their people the need of social revolution prepares us for constructive possibilities. If these nations do not find alternatives to the Communism sponsored by Russia and China, no military power will avail much in preserving the free world.[14]

[14] As this book is going through the press the international situation is especially critical, but specific comments on it would soon be out of date. There is, however, one change of emphasis in the presuppositions on which

The other area of policy which I shall emphasize is the fashioning of the institutions of world order. As I have suggested, what Christian theologians have said about the national state as the instrument of order applies to the international institutions of which the United Nations is the center. A few years ago there was a tendency in Church circles to regard the United Nations as itself the solution of international problems, but today it is a service to the United Nations if one does not create false expectations. The United Nations cannot change the location of power in the world. It cannot by the exercise of the power of a super-government bring the conflict between the Communist and non-Communist worlds to an end and that conflict does greatly hamper its effectiveness. If other factors reduce this cold-war tension the United Nations may well enter a period of increased effectiveness.

Meanwhile the United Nations performs functions of great

national policy is based that has become clearer to me since the manuscript of this book was completed. American policy in the cold war has presupposed mortal conflict with Russia and China, nations in which Communism is well established, until there is victory for our side. That assumption may not now be explicitly acknowledged, but it has deep roots in our national feeling. I doubt if such an assumption is any longer relevant. Instead, we must assume that Communism in those two nations is a gigantic human experiment that will run its course. It is irreversible, but fortunately it is not unchangeable. We should continue to seek to limit the extension of Communist power, especially by helping vulnerable nations find constructive alternatives to Communism. There remains a long spiritual struggle with Communism as a faith and as a world-view. But we must accept for an indefinite period the reality of competitive co-existence and make clear that we do so, for the only alternative is mutual destruction. In doing so, the United States should take more seriously than has been the case the natural fears and legitimate aspirations of these Communist nations as nations. There is a vicious circle of hostility and fear in international relations to which we have contributed because we have had so little empathy toward the feelings of insecurity which our system of bases and the missile race bring to the Russians. An intransigent policy in these matters seems to drive uncommitted peoples closer to the Communist camp. The hope for the future lies not in victory over Communism in Russia or China, but in the changes in Communism which come with a new generation that is more concerned about the building of their own society than with ideology or world-revolution.

value. It provides the machinery for continuous consultation and negotiation; it provides a forum for an emerging world public opinion; and even though it does give opportunity for the making of much propaganda, it creates an atmosphere in which prestige goes to the moderate and reasonable leaders of nations rather than to the bullies who throw their weight around; it keeps the spotlight on areas where conflicts arise and it can gain time, provide information about the causes of the conflict and even, as in the case of Israel and Egypt, use a police force to keep the parties from attacking each other; it enables some of the less powerful nations to have moral influence far beyond their power; it brings the new nations of Asia and Africa immediately into the world community and gives them dignity and a chance for international experience. The specialized agencies of the United Nations and allied organizations can deal helpfully with the social and economic conditions and often, because they are multi-lateral, their activities are more acceptable to nations that are aided than the efforts of single nations, though, because of the volume of the need and of our own relative wealth, they cannot fully replace American economic aid.

It would be a mistake to try to transform the United Nations into a super-government in terms of an *a priori* blue-print. The veto in the Security Council at present is a reflection of the real situation in the world and if it were abandoned it would either cause some great powers to lose interest in the United Nations or it might even enable the United Nations to become the instrument for organizing one part of the world against another and this might bring about the war that it was designed to prevent. There are frustrations here with which we must live. Also, it is difficult to know how to solve the problem created when two-thirds of the over eighty nations in the Assembly vote for action which only a few nations have the power to implement and for which these few would incur the risk and the cost. This separation of votes and responsibility is another problem for which no solution is in sight. To ask nations to give up their sovereignty to such a body is to ask the impossible and, even if it were possible, the wholesale transfer of sovereignty would lead to too great centralization of power in the world. National sovereignty can be abridged as particular functions, especially those affecting the limitation and supervision of armaments and collective security, are delegated to an international body and we may well work and pray for developments along this line. All that was said earlier about the limited state applies even more to any future international political organization. The development of the realities of non-political world community and the safe-guarding of the self-government of peoples and their spiritual and cultural freedom need to accompany all advances in the political embodiment of world order.

The ecumenical Christian community parallels the United Nations though, of course, its strength varies a great deal among the nations and it has little leverage at present on the policies of Communist governments. It should recognize in the United Nations a providential instrument for the realization of its own purposes for world order and justice. It preserves among its member Churches both vision of universal human community and awareness of the special problems and aspirations of particular nations. Even Christians from nations where the Church is a small minority do represent to Christians in other countries the needs and the responses to world events among their people. Spokesmen for the ecumenical community can at times bring to the United Nations what Churches within a nation bring to their government. This community can speak a word of God which transcends the partial vision of particular national Churches; and it does bring to the political institutions of world order sources of judgment, inspiration and grace that come only from the Gospel.

PART THREE

CHURCH AND STATE

Presuppositions about the Church

As a background for any discussion of the relationship between Church and state it is necessary to consider what the Church is in the light of its own understanding of itself. The Church as a social institution and as a community is subject to sociological investigation. But unless account is taken of the Church's own faith concerning its nature and purpose, such investigation will be limited in its results. The same is true of any political theory about the relation of the Church to the state and to society that does not reckon with the faith and the important tives which are at the heart of the Church's inner life.

As an association among associations, the Church is in appearance a "voluntary society." John Locke, in order to make way for religious toleration, so defined the Church. He also described the relations of the Church and the Commonwealth in such a way as to make most discussions of the problem of Church and state seem irrelevant. He says that "the Church itself is a thing absolutely separate and distinct from the commonwealth. He jumbles heaven and earth together, the things most remote and opposite, who mixes these two societies, which are in their original end, business and in everything perfectly distinct and infinitely different from each other." Locke had a good motive for wanting to keep Church and state so far apart from one another. He lived near the end of the long and repellent history of religious persecution and he

¹ Letter on Toleration (The Library of Liberal Arts, 1955), p. 27.

CHAPTER XIII

Presuppositions about the Church

As BACKGROUND for any discussion of the relationship between Church and state it is necessary to consider what the Church is in the light of its own understanding of itself. The Church as a social institution and as a community is subject to sociological investigation. But unless account is taken of the Church's own faith concerning its nature and purpose, such investigation will be limited in its results. The same is true of any political theory about the relation of the Church to the state and to society that does not reckon with the faith and the imperatives which are at the heart of the Church's inner life.

As an association among associations, the Church is in appearance a "voluntary society." John Locke, in order to make way for religious toleration, so defined the Church. He also described the relations of the Church and the Commonwealth in such a way as to make most discussions of the problem of Church and state seem irrelevant. He says that "the Church itself is a thing absolutely separate and distinct from the commonwealth. The boundaries on both sides are fixed and immovable. He jumbles heaven and earth together, the things most remote and opposite, who mixes these two societies, which are in their original end, business and in everything perfectly distinct and infinitely different from each other."[1] Locke had a good motive for wanting to keep Church and state so far apart from one another. He lived near the end of the long and repellent history of religious persecution and he

[1] *Letter on Toleration* (The Library of Liberal Arts, 1955), p. 27.

had much to do with the coming of religious toleration. Yet we may say that though the Church was at fault in the way in which it had exercised its responsibility for the commonwealth, Locke was wrong in denying that it had such responsibility. Many Americans influenced by Locke's idea see no reason why the formula of "separation" should not solve all Church-State problems and bring an end to books on the subject.[2]

But the Church is not in its understanding of itself a "voluntary society" and it does have responsibility in relation to all phases of the life of the "commonwealth." It may have legal independence of the state and this can be called "separation" if it is properly understood but it cannot be separated from society or keep out of many activities which touch the life of the state. I shall have much to say in the next chapter in defense of the legal independence of Church and state but this independence does not solve for all time the problem of the Church and state because the Church by its very nature is involved in most phases of life in which the state also is involved.

It is true that the Church is a voluntary society in this country in the sense that there is no national church to which all citizens belong unless they deliberately renounce their ties with it. In some nations infant baptism is so universal that while all citizens are not born into the Church, they are almost automatically baptized into the Church, but that is not the case here. Even churchmen who emphasize the voluntary character of the Church because they believe that true baptism

[2] Locke himself did not carry through the logic of this position as he still accepted the Anglican establishment and reflected in many ways the thought of Richard Hooker. Americans such as Madison and Jefferson, who were much influenced by Locke, carried this idea of distance between Church and Commonwealth to its limit. Madison's "A Memorial and Remonstrance on the Religious Rights of Man" is a classic statement of this position. This is published in Joseph L. Blau's *Cornerstones of Religious Freedom in America* (The Beacon Press, 1949), pp. 81-87.

must be believers' baptism also believe that God calls his people into the Church. The Church may be considered voluntary in the sense that its members do at some stage decide to become or to remain members of the Church. But the Church is not voluntary if this means that it understands itself as a human creation, as an organization which exists because its contemporary members choose to associate with one another to form churches. They do associate together, but they associate together because of their response to what they believe to be an act of God and they acknowledge that the Church is a given reality by which their own faith has been nourished.

I once heard Dr. Harry Emerson Fosdick in an address say that, while there was a time when he would have said that "we make the Church," he now believes that the "Church makes us." Since Dr. Fosdick comes from the Baptist tradition and generally represents in his views what we may call the ecclesiastical "left," this statement seems to me to be very significant. It expresses well the inadequacy of the conception of the Church as a voluntary society from the point of view of its own understanding of itself even though sociologically that conception may have much in its favor. To the religiously indifferent, both the Roman Catholic Church and a Baptist Church appear to be voluntary societies, for they have voluntarily chosen to remain aloof from both.

In recent decades there has been a rediscovery of the Church among Protestants who had in the past thought of Christianity in individualistic terms. Experience of the ecumenical Christian community has greatly enlarged and deepened their conception of the Church. They have learned from Biblical studies that Christianity was from the beginning a religion of the Christian community. The structure of the New Testament Church was not clearly articulated. There was no universal church government over the local churches, but there was a Christian community in those early years that transcended the local churches. New Testament Christians thought of themselves as a people, as the people of God. Paul defined the Church as the Body of Christ and he meant by this something so objective that it is difficult for our minds to grasp his full meaning.[3] We can understand the idea that the Church was the instrument of Christ in the world. We can understand Paul's conception of the corporate nature of the Church which is developed with such vividness in his figure of the body with its many members. New Testament Christians saw in the Church a new stage in the life of "the people of God" established by the Old Testament Covenant. Shortly after the period of the New Testament, Christians were able to think of the Church as a "third race," a figure of speech which makes even clearer to us the idea of the people of God.

Two passages in the New Testament express the Church's maximum understanding of itself with peculiar power and they may well seem pretentious nonsense to those who do not share the Church's faith. The author of I Peter writes to a group of Christians: "But you are a chosen race, a royal priesthood, a holy nation, God's own people, that you may declare the wonderful deeds of him who called you out of darkness into his marvelous light."[4] The author of the Epistle to the Ephesians writes that God had raised Christ from the dead "and made him sit at his right hand in the heavenly places, far above all rule and authority and power and dominion, and above every name that is named, not only in this age but also in that which is to come; and he has put all things under his feet and has made him the head over all things for the church, which is his body, the fullness of him who fills all in all."[5] It would be impossible for a Church which starts with this understanding of itself to think of itself as "absolutely separate and distinct from

[3] J. A. T. Robinson, *The Body: A Study in Pauline Theology* (S.C.M. Press, London, 1952), p. 47.
[4] I Peter 2:9.
[5] Ephesians 1:20-23.

the commonwealth." It would also be natural for those who are outside the Church and who can make no sense of such claims to fear that the Church will always seek the power to lord it over them. In the past this is what it has often done. No wonder the United States, since it was able to make almost a fresh start and was inhabited by so many refugees from state churches, decided that this would be one country where no Church would be allowed to use the power of the state to interfere with the religious liberty of any citizens.

There is so much disagreement about the doctrine of the Church among Christians, especially between those who represent a Protestant and those who represent a Catholic interpretation of Christianity, that I cannot do more here than state some of the major convictions about the Church which are widely held. My statement of them will not be wholly acceptable to Catholics (Roman, Orthodox or Anglican), on the one hand, or to those who represent a consistent independency (a minority of Congregationalists and a majority of Baptists), on the other. But Christians at both extremes can accept much of what I shall present.[6] At least the following elements in the doctrine of the Church should be emphasized as we approach the discussion of the relations between Church and state.

(1) The Church is the human community which relates us to the revealing and redeeming acts of God in Christ. We should extend our conception of the acts of God in Christ to include both the preparation for his coming recorded in the Old Testament and the witness of the apostles in the New Testament. The founding of the Church may itself be regarded as a part of the divine strategy of redemption. This emphasis upon the divine initiative in the Church would be accepted by both Catholics and Protestants.

[6] Catholics will differ on the location of the Church. Roman Catholics will admit that there are Christians in the Protestant Churches but not that the Protestant Churches are Churches.

(2) There is in the Church something that is already *given* as an essential part of the Christian gospel. This given element for all Christians is the community itself. For Catholics it is also a particular structure of the community but that difference has little importance in principle for the problems of Church-State relations. In this sense the Church is not properly understood as in all respects a voluntary society.

(3) No local Church, or denomination, is a true Church in isolation. The Church is by its very nature a universal community. There is continuity in its life as a community with the Church of the centuries and with the contemporary Church in the whole world. The ecumenical movement with its structure in the World Council of Churches signalizes the coming into clearer visibility of the universal Christian community. One of the essential marks of the freedom of the Church within a nation or under a state is its capacity to preserve close relations with the ecumenical community. Membership in a local Church means membership in the larger Church.

(4) The Church is not its own authority. It stands under the authority of the revelation of God in Christ. That revelation comes to it through the Bible. An essential element in Protestantism is that the Church stands under the Word of God. It is in perpetual dialogue with this Word of God which is mediated through the Bible which the contemporary Church must interpret but which still presses upon it as an independent authority that the Church cannot control. Obviously there are great differences between Catholicism and Protestantism here and Protestants must reject the Catholic tendency to put the continuing tradition of the Church on the same level with the Bible and to allow it in practice to control the original revelation. But Catholics and Protestants can at least agree that the final authority for the Church transcends every state and is a source of judgment upon the life of every nation. A purely contemporary Christianity or a purely American Chris-

tianity is always a great distortion. Most Protestants today would say the same about a purely denominational or confessional Christianity.

(5) The Church by its commission has responsibility for the life of society as a whole. It is called to mediate the love and the judgment of God to every phase of human life. Its members are citizens of the nation and as citizens they have a vocation involving obedience to God's will for the nation. As members of the Church they should be helped to find guidance for this vocation. Christian faith brings wisdom that illumines the presuppositions and the goals of life and many of the more specific social tasks. It should not over-ride all the relative autonomies of politics and economics, of the sciences and the arts and prescribe Christian solutions for all problems but those who pursue these interests should be helped by the Church to fit them into their total view of life, bringing richness to that total view and being illumined by it. The Church has pastoral responsibility wherever there is human need not otherwise met. This means that the Church has been the great pioneer and initiator in many areas of life where now other agencies have assumed major responsibility, but we can never say in advance where that pioneering and initiating will no longer be needed. Circumstances may at times greatly limit what the Church can do outside its own doors but it can never accept such limitations as final and if driven underground, it must seek ways of coming above ground again and work once more to bring light and love and healing to society as a whole.[7]

[7] This conception of the Church's responsibility that I have outlined fits neither the role of the "sect" nor that of the "church" in terms of Ernst Troeltsch's famous analysis of types of Christian institutions. The "sect," as he describes it, is too exclusive and perfectionist and it is too much separated from the world and the problems of the culture. Actually, sects do not remain so exclusive for more than one or two generations and most American Churches have become inclusive Churches regardless of their origin as sects. When Troeltsch thought of the "church-type" of Christian institution he had in mind the inclusive and conservative national churches of Europe which brought objective means of grace to the whole

The Church cannot be content with either the inclusive or the exclusive ideal alone. Its members are not limited to those who are righteous or who have arrived religiously; they are sinners—forgiven sinners. But this does not mean that there are no conditions of membership in the Church for the Church should be a community of people who know that they are sinners in the light of a particular allegience and who together are looking to the same source for forgiveness, for guidance, and for the grace that empowers.[8]

(6) The Church is never a self-enclosed whole. This is obvious from the fact that it is not its own authority. But I want to emphasize here more broadly the way in which the Church exists to be invaded by that which comes from God. Whenever the Word of God is preached within it there is the opportunity for this invasion. The experience of the Holy Spirit in the Church is another way of expressing the same truth. The Church to be true to itself must always point beyond itself to the sources of its renewal. Its worshipping and its listening involve this. This structure of the life of the Church is of enormous importance when we compare the visible, empirical Churches with what the Church claims to be. We

community. Almost the whole nation was baptized and was counted as belonging to the Church. In contrast to that view of the Church, I am emphasizing voluntary participation in the Church based upon the beginnings of faith with the Church as a nourisher of faith.
See Ernst Troeltsch, *The Social Teaching of the Christian Churches* (Macmillan, 1931), Vol. I, pp. 331-349.

[8] There is a very illuminating passage in Bonhoeffer's *Ethics* based upon the experience of the Confessing Church in Germany. He says that Christians in Germany often found that outside the Christian circle the name of Christ had "an unforseen power" and that they felt kinship with many non-Christians who stood for "justice, truth, humanity and freedom." But they also found that unless they drew clear lines concerning the meaning of the Gospel within the Church, the Church was threatened with "inner disintegration and disruption." The "neutrality" of its members became "hostility to Christ." He says that "in isolation the claim to exclusiveness leads to fanaticism and slavery; and in isolation the claim to totality leads to secularization and self-abandonment of the Church." Pp. 179-180.

should be thoroughly realistic about these visible, empirical Churches but we should not appeal from them to an invisible Church which is to be distinguished from them. If we realize that the visible, empirical Churches have as a part of their structure this openness to invasion from God's Word in Christ, by God's Spirit present in Christ, we are able to keep our realism about the actual churches of our experience, and witness to the Church in the light of God's intentions for it.

(7) Some readers may wonder why I have said nothing about the Kingdom of God. Ideas of the Kingdom that were dominant in American Liberal Christianity a generation ago almost displaced the Church as the central expression of the social nature of Christianity. Perhaps that was natural when the expectation of the Kingdom as in large measure embodied in the total society of the future was so vivid. This expectation of the coming of the Kingdom of God as a new social order was bound up with ideas of over-all and secure progress which are now unconvincing. This is not to deny the possibility of advances in any area of life or the possibility of finding solutions of many problems. But today we are aware of the possibilities of regression or of nuclear destruction which make all progress insecure and we also are aware that solutions of old problems do bring new problems that are often unexpected and for which there is no preparation. Neither a dogmatic optimism nor a dogmatic pessimism has any place in Christian thinking about the future.

This view of the future that I have briefly outlined means that the Kingdom of God can be partially embodied in society but that it will also be a source of judgment upon society. There is no basis in the New Testament for identifying the Kingdom with a new social order and there is no basis in our experience for doing so either. But the Kingdom is relevant to all social orders and Christians serve the Kingdom whenever they seek "justice, truth, humanity, and freedom" in any social order. Looked at in this way, we may say that the Catholic is wrong when he almost identifies the Church with the Kingdom and that the liberal Protestant is wrong when he almost identifies a future social order with the Kingdom. The Kingdom is present in the Church and it is more precariously present in embodiments of justice and freedom in the larger society, but it transcends both and it can be present in its fullness only in God's own ultimate consummation of all things in heaven and on earth. The Church exists to serve the Kingdom and to be the mediator of the powers of the Kingdom.

CHAPTER XIV

Patterns of Church-State Relations—

Grounds for Separation

THERE is no Protestant doctrine concerning Church-State relations. There is a Baptist doctrine that is very clear and that has always had great influence in this country. There is an American doctrine which has been developing since the beginning of the Republic and some aspects of it are still being clarified by the courts.

The dominant Protestant as well as the dominant Roman Catholic and Eastern Orthodox view of Church-State relations in Europe still involve a close tie between Church and state. Sometimes this means that there is a national Church which is almost identical in its membership with the nation as in the Scandinavian countries. In England there is a State Church which includes no more than half of the people who are active as communicants or church members but which is still the means by which the state expresses the historic faith of the nation and it is subject to certain types of state control.

The extent to which these Protestant established or national Churches have freedom varies a great deal. In Norway, for example, every local pastor is appointed by the government though nominations are made by representatives of the Church. The Bishops are appointed by the government and there is in the country no synod or Church council other than the meeting of Bishops, and the national parliament has recently acted to prevent the formation of such a Church body. In Sweden there is a Church Assembly that can recommend legislation to the parliament and while the Bishops are chosen by the government, the local pastors are not. At the other extreme is the Church of Scotland which is a national Church and which is the means of religious expression for the nation but which is entirely free from any control by the government. Its General Assembly is as free a body as the synods of Churches in the United States. In all of these countries the smaller free Churches feel the pressure of great dominant Churches but their religious freedom as Churches is protected even if they do not share the public privileges of the national Church.

The most wonderful combination of things is to be found in the Anglican establishment. The Church of England itself is not supported financially by the state, but it has its own endowments. Its leadership is appointed by the government. This is true of its Bishops, Deans, Canons and some theological professors. Yet for the most part, the government exercises restraint and allows the Church itself to have decisive influence over its appointments. On the other hand, it is true that even in this century there has been at least one case in which the Prime Minister has appointed a Bishop against the advice of the ecclesiastical authorities.[1] My understanding is that this is not likely to happen now but that is only because of extra-legal traditions and restraints. The Parliament still has a veto over legislation affecting the inner life of the Church. It exercised this veto in 1927 in the case of the Prayer Book that had been agreed upon by all of the organs of the Church. The Church since 1919 has had a National Assembly which can pass legislation that is still subject to the Parliament's veto, though, except for four occasions since 1919, this veto has not

[1] I do not know whether there have been others, but one well-documented case was the appointment of Hensley Henson as Bishop of Hereford by Lloyd George in 1917. (See G. K. A. Bell, *Randall Davidson*, Chap. LIII.)

been exercised.[2] So the Church has been able to achieve substantial freedom even though formally it gives the appearance of being very much under government control. Freedom for religious witness and for prophetic utterance certainly does exist for all who have tenure in any ecclesiastical office. There is hardly a man on earth who has more freedom to speak than an Anglican parson or Church dignitary. The Dean of Canterbury is a living proof of this! One may wonder whether the congregations have enough freedom! A number of the Bishops belong to the House of Lords, and though this House has very little legislative power, the position does enable them to speak a Christian word in the context of the state.

The non-Anglicans in England also have religious freedom from the state and from the established Church. Until 1828 they could not even hold public office. There are now almost no disabilities remaining, though they do take second place on all ceremonial occasions. Their freedom from disabilities has come gradually since 1688, the date marking the beginning of toleration.[3] Today their situation is such that there is no great pressure for disestablishment among the free Churches. There is much more of such pressure in the Church of England itself, but usually there is a tendency there to wait until Parliament again vetoes such important Church legislation as the adoption of a new Prayer Book. It is often said that bad as the formal processes of appointment are, suggesting as they do a humiliating control of the Church by the state, the effects of this system have been good on the whole, that the choice

[2] Cyril Garbett, *Church and State in England* (Hodder Stoughton, London, 1950), p. 119. (Dr. Garbett was Archbishop of York when he wrote this book.)

[3] It is hard to realize how recently some of the disabilities have been overcome. For example, my own teachers at Mansfield College, Oxford, in 1925 belonged to the first generation of non-conformist students who were allowed to enter Oxford and Cambridge because of religious tests. Also, the non-conformists were until very recently the victims of a most unlovely combination of ecclesiastical pretensions and social snobbishness, especially in the small towns and villages.

of Bishops by election would favor the selection of safe dark horses whereas many of the Bishops have been men of great gifts, of decisive convictions, and of scholarly eminence. Also, it is often said that the whole system does provide through the participation of parliament and the government in Church affairs a lay influence that is salutary. This is one ground for the complacency of non-Anglicans because a fully self-governing Church might, as they believe, become more clerical. Yet it will never be anything but absurd in the abstract to have the leaders of a church appointed by a Prime Minister who may be a Unitarian or an Agnostic, and for great decisions in regard to the inner life of the Church to be made by a Parliament that contains only a minority of members of that Church.

I have described briefly these situations in other countries as a back-drop for the discussion of Church-State relations in the United States. It is obvious that no country that has had to make a fresh start in the modern period could create such institutional configurations as we find in most European countries. The inconsistencies which we see in England are the result of centuries of growth and change; no one could plan things that way. But this kind of growth has a way of rubbing the edges off the contradictions in practice and in the English context there may be no adequate reason to desire a radical change. At least that is one decision that American churchmen do not have to make.

In our own history there were also religious establishments in some of the colonies. At least five outlasted the Revolution and two—in Connecticut and Massachusetts—lasted until the years 1818 and 1832 respectively. But at the time of the Revolution the trend was undoubtedly away from religious establishments because of two powerful forces in the life of the young nation. One was the influence of the "sectarian" religious bodies such as the Baptists who had always been opposed to all ties between Church and state and had often suffered persecution under state Churches. The other influence was that of the intellectuals influenced by the Enlightenment, especially Thomas Jefferson and James Madison, who were powerful advocates of religious liberty and who sensed threats to liberty in every form of religious establishment. Jefferson and Madison had succeeded in ridding the state of Virginia of an Anglican establishment which was oppressive to minorities and the struggle to do so sharpened their minds on the subject. But it cannot be said too strongly that the American system of Church-State separation was not the result of hostility to Christianity or of the desire to put the Churches at a disadvantage. It was the result of the competition of many Churches and of the sincere belief of many churchmen that Churches were better off when they were on their own. Jefferson was not hostile to Christianity and he believed in the importance of a broad religious faith for the national life.

When the Federal Government was formed, it was possible to begin with a clean slate so far as its relation to Churches was concerned. Today the idea of separation of Church and state is so much taken for granted in this country that it is difficult to realize what an adventurous step it was. The Constitution itself prohibits all religious tests for federal office holders and this was an important start in separating the Church from the state though of itself this is not inconsistent with some forms of religious establishment. Religious tests were abandoned in Britain over a century ago. The very general words of the First Amendment to the Constitution laid down the lines along which our institutions were to develop: "Congress shall make no law respecting an establishment of religion, or prohibiting the free exercise thereof." This amendment did not apply to the states but only to the actions of Congress, and it was not until 1923[4] that in matters of religious

---

[4] Stokes, *Ibid.*, Vol. I, p. 591.

liberty the guarantee of liberty by the Fourteenth Amendment ("Nor shall any State deprive any person of life, liberty, or property, without due process of law") was extended to actions by the states.

It should be noted that the word "separation" is not in the Constitution. It was Jefferson's word and it came to be the popular American word for this constitutional provision; later the Supreme Court was to use Jefferson's metaphor, "wall of separation," as a fitting description of the American Church-State pattern. I agree with those who believe that this is an unfortunate metaphor because there can be no such wall between institutions which have to so large an extent the same constituency and which share many of the same concerns for the same national community. I also believe that it would have been better if the popular word for the American system were "independence" rather than "separation."[5] But, I am not quibbling over that and in what follows I shall speak of the separation of Church and state. In the next chapter I shall deal with the most important conflict in the interpretation of its meaning. In the remainder of this chapter I shall discuss the major reasons for the separation of Church and state as this is understood in general terms. I doubt if the conflict of interpretation to be discussed in the next chapter affects the significance of any one of these reasons except marginally. There are three reasons why I believe that this general pattern of "separation" is best for both Church and state and that changes in other countries which have established Churches should be (and, in fact, are) in this direction.

(1) The first reason for emphasizing the separation of Church and state is that it is the only way of assuring the complete freedom of the Church. Established Churches in Europe are all attempting to gain the substance of freedom

---

[5] This position is well stated in Merrimon Cuninggim's *Freedom's Holy Light* (Harper, 1955), Chap. IV.

but this still remains a difficult struggle. Anglican leaders now declare that if the British Parliament ever again uses its acknowledged legal right to interfere with the doctrine or worship of the Church, the Church must insist on its freedom even at the cost of disestablishment.[6]

In this country the freedom of the Church from state control is not a real problem. Freedom of the Church from control by the community or by movements of public opinion is a problem, but I am not discussing that here. The Church-State problems that call for solution in this country are basically in a different area, but they usually raise the question as to whether the Church should relate any of its efforts or its institutions to the state in such a way that the state might come to exercise control over them. But no one suspects any agency of the state in this country of trying to dictate to the Churches. I remember how great a furor there was when Mayor La Guardia of New York, who was in charge of civil defense during the Second World War, sent around to the clergy some very innocent suggestions concerning a sermon that might be preached. This was a blunder on his part, as he soon learned, but he obviously had no intention of trying to dictate to the clergy. The American Churches are extremely sensitive on matters of this sort. For example, it took a long time for enough of them to agree to have the Federal Social Security

[6] Archbishop Temple wrote in 1928: "If Parliament uses its unquestioned legal right to restrict the Church's freedom in this field (the determination of its own modes of worship), the Church must act through its own organs, and leave the State to do what it thinks right." I have heard Archbishop Temple say that establishment was good for the state but bad for the Church. It is obvious that if it is too bad for the Church it is not good for the state. (See Temple, *Christianity and the State*, pp. 195-196.)
Archbishop Garbett, writing in 1950, took the same view about the freedom of the Church. He said: "If these freedoms (such as the freedom to control its own worship) should be deliberately and decisively refused by Parliament, then the Church would be compelled to ask for disestablishment with full knowledge that some disendowment will accompany it." *Op. cit.*, p. 157.

made *optional* for ministers on the basis of self-employment to enable this to become law, though it is difficult to see how this can threaten the freedom of the Church. If any Churches become lax on matters affecting their freedom they get a strong reminder from the Baptists who are in a special way watch-dogs concerning the freedom of the Church, and it is good to have them perform this function.

Though the freedom of the Church from state control is not a serious problem in this country, in many countries it is the most serious external problem confronting Churches. In the Communist controlled countries, the Churches have no freedom to function outside their own sanctuaries in relation to the problems of state and nation, and they have to struggle to remain free even in their own worship and witness and especially in the religious education of their own children and youth. Usually so far as education is concerned, even if they still have some internal freedom, the pressure of the school and of the party organs upon the youth creates a severe spiritual struggle for them and for the Churches.

Patterns differ from country to country depending upon the strength of the Churches and on other conditions, and the Communist governments change their tactics from time to time. There are two generalizations which are safe. One is that the pressure of the state and the party organs on the Christian youth is everywhere a problem. The Communists expect that the future will be with them because they believe that the Churches will languish and die if only the party can influence the younger generation. The Communists have had some success here and everywhere they create agonizing conflicts for the young people themselves, but they are not winning in the satellite nations, and even in Russia the younger generation from time to time shows a very heartening independence. But whatever the degree of their success, this is the number one problem of the Church.

The second major problem of the Churches in Communist controlled countries is the freedom of the Churches to avoid being used for purposes of propaganda, especially in international relations. The state can sometimes compel the Churches to accept top leaders who are willing to be so used. Where the Church is so strong and united as it is in East Germany, this is not possible but it has been possible in Hungary and Czechoslovakia. In Russia and China the leaders of the Church have performed this function. I am making no judgments about the integrity of such leaders. Especially in Russia there is a tradition of uncritical support of the state in the Russian Church, and leaders in that Church have lived so long behind walls of censorship that they may not be conscious of being used any more than leaders of the American Churches were conscious of being used in the First World War. The Chinese Churches faced special problems in the fact that they were so weak, and in their ties with western countries, especially the United States, which made them peculiarly vulnerable to attack by the Communists. The few Chinese Christian leaders who have had any contacts outside of China have represented the outlook of their government, probably in part from inner conviction. Those of us who live under free conditions and yet who have our own ways of being colored in our thinking by a narrowly western or American point of view are in no position to criticize the motives of individuals who seem to us to be quite mistaken in giving Christian sanctions to the policies of their governments. This is especially true when they have been cut off for a long time from any informal contacts with people outside their own country.

It might be said that these Churches in Communist countries are separated from the state, but in all external matters they are dependent on the state. In such countries Churches live on sufferance and sometimes they still get state support. In so far as there is separation it is a very one-sided form. The

Churches are not allowed to influence the state, but they are under state control in all but their worship and their teaching within the walls of the Church, and even the latter is under supervision lest it encroach, as Christian teaching should, on matters of social life and state policy.

In this country the Churches live independently with a friendly state and the American form of separation is in the first instance as good a guarantee of the freedom of the Church as Churches have ever had in their long history.

(2) The second reason for believing in the separation of Church and State is the preservation of the state from control by the Church. This freedom from control by the Church takes two forms. One is freedom from ecclesiastical pressure on the state itself on matters of public policy. In a later chapter I shall discuss what forms of influence or even pressure by the Churches upon the state are not open to objection. Much of this influence or pressure is a part of the democratic process itself. When the constituencies of Churches express their views on public questions, this is a part of the process of the formation of public opinion. There is nothing about the role of the Church here that need be regarded as unfair pressure or ecclesiastical manipulation. It is true that Churches which are governed by hierarchies which carry on their debates in secret and which are believed to be able to "deliver" large blocs of votes on some candidates or issues raise a different problem. It is the right of such Churches to be so governed; this belongs to their guaranteed religious liberty. It is the right of their members to heed the guidance of their leaders on political matters. I shall discuss the problem that is raised here in a chapter on Protestant fears of Catholicism. I think that whatever may be the truth about the influence of the hierarchy, about the range of issues on which it takes a stand, about the bloc voting of Roman Catholics, this type of Church structure does create a real problem for democracy even though most of those within the Church,

from Cardinals down, may sincerely believe in democratic institutions in the state as contrasted with the Church.

There is another aspect of this freedom of the state from
Church control which is related to the ecclesiastical pressure
upon government but it is in itself so central in the concern of
Americans that I shall lift it up for special emphasis: the freedom of all religious minorities, and of those who reject all forms
of religious faith, from pressure from any Church or group of
Churches of the kind that comes through the use of the power
of the state.

Today when Church-State problems are discussed in this
country the one concern that ranks above all others is the fear
that one Church or a group of Churches may finally be able to
use the state to bring about discrimination against citizens on
grounds of religion or to limit the freedom of any religious
bodies. The people who belong to no religious body are afraid
that all religious bodies may combine against them. The Jewish
community usually takes their part because it fears that if there
is any such combining of religious bodies, the Christians will
control the combination. So, Jews take their position with the
Baptists as watch-dogs in all matters that affect religious liberty.
Both in practice often make common cause with the various
forms of secularists. We must not forget that secularists often
do most of the struggling for religious liberty in countries where
there are no important religious minorities. Protestants, while
not a religious minority in the nation as a whole, are a minority
in many great cities, and in some states they have a minority
consciousness because the Catholic Church is so much stronger
in organization and more effective in strategy. It is quite natural
that fear of Catholicism should provide most of the feeling
expressed in current Protestant discussions of Church-State
relations. Protestants are especially worried when they read and
hear that the Roman Catholic Church still regards as normative
a union of Church and state and accepts the American pattern

of separation only as a matter of expediency. If the Roman Catholics could effectively reassure Protestants on this point, it would be possible to deal more objectively with many of our problems.

Protestants are fearful that at the very least a Catholic majority in various states soon and perhaps later in the nation as a whole would shape public education along Catholic lines, that it would pass laws on such matters as marriage, birth control, medical practices dictated by Catholic interpretations of natural law. These are the fears concerning what the Church might do through extensions of what are now seen to happen in some places. Beyond them there is a vaguer fear that a large Catholic majority, first of all on a state level, might find ways of limiting the public activities of non-Catholics in the sphere of religion and morals. I believe that these fears are exaggerated, but they do have substance and unless Catholics who believe in democracy and religious liberty take them seriously, they will neither understand much of the opposition to them nor will they do the things that they can do to provide for a sound development of our institutions at the point where Catholic and non-Catholic interests meet.

The religious liberty which we have in this country and which we should seek to preserve here and to encourage in every country is, of course, not only liberty within the walls of the church. Religious liberty should include in addition to this the liberty of public witness, of evangelism. It should be the liberty not only to convert, but also to be converted in the sense of changing one's religious affiliation. It should be the liberty of public teaching not only about religious matters in the narrow sense, but also about all social, economic and political questions concerning which there is a religious judgment. It should include the liberty of Churches and other religious institutions to do all that is necessary to preserve their freedom as organizations, to hold property, to choose their own leaders. It is significant that the First Amendment in the very sentence that speaks of religious liberty also mentions freedom of speech, of the press, of "the right of people peaceably to assemble, and to petition the government for redress of grievances." It is fitting that religious liberty should be related so closely to these other liberties for there can be no religious liberty unless there is religious freedom to speak, unless there is freedom for religious books and periodicals, unless there is freedom for congregations and many other religious groups to assemble, and unless there is freedom to petition on all matters that affect the rights of Churches or of the individual conscience. Whenever any state clamps down on these rights of citizens on political grounds, religious liberty even in the narrowest sense is in danger for there is always the possibility of claiming that religious teaching is politically subversive. And when governments clamp down on religious liberty, any group of citizens who express political ideas that are regarded as subversive may be accused of religious heresy. So interdependent are all these freedoms of the mind and spirit.[7]

(3) The third reason for emphasizing the separation of Church and state is that it is best for the Church to be on its own. Here we can distinguish between two considerations.

The first is that in contrast to the experience of the national Church, it is important to have a Christian body that is distinguishable from the national community. Where the national Church does include almost the whole nation it is difficult to find any such body at all except the clergy. They in their training and function are set apart; they are the visible churchmen. I have referred to the fact that there is in some national Churches no synod representing clergy and laymen and the reason for this is that the national parliament is supposed to act in that capacity for most of its members are baptized church-

[7] For a careful analysis of all these elements of religious liberty see, M. Searle Bates, *Religious Liberty: An Inquiry* (Harper, 1945), especially pp. 300-310.

men. Once there was reality behind this arrangement, but now it is fictional and very bad for the Church. I should emphasize the fact that most national Churches are fully aware of the problems to which I refer and changes are rapidly taking place.

Soren Kierkegaard exposed the weakness of the national church mercilessly. There is a volume of his articles on the subject entitled *Attack on Christendom* which is a brilliant and devastating and one-sided attack on the Church of Denmark. I quote here a sample of his criticism from his greatest philosophical work, *Concluding Unscientific Postscript*. He is describing the situation of a Dane who, when he raises the question as to whether or not he is a Christian, is likely to get from people the following answer:

"How tiresome to make such a fuss about nothing at all; why can't he behave like the rest of us who are all Christians? . . . And if he happened to be married, his wife would say to him: 'Dear husband of mine, how can you get such notions into your heart? How can you doubt that you are a Christian? Are you not a Dane, and does not the geography say that the Lutheran form of the Christian religion is the ruling religion of Denmark? For you are surely not a Jew, nor are you a Mohammedan; what then can you be if not a Christian? It is a thousand years since paganism was driven out of Denmark, so I know that you are not a pagan. Do you not perform your duties at the office like a conscientious civil servant; are you not a good citizen of a Christian nation, a Lutheran Christian state? So then, of course you must be a Christian.' "[8]

There is a tendency for a national Church to be an institution manned by the clergy which provides sermons and sacraments for the whole national community without itself being a community. Often the vast majority of the people become indifferent to both sermons and sacraments though they are still glad to know that they are there. Advantage is taken of the Church when people are baptized, when they marry and when they die.

[8] Translated by David F. Swenson (Princeton University Press, 1941), p. 46.

At one point they are confirmed, but the saying is in some places, "confirmed out of the Church."

This is a very one-sided view and I am purposely avoiding references to particular countries; I am interested in it only as representing a trend that is present in national Churches. During the Second World War and since the War, there has been a great awakening to the dangers in this trend and the European Churches are emphasizing the substantial independence of the Church in spite of its ties with the state; they are emphasizing in a remarkable way the role of laymen. It was these national Churches which were very much tested during the National Socialist period and some of them proved that there was iron in them, after all; they proved that Kierkegaard's picture of the national Church was probably grossly unfair to a Church that had not been fully tested.

During the war years and immediately after the War there was much talk of "the renewal of the Church" and, while there has been some disappointment that the degree of Christian commitment that seemed to be present during the days of greatest testing is now less widespread in the various nations, this commitment continues in a very considerable Christian body that is distinguishable from the national community. The nation in which the Church was most tested, Germany, shows much evidence of this renewal and its Evangelical Academies and its Kirchentag have been extraordinary expressions of this lay interest in a vital Christian faith. The World Council of Churches with its Ecumenical Institute, and in other of its activities, has been a great source of inspiration for this renewal of the Church. Karl Barth, who always seems to be bolder than others, has shocked the European Churches by opposing infant baptism on Biblical grounds. Whatever one may think of this ultimately as a matter of doctrine, it does represent an attack on the idea of an almost automatically baptized nation which should be taken seriously. Those who do not agree with Barth are concerned to take a more responsible attitude toward infant baptism than has often been the case so that it is in effect a real initiation into the Christian community and not initiation into a national community with a formal religious sanction.

In my emphasis upon the renewal of the Churches in Europe I may seem to go against my own argument for the separation of the Church from the state. I shall come back later to the ways in which European churchmen defend the national Church today, but now I shall express my own conviction that this renewal of the Church may have taken place more in spite of than because of the structure of the Church. In so far as it does succeed in developing a distinctive Christian body within the national community and in so far as it preserves the full Christian freedom of this body, a situation has been created that is certainly difficult to harmonize with the structure of the national Church. If this can take place, it is not for any Americans with a doctrinaire view of the matter to say that it cannot take place or that it may not be better to preserve continuity with history than to create a new structure. Where this historical background does not exist, it is clearly impossible to have the combination of things which are possible in some European countries. It is difficult for me not to believe that if the national Churches of Europe are to hold the gains they have made, they will move in the direction of the separation of Church and state in some form.

The second consideration which is involved in the proposition that it is best for the Church to be on its own is that a free Church must support itself. It cannot rely on funds from the state or on the remarkable system of church-taxes which are compulsory for all who acknowledge membership in the Church even though such membership is not compulsory. It is our experience in the United States that the activity of the laymen in their financial support of the Church has created an extraordinary momentum of lay interest in the Church. It is significant that the Churches that have to support themselves have the greatest resources available for missions and other benevolences. At the present time, the vitality of the American Churches amaze all who observe it and this vitality is in considerable measure the result of the very active and often sacrificial interest of the laymen. The Church's use of laymen increases their sense of responsibility and their loyalty to the Church. I realize that there is much debate as to how much depth or how much understanding of the Gospel or how much distinctively Christian commitment there is in all of this lay activity. Certainly it is all very mixed. The popularity of the Church does tend to lead to the secularizing of the Church and it is ironical that Churches that are not national Churches in this country actually seem more organic to the community as a whole than do national Churches. But after all of the criticisms of this vitality in the American Churches, one can hardly deny that it provides a tremendous opportunity for the Churches to mediate the truth and the grace of the Gospel to people.

Professor Winthrop Hudson in his book *The Great Tradition of the American Churches,* emphasizes the value of the Church's self-support. He has a very interesting chapter on Lyman Beecher who was one of the most influential leaders of the Congregational Churches in Connecticut when they were disestablished in 1818. Beecher fought hard against the disestablishment of the Churches but after it had taken place, and after the Churches had been for some time on their own, he admitted that he had been mistaken. Professor Hudson describes Beecher's change of mind in this passage:

"He found himself forced to acknowledge that what he feared as the worst thing that could happen had turned out to be 'the best thing that ever happened in the State of Connecticut.' For, as he said, 'it cut the churches loose from dependence on state support,' and 'threw them wholly on their own resources and God.' Before the change, he declared, 'our people thought that they should be destroyed if the law should be taken away from under them. . . .

But the effect, when it did come, was just the reverse of the expectation.' 'Being "thrown on God and ourselves," there was created
that moral coercion which makes men work. Before we had been
standing on what our fathers had done, but now we were obliged
to develop all our energy.' There were some who felt that ministers
had 'lost influence', but 'the fact is,' asserted Beecher, 'they have
gained. By voluntary efforts, societies, missions, and revivals, they
exert a deeper influence than they ever could by queues, and shoe
buckles, and cocked hats, and gold-headed canes.' "[9]

What do those who still believe in the National Church say
about this claim that it is best for the Churches to be on their
own? There are at least three points that I have often heard
made and each one of them does suggest a weakness in the
free Church, and American churchmen should consider them
not as arguments for changing the American system, but as
warnings to be taken seriously.

(1) There is a danger that the Church will seem to be a club
owned by those who support it. This is all the more true when
the Church gathers to itself socially congenial people with the
same background and social outlook. Whereas a national
Church is threatened by state control, a free Church is threatened by control by its living donors. There is great advantage
when the donors are many rather than few but even then waves
of public prejudice can cause many donors to try to control
the Church for essentially secular purposes. I recently heard
a Scotsman describe the Churches in his village. It helped me
to realize the difference between living with a Church that has
been in the village for many centuries and being a part of a
Church that was recently founded and for which one's own
generation has built the building. In the first case it is easier
to feel that we receive the Church; in the second it is a temptation to think that we have made the Church.

(2) The most insistent criticism of the American pattern
that I hear is that the Church's dependence upon lay financial

[9] Harper, 1953, pp. 64-65.

support leads to a one-sided conception of lay participation in the Church. Not only does it overstress financial support; it also overstresses what the laymen do for the Church within the doors of the Church rather than what the laymen might do for the Church in their various occupations in the world or as Christian citizens. One does get the impression that many American churchmen assume that the most successful Church is one that provides either the most responsibilities or the greatest number of attractions to keep the laymen *in church* during the week. I think that this criticism has some justification and Americans can learn a great deal from the European emphasis on the importance of the layman's vocation in the world. On the other hand, I think that the criticism is over-drawn and fails to take account of the great role of American laymen in Christian education, and in activities which are not just busy-work to keep its members in Church, but which are ways in which the Church serves people. I have in mind especially the way in which it helps to provide, in its own life, a kind of community for our mobile population which loses its roots in the larger community. Criticism of American Churches at this point is in part the result of a failure to understand some of our cultural needs and what Churches actually do to meet them. But this defense should not, for a moment, divert us from the real stimulus and inspiration in the best European emphasis upon the role of laymen.

(3) A third criticism that is directed against the whole pattern of American church life, really against our whole history, is the criticism of our large number of denominations. If there is one dominant national Church, this favors concentration on that Church and the free Churches that live with it do not greatly alter the pattern. This is less true in England than it is in Scotland and on the Continent, but our denominationalism horrifies many English observers. If we were interested in scoring points against the European critics we might say that most of our

denominations are transplanted from Europe (some of them were national Churches in the "old country") and that we are chiefly victims of European religious history. Also, there is a tendency for the European observer to exaggerate greatly the divisions in American Protestantism. Most American Protestants are in a comparatively few denominations and between these there is far more Christian unity than the outsider can easily imagine. It would take us too far afield to discuss the problems of church union in the American context. At present our Church-State relations are really irrelevant to this problem. Our many denominations are the result of the religious liberty which most critics also prize and would try to make room for in any system of Church-State relations which they do favor.

There is one consideration that I owe to Professor James Hastings Nichols[10] which, while it does not justify the continuation of so many competing denominations, should give pause to those who put all the emphasis upon the idea of a unified national Church. People in many European countries often found that they had to choose, on the one hand, between a National Church which in its orthodoxy offended their feeling for intellectual honesty or which seemed to be on the wrong side in the struggle for social justice, and, on the other hand, either atheism or an anti-clericalism which cut them off from the Christian community. In Britain and in America this was not the case because of the existence of the free Churches. It is not enough to say that it is a kind of "cafeteria conception" of Christianity to allow people to take their choice among Churches. A dominant Church may hide the Gospel from many people. If it does that, it is better for them to be able to find an alternative Church than for them to reject Christianity. It is a tragedy when this takes place under conditions which cause the Churches to reject each other as Churches. Those conditions have been in

[10] "Atheism has progressed in the modern West in inverse proportion to schism." *Democracy and the Churches* (Westminster Press, 1951), p. 61.

large measure overcome within Protestantism by the ecumenical movement. But as the Churches move closer to each other they should remember this fact about their history as a warning against the uniformity that may unnecessarily turn people away from Christ.

In this chapter I have set forth the main reasons for believing in the separation of Church and state. I have always kept in mind the fact that these reasons have a special application to the United States but, while they do not necessarily suggest that the American form of separation is good for all countries, they do suggest that older forms of the national Church should everywhere give way to new patterns which do justice to the freedom of the Church, to the religious liberty of all citizens and to the need of developing distinctively Christian communities characterized by lay initiative.

In the next chapter I shall raise the question as to what the separation of Church and state means in the light of one important controversy which divides Americans who accept the general principle of separation.

CHAPTER XV

A Major Controversy Concerning the
Meaning of Separation

IN RECENT years there has been a significant debate concerning the meaning of the First Amendment. This controversy divides the Protestant community, and, in general, the Jewish and the Catholic communities are on opposite sides. One can quote historians, judges and theologians on both sides. In fact it seems to many people, not least to a Supreme Court minority, that the majority of the Supreme Court has taken both sides of the argument in the course of four years.

The issue is this: does the First Amendment rule out not only preferential treatment by the state of any religious body (or bodies) or discrimination against any religious body (or bodies), but also all aid to or helpful cooperation with all religious bodies on an equal basis? The debate was sharpened by some words in the opinion of the Supreme Court in *Everson v. Board of Education* (New Jersey bus case) in 1947 which were repeated in the opinion of the Court in *McCollum v. Board of Education* (Champaign released-time case) in 1948. The words are as follows:

"The 'establishment of religion' clause of the First Amendment means at least this: Neither a state nor the federal government can set up a Church. Neither can pass laws which aid one religion, aid all religions, or prefer one religion over another."

The phrase "aid all religions" is the critical phrase. These words were applied by the Court, not to any financial aid to "all reli-

gions," but to the arrangements for released time religious education in Champaign, Illinois. These arrangements did involve the
use of school buildings for religious classes and to this degree
there was material aid to all of the religions involved. But many
opponents of released time, including several Supreme Court
Justices, oppose any use of the processes of public education to
facilitate released-time classes which are administered and supported by the Churches.

I shall discuss the problem of released time in the next
chapter. Here I am interested in this and other statements of
the Court which have a much broader application. It is remarkable that in 1952 the Supreme Court in a decision which upheld
the New York State system of released-time religious education
(*Zorach case*), said quite different things about the problem of
the relation between the state and the various religious bodies.
This decision was written by Justice William O. Douglas and it
included the following statements:

"When the State encourages religious instruction or cooperates
with religious authorities by adjusting the schedule of public events
to sectarian needs it follows the best of our traditions. For it then
respects the religious nature of our people and accommodates the
public service to their spiritual needs. To hold that it may not would
be to find in the Constitution a requirement that the government
show a callous indifference to religious groups. That would be preferring those who believe in no religion over those who do so believe.
Government may not finance religious groups nor undertake religious instruction nor blend secular and sectarian education nor
use secular institutions to force one or some religion on any person."

Perhaps the most important sentence in this opinion of the
Court is that:

"The First Amendment, however, does not say that in every and all
respects there shall be separation of Church and State."

Three of the Justices who had approved the statement about no
aid to all religions and who had approved the use of Jefferson's

metaphor, "wall of separation," also approved this opinion of Justice Douglas. The separate opinions that have been filed by members of the Court are remarkable examples of judicial indignation and eloquence.

Writers on this subject always find their differing judgments of policy supported by the history of the First Amendment. Those who emphasize restrictions on aid to all religions on an equal basis read the Amendment in the light of one side of the thought of Madison and Jefferson. The general tendency of the thought of both was on the side of a strict interpretation of separation; they both supplied both the formulae and the rhetoric for this interpretation.

Jefferson was not involved in the drafting of the First Amendment as he was the Minister to France at the time. He did, however, combine with his emphasis upon "the wall of separation" a willingness to make practical adjustments to the needs of Churches, notably in the case of his plan for denominational schools on the edge of the campus of the University of Virginia which would be independent of the University and yet would have the advantage of many forms of cooperation with the University.[1] He also planned to have a professor on the faculty of the University who would teach Natural Theology and Ethics, and a "special room for religious worship."

Madison did have a major part in the drafting of the First Amendment. Those who seek to provide an historical basis for the strict view of separation make much of his role and they connect it with the evidences of his extreme views on this subject, such as his opposition to the payment of Chaplains in the armed forces by the government and his opposition to the appointment

[1] *Cf.* Anson Phelps Stokes, *Church and State in the United States* (Harper, 1950), Vol. I, pp. 337-338.
If it were not for Canon Stokes' massive volumes it would be difficult for one who is not an historian to find his way on this subject. Canon Stokes' thoroughness and his fairness of judgment make his book an indispensable guide.

of Chaplains for the Houses of Congress.[2] Madison's famous "Remonstrance" is one of the documents most often quoted in favor of the strict interpretation of separation. Yet in his work in relation to the First Amendment, Madison can be quoted in favor of a more flexible interpretation. The report of the debates says of him: "He believed that the people feared one sect might obtain a pre-eminence, or two combine together, and establish a religion to which they would compel others to conform. He thought that if the word national was introduced, it would point the amendment directly to the object it was intended to prevent."[3]

This report about Madison is important in two respects. It shows that he was thinking chiefly about the danger that one or more Churches might gain pre-eminence and it also shows that he did not have the states in mind but only the problem of a national establishment. On another occasion he introduced the proposal that "no State shall violate the equal rights of conscience, of the freedom of the press, or the trial by jury in criminal cases."[4] But this proposal was not adopted and even the part of the First Amendment dealing with religious liberty did not become applicable to the states until it was applied to them through the Fourteenth Amendment.

I see no reason to allow the historical case for a flexible interpretation of the First Amendment to stand or fall with the outcome of an argument over the various aspects of Madison's thought. There is one fact about the period in which the Amendment was adopted that seems to me, as one who is neither historian nor judge, to compel the conclusion that the First Amendment, whatever Madison himself believed, was essentially a compromise and that it is a mistake, therefore, to impose upon it the most one-sided interpretation. That fact is that five of the states at the time had some kind of religious establishment.

[2] Stokes, Vol. I, p. 347
[3] Quoted by Stokes from the *Annals of Congress*, Vol. I, p. 543.
[4] Quoted in Stokes, Vol. I, p. 541.

There were two views of this matter that went into the drafting of the Amendment. The very vagueness of the language "no law respecting" can be interpreted to mean that Congress was to pass no law that would have an unfavorable effect on the establishments that existed in the states as well as no law that would lead to a national establishment.

Professor Corwin's much-quoted article on this subject states flatly that "respecting" was a "two edged word, which bans any law *disfavoring* as well as any law *favoring* an establishment of religion."[5] He quotes in support of his position the *Commentaries on the Constitution* by Joseph Story (1833). Those who take the opposite view dismiss Story as a prejudiced witness because he was a Massachusetts[6] man who did not believe in the separation of Church and State anyway.[7] It is hard for me not to think in view of this argument that the vague words are favorable to a more rather than a less permissive interpretation of the Amendment. Great as were the Virginians, they had a strong bias and we should not listen to them alone in interpreting the history. Whether their position was wise as a matter of policy is a question to be discussed on its own merits.

Professor Freeman Butts,[8] who has written a very able and thorough account of the First Amendment with much use of Madison's views, emphasizes two things that need to be considered. On the one hand, he points out that, though establishments still existed, the trend was certainly against establishment at that time in the nation as a whole. He shows that even in

[5] "The Supreme Court as National School Board" in *Thought* (1948), p. 665. I have used a revised edition of it published in *Law and Contemporary Problems* published by the Duke University School of Law, Winter 1949, p. 12.

[6] The date of this book was the year after disestablishment was effected in Massachusetts.

[7] Leo Pfeffer, *Church, State and Freedom* (The Beacon Press, 1953), p. 143.

[8] R. Freeman Butts, *The American Tradition in Religion and Education* (The Beacon Press, 1950).

Massachusetts and Connecticut, where the establishments were more substantial than in South Carolina, New Hampshire or Maryland, there had developed a system of "multiple establishment." This meant that state support was given on the basis of equality to several Churches. He also makes much of the fact that Congress in the process of drafting the Amendment turned down a resolution that would have favored a merely non-preferential interpretation of the Amendment.[9] He says that it is this non-proferential interpretation that is really involved in the view of the Amendment that would enable the state to "aid all religions" on an equal basis.

The fact that there was a trend toward disestablishment does not, of itself, alter the compromise character of the wording of the Amendment. My chief difficulty with Dr. Butts' argument, however, is that he tries to force all interpretations of the First Amendment into one of two categories: absolute separation, which underlies the opinion of the Supreme Court in the Mc-Collum case, or "multiple establishment." He allows for no aid to all religious bodies by the state which is short of giving all such bodies the status of "establishment." This seems to me to be an attempt to force a very rigid pattern of alternatives on a document that carefully avoids precision.[10]

There is another aspect of this historical discussion that does not usually get sufficient emphasis: it is the fact that the First Amendment did not apply to the states but became applicable to the states only after the adoption of the Fourteenth Amendment, and that the Fourteenth Amendment clearly is applicable to the part of the First Amendment that refers to the "free exercise" of religion but less clearly applicable to the prohibition of

---

[9] Canon Stokes concurs with this. In relation to one proposal voted down, he says: "This action was significant in showing that Congress was not satisfied with a proposal which merely prevented an advantage to any one denomination over others as far as Church-State separation was concerned. It wished to go farther." Vol. I, p. 546.

[10] Cf. Merrimon Cuninggim, *Freedom's Holy Light* (Harper, 1955), pp. 135-140.

laws respecting the establishment of religion.[11] I recognize that the relation of these two parts of the Amendment to each other, and the relation of the Fourteenth Amendment to them, are among the very moot points of constitutional interpretation. It is significant that Leo Pfeffer, whose book is the most solid study of these matters from the point of view of extreme separationism, does distinguish between these two aspects of the Amendment (though with some difficulty he applies the Fourteenth Amendment to both) and that he finds "the religious liberty" clause more permissive than the establishment clause and on that basis favors chaplains for the armed forces which are questionable from the point of view of the establishment clause. He sees the religious liberty of conscripted citizens to have access to a religious ministry at stake.[12]

There is obvious doubt concerning what the combination of these two Amendments really requires. The combination is interpreted loosely and interpreters get out of it what they want. When the First Amendment was adopted, the Fourteenth was not in sight and efforts of Madison to have the application of the First Amendment to the states incorporated in it was voted down.[13] Why is it not better, when there is doubt of this kind, to give the benefit of that doubt to states and communities in experimenting with solutions of a very difficult problem?[14] These

[11] Professor Corwin says that "it is only liberty that the Fourteenth Amendment protects," and he distinguishes sharply between liberty and the question of the establishment of religion. (P. 19.) Professor Mark DeWolfe Howe seems to agree with this limitation of the Fourteenth Amendment. See *Religion and the Free Society* (Fund for the Republic, 1958), p. 56.

[12] Pfeffer, *op. cit.*, p. 151. This distinction is rejected by interpreters who say that the only point in ruling out establishment is to protect liberty, but such a view would favor a more limited test of what constitutes establishment.

[13] Stokes, Vol. I, p. 541.

[14] I realize that this argument might be turned against the Supreme Court's decision on racial integration in public schools. It does favor strongly the Court's emphasis upon "deliberate speed" that takes account of regional differences. But if the Court was right, as I believe it was, in

experiments should be subject to the protection of the religious liberty of all citizens—both the liberty of citizens to be free from any form of religious discrimination or coercion and the opportunity for citizens to exercise their religious liberty in positive ways. The tension between these two forms of religious liberty is the source of the deepest problem here and it is a mistake to try to solve the problem by one-sided federal prohibitions which take account only of the negative form of religious liberty. Professor Butts says that " 'cooperation' of Church and State is just as inimical to the equal rights of conscience as free exercise is necessary for them."[15] But, what if positive free exercise of these rights depends upon "cooperation" between Church and state?

The difference between the kind of aid to all religions which I am defending and the aid that might be regarded as a mark of "multiple establishment" may be that in the latter case the state goes out of its way to aid Churches for their own sake whereas in the former case the state finds itself involved in activities, such as education, in which the Churches have a special stake and it may therefore seek to arrive at some adjustment that limits the injury to the interests for which the Churches stand. Interpretations of the separation of Church and state which rule out such adjustments on *a priori* grounds are unfair and are inimical to the free exercise of religion. Advocates of such interpretations who are themselves advocates of secularism as a view of life in place of the historical religions fail to understand this claim that there is injury or unfairness or deprivation of freedom

seeing injurious discrimination against a whole race in a system of compulsory segregation, the rights and dignity of these millions of American citizens are at stake. In the case of these educational experiments connected with religion there is no comparable injury or affront to any group of citizens. I realize that those who take the strongly separationist position in this matter fear that there will be such injury and affront to religious minorities but they can hardly say that these are inherently involved in non-discriminatory provisions for religious education as they are in segregated education. The fear itself does not seem very substantial and it is surely possible to guard against its realization.

[15] *Op. cit.,* p. 91.

because schools which have no place for religion favor in practice freedom for their faith. There seems to me to be here an area of real misunderstanding since this extreme view of separation is sincerely believed to be based upon a concern for fairness and freedom. Doubtless there is involved here a judgment upon the Churches for their own unfairness in the past in dealing with dissenters.

The military chaplaincy can be seen as an embodiment of the intentions of the American people in regard to religion. It is a form of actual aid, even financial aid, in effect, to the Churches, to all Churches on a proportional basis. It is an example of co-operation between Church and state at a point where *both* have a stake in such cooperation. The Churches have a stake in providing pastoral services for their members and for all who will receive them. The state has a stake in the religious liberty of the citizen to engage in the "free exercise" of religion in positive terms when he is in military service. A reasonable and impartial method of cooperation is called for by the situation and it is permitted by the words of the Constitution. There are other forms of cooperation of the kind that Justice Douglas mentions when he speaks of the "adjusting the schedule of public events to sectarian needs."

Tax exemption of Church property and the generous exemption for gifts to religious institutions is perhaps the most remarkable of all forms of aid to all religious bodies on a non-preferential basis. It goes beyond the aid that represents an adjustment to avoid injury. There are leaders of the Churches who now raise the question as to whether such tax exemption is a good thing. I am sure that they would apply this only to property and not to gifts. While it is arguable that it might be better for Churches to be more completely on their own by having to pay taxes, along the lines of my argument in the previous chapter, I wonder if it is not good for the state, perhaps more than for the Church, to signalize in this way the high place given to religion. More broadly there is much to be said for the state's going out of its way to encourage voluntary associations of citizens which are important for the welfare of the community.

The controversy that I have discussed in this chapter comes to a head in the area of the relations between the state, the Church and education. That is today the most troublesome and baffling area in all American thinking about the separation of Church and state. In the next chapter I shall deal with it—with no little "fear and trembling"!

CHAPTER XVI

Church, State, and Education

THE purpose of this chapter is not to argue in favor of any particular type of solution for the problems that are involved in this highly controversial area, but to emphasize the importance of encouraging many different experiments instead of insisting on very narrow and rigid limits to what is permitted. I shall deal with particular methods and proposals rather for the sake of illustrating this general principle than to offer easy judgments concerning what are likely to have the best results.[1]

It is necessary to see what the problem is. The first element in it is that the state in moving so heavily into the field of education has itself crossed any line that might be thought to separate the sphere of the state from the sphere of the Church. Both Church and state are interested in the formation of the minds and spirits and characters of children. Some interpreters of the state's functions may draw back from that but they must admit that education is concerned with all three.

It is impossible to separate that which is purely secular in the field of education from that which has religious implications. It is widely recognized that when all specific forms of religion are omitted from the world of the school, this is itself a negative form of religious teaching; it strongly implies that religion is

---

[1] Dr. F. Ernest Johnson has said this well in the following passage: "Personally, I should like to see a national policy adopted that would permit a wide range of local experimentation, with courts standing guard and ready to intervene only when there is a 'clear and present danger' that some violation of religious liberty will occur." *American Education and Religion* (Ed., F. E. Johnson. Harper, 1952), pp. 8-9.

peripheral and dispensable as a matter of human concern. Leaders of public education now emphasize their belief that public education is concerned with moral and spiritual values. The discussion of these values without any reference to their historic religious roots is certainly artificial and again it creates a false impression about the meaning of religion. A curriculum that deals only with the most external secular subjects and that avoids any reference to moral and spiritual values may be less misleading religiously than a curriculum that does include many matters that have to do with character and the life of the spirit and carefully abstracts them from their religious context.

The fact that the modern school takes so large a part of the time and interest of the child—at least where there are enough schoolrooms so that the educational program is not limited to a half schedule for reasons of space—is a serious handicap in providing for adequate supplementary religious teaching outside of school hours. Also, such supplementary religious teaching has the disadvantage that there is no chance to relate it to other subjects. Protestants are often very critical of the Roman Catholic emphasis upon parochial schools, but they should admit that the Catholics face this aspect of the problem more realistically than most Protestants. I think that they may overdo it if they deny relative autonomy to some disciplines. There is obviously no Christian arithmetic and no Christian physics, and such subjects can be taught so far as their own materials are concerned in a wholly secular manner. But even if that is the case, the way in which such subjects fit into the whole educational pattern does depend upon the atmosphere of the school and the total outlook of the teachers. It makes a great difference whether or not natural sciences are taught in such a way as to point to mystery, to the conviction that nothing about which we know is self-sufficient. It is not necessary to bring in religious dogmas as answers, but it is most important not to bring in secular dogmas as answers either. There are other subjects which can only be taught meaningfully if the relation of their content to religion is allowed to appear throughout—such as history, literature, art, and studies of contemporary society.

There is one other factor in the American situation which creates a problem for all who represent the Christian or Jewish faiths: it is the development during this century of a widely influential philosophy of education which is based upon wholly secularist presuppositions. It may be that those who share this philosophy have a positive place for what they call religion as the attitude of commitment toward particular personal and social goals, goals which are democratic and involve respect for the person. But the difficulty is that those who hold views of this kind have no place in their thought or feeling for the content of revealed religion in any form. If this position were really neutral religiously, it would not create such a problem but it is not neutral in its attitude toward the great religious traditions. It rejects them all implicitly or explicitly as authoritarian and inimical to the democratic educational process. I do not doubt that much of this type of thinking has brought correctives to some religious attitudes and to traditional educational methods. It became a problem only as it developed a pretentious ideology that offered its own answers to religious questions.

The religious vacuum in public education is often filled by a religion of democracy that is thought to be more enlightened than the historic faiths. The fact that this kind of approach is not connected with any of the traditional Churches means that it can be presented in schools without being spotted as religious teaching that raises Church-State problems. Constitutional inhibitions do not apply to the teaching of a new and unrecognized religion as they do to one with traditional symbols. Justice Douglas in the Zorach decision spoke of the danger "of preferring those who believe in no religion over those who do so believe."

I have sketched the problem. It leads to a very practical dilemma for a large proportion of American parents. They usually must send their children to a public school, and for many good reasons they want to do this. They know that this school has become secularized even though the teachers and the administrators may as individuals hold religious convictions. They would like to see some modification and supplementation of public education that would permit religious teaching, but every effort that is made in this direction is opposed as divisive or as unconstitutional by portions of the community. The same voices that condemn most strongly every concession to parents who send their children to parochial schools often condemn with equal strength every experiment to relate education to religion under the aegis of the public school. All of this goes under the name of religious liberty but it might well be called the denial in specific terms of the positive religious liberty of the parents in the interests of a hardened conception of negative religious liberty.[2]

I have stated the problem in dogmatic terms, but I am not as dogmatic about solutions. It is a safe generalization that all the proposed solutions create difficulties and probably none of them would be applicable to all communities.

All discussions of the subject mention at least three possible patterns of religious teaching related to public education. I shall say something about each of these and then comment on the place of parochial schools.

(1) The first of these patterns involves the teaching by the school of a "common core" of religious faith which belongs to the Judaeo-Christian tradition. Since this is the traditional faith

[2] *Cf.*, Henry P. Van Dusen, *God in Education* (Scribners, 1951). Dr. Van Dusen says: "It lies within the power of the American people, and it is their duty, to make clear that they continue to desire for their children, as their forebears prevailingly did, the influence of religion in the schooling offered the youth of the land in publicly maintained institutions; and that they desire their national Constitution to be interpreted as its authors intended, and as it has in fact been interpreted throughout the nation's history, so as to make possible a wide variety of provision of religious instruction and religious worship in public schools and colleges." P. 118.

of the people, it is believed that it can be taught by the school as school without raising any problem of cooperation with Churches. This common core is, as described by one of the proponents[3] of this pattern, "an out and out theism," but it does not involve anything "distinctively Christian" as opposed to Jewish convictions. The most authoritative statement of this view says: "As far as the school can, in view of the diversity of our people, judicial opinions, and our American traditions, we expect it to teach this common religious tradition as the only adequate basis for the life of the school and the personal lives of teachers, students, citizens in a free and responsible democracy."[4] This view has considerable support among Protestant leaders. It has had official approval of the leaders of Christian education representing Protestant Churches. It has been strongly supported by such leaders of theological education as Dean Luther A. Weigle and President Henry P. Van Dusen.

I do not see how this "common core" can be included in the curriculum of a school in a way that avoids both of two dangers. One is that it be in fact Christian rather than Jewish, or Protestant rather than Catholic. It may be this less in what is said than in the emphasis with which it is said and in the exact line that is drawn concerning what should be omitted. Biblical teaching which included only the Old Testament would create a false impression, but the New Testament does not belong to the "common core." Even if such sectarianism can be avoided, I believe that there is great danger here of allowing the "common core" to develop into a common denominator religious tradition that is put beside the other traditions.

If we look at this pattern in the light of the emphasis of my chapter on the place of religion in our pluralistic society, it might

---

[3] Nevin C. Harner, "A Protestant Educator's View" in Johnson, *American Education and Religion*, p. 88.

[4] From Report of the Committee on Religion and Public Education of the International Council of Religious Education (1949), quoted by Harner.

be possible to distinguish between *religious acknowledgement* and *religious teaching*. The school as school often does make provision for this and in most states it is constitutional to have readings from the Bible without comment (though this does create difficulties because of Catholic and Protestant versions). The religious symbolism that is used by the nation could be present at some point in the life of the school. This acknowledgement of God can, of course, be perfunctory or it may look like an effort to make worship compulsory; but, there should be room for local experiments. The moment this becomes religious teaching and there is any elaboration of the "common core" it would be almost impossible to avoid either sectarianism or the development of a public school religious doctrine. It would also in many situations threaten the academic freedom and the religious liberty of teachers who personally reject the "common core." If these criticisms are sound, even though some place may remain for what I have called religious acknowledgement, this view does not point the way to a substantial contribution to religious education.

(2) The second type of proposal seems to me to have more promise. It is the much discussed teaching *about* religion that has been strongly recommended by various educational bodies.[5] This involves the attempt to teach the facts about religion without any effort to indoctrinate, and to expose children to the Bible and other religious literature as this is often done in academic institutions on a higher level—with an attempt to be objective but with appreciation. It might also include the very

[5] See Report of the American Council of Education Committee on Religion and Education: *The Relation of Religion to Public Education— the Basic Principles* (1947) and the Report of the Educational Policies Commission of the National Education Association and the American Association of School Administrators: *Moral and Spiritual Values in the Public Schools* (1951).
There is a careful discussion of the principles involved and a body of suggestions for curricula based in part on local experiences in Virgil Henry's *The Place of Religion in Public Schools* (Harper, 1950).

definite attempt to describe the major faiths that are actually
represented in the school. This type of teaching would come into
the teaching of other subjects where it belongs naturally. But,
this would involve coherent units of teaching about religious
materials even though they might come under the general head-
ing of literature or social studies.

There are obvious limits to this approach, and it also raises its
own problems. It is much less than many people want in terms
of direct religious education. Teachers would find it difficult to
be objective enough to satisfy the religious groups and, in some
cases, their very objectivity might be resented. On the other
hand, there would be a great gain if the religious writings are
allowed to make their own impression. In some communities the
teachers would be under constant surveillance to make sure that
they neither taught their own faith as true nor belittled one of
the other traditions. In the homogeneous communities where
this approach might meet with least opposition, there would be
a temptation to indoctrinate as much as the traffic would bear.
I think that no one of these difficulties points to anything that
is inherently wrong or impossible about this approach. It is important to realize that some communities are not ready for it
and that it should not be pushed in communities where it would
be most likely to be abused or where it would be most divisive.
But it is the whole point of this chapter that we should be content with many experiments, usually on a local basis, and not
look for over-all solutions. This approach, if it were followed
through with measurable success, would expose children to books
and to persons in history that would make their own impression
and it would overcome the difficulty that when religion is not
given a place in a curriculum it is made to seem unimportant.
It might make possible much greater mutual understanding as
between the faiths.

(3) The released-time method of religious education has had
the greatest amount of attention in the public controversies. It is

strongly opposed by important segments of the community as religiously divisive. The Zorach decision did give assurance that some forms of released time are constitutional, but I have noticed a strong tendency among Protestant leaders to suggest that released time is ineffective and hardly worth much emphasis.

There is one general consideration about released time that is independent of the question concerning the success or failure of particular programs. The Court's upholding of the principle is a very important symbol of the positive religious liberty of parents to find ways to supplement public education during the regular school day. Released time does offer an area of experiment and maneuver which should not be closed off by judicial fiat on a national scale.

Another major consideration on released time is that it may still offer a chance for a substantial amount of religious education during the week that does not have the limitations of teaching by the school, if the Churches take it seriously. The Churches could decide to give it a much higher priority than has been the case. It may be impossible in some communities, but a staggered system of released time enables the Churches to develop a staff of highly trained teachers on a full-time basis. Since released-time classes cannot be held in the school building, such a staggered system raises practical problems because church buildings may not be near the school. But is it impossible to think of the construction of part-time parochial schools near the public school? They might all be in the same building as is sometimes the case with Army chapels and with religious centers on some university campuses. Another device is the use of buses which are fitted up as classrooms. I used the words "part-time parochial schools" here purposely because it might be possible to persuade Catholics in some communities to substitute such part-time parochial schools for full-time parochial schools with advantages to the community. Such a proposal would be anathema to those who think in rigid terms about separation of Church and state and who fear all activities that seem to divide people. But such rigid thinking about separation is not required by the American system and people are divided religiously anyway and know it. They should not be ashamed of the public recognition of the fact of their division if they regard religion as important.

There is a serious problem of divisiveness when one of the groups is a very small minority. This minority might be opposed to the historic faiths. Such a situation calls for tact and consideration, but I doubt if it should of itself be the one factor that prevents this kind of experiment. Perhaps when a staggered system of released time is impossible, "dismissed time"—involving the dismissal of all classes early with no problem of what to do with those who do not choose to go to religious classes—would be preferable. If, however, a more ambitious program of religious education near the school is physically possible, it ought to be one of the permissible areas of local experiment.

I have discussed briefly the three major proposals for doing something about religious education in the context of the public school. It is now necessary to consider the other major approach to week-day religious education: the parochial school. It is here where the most bitter feelings arise.

There is nothing un-Protestant about the idea of parochial schools. Some Protestant denominations have them, but their total number is still small. Some Protestant leaders today say that unless something can be done about the largely unintended negative religious influences which they see in public education, they will advocate the extension of Protestant parochial education. The Supreme Court's decision in the McCollum case stimulated this feeling among Protestants.

There is a clear acceptance of the legal right of parents to send their children to parochial schools. A celebrated decision of the Supreme Court (*Pierce v. Society of Sisters*) in 1925 established this principle by declaring unconstitutional a law of the state of Oregon that required parents to send their children for a number of years to the public school. This action was important, not only on account of its bearing on religious schools, but also because it discouraged a tendency toward a state monopoly of education. It emphasized the right of parents to control the education of their children. Roman Catholics have been clearer on this right than Protestants who are much vaguer in their thinking about the division of responsibility between state, Church, community, parents, and the teaching profession in education. They have often had to be reminded by Catholics that though the state provides opportunities for education it should not be regarded as the educator. There are many secularist educators who cannot seem to see the connection between the idea of the state as the educator and the totalitarianism which they abhor.

Roman Catholic parochial schools have been in part a reaction against the Protestant character of much public education in communities that had formed the habit of acting as though they were homogeneous Protestant communities. They have also been in part a reaction against secularized public education though it is only fair to say that Catholics, for understandable reasons, have made experimenting with any recognition of religion in the schools all the more difficult and contributed in part to the secularization which they criticize. Now when the Catholics are strong in communities they are in favor of such experiments. The Catholics do have a philosophy of education which makes them dissatisfied with any educational program which allows religion to be only a supplement. They prefer an organic connection between religion and the total program of the school. Many Protestants would agree with this philosophy in theory but are more willing to compromise because they believe so strongly in the value of the public school system. Also, few Protestants emphasize this philosophy of education so much that they would be willing to make great sacrifices for a system of religious schools. But Protestants can hardly deny that there is great truth in this philosophy of education and they should respect the Catholic willingness to pay a great price for it even though they may regret some of the social consequences of the policy.

What should be the attitude of Protestants to the desire of Catholics to get various kinds of public aid for their program of education?

There is no doubt that Protestants in America are almost unanimously opposed to any direct aid to parochial schools. This is not a matter of Protestant doctrine, for Protestants in other countries favor plural systems of education supported by the state; it is a matter of American experience. It stems in part from the fact that only Catholics have an extensive system of parochial schools and so aid to them would not seem to be consistent in practice with the idea of non-preferential aid to religious bodies. Also, direct financial aid to parochial schools would seem to cross the line that divides the separation of Church and state as it has developed among us from the idea of multiple establishment which, when it has stood out as a fairly clear alternative, has been rejected. There are areas of fuzziness here, but in spite of some confusions, an articulated system of multiple establishment would be rejected by almost all Protestants and it would have no chance with the courts.

I believe that even more important is the consideration that decisive encouragement of parochial schools through public financial aid would have a destructive effect on the public schools and on education generally. If in practice the aid went almost entirely to Catholic schools, that would for a time be preferential in practice, but if it encouraged the formation of aided systems of Protestant and Jewish parochial schools, it would be educationally disastrous. I am told by those who have studied the matter most closely that we could not expect to have fewer than five or six systems of parochial schools competing for the resources of the community in the large or middle sized cities. This would be divisive; it would be expensive; and it would also mean that every system would be educationally weak. It would mean a scattering of our available personnel and of our available funds. The Catholic schools would have a better chance than Protestant schools because Catholics have a surer basis for believing in them and they would also have their orders of nuns to do the teaching on a subsistence basis. Such a development would drain off from the public school the teachers of strongest religious commitment and so public education would be more secularized than it is now.

These are sufficient grounds for not encouraging the development of systems of parochial schools. But they do not cancel the fact that there is already a large system of Catholic parochial education, that large numbers of our Catholic neighbors conscientiously believe that they should send their children to parochial schools. They differ with most non-Catholics concerning the claim for at least limited public support for their system. Catholics are not agreed as to how much support they would regard as just or, even from their own point of view, desirable. They know that public support might mean more public control than they would be willing to accept. Also, there are many Catholics—how many I do not know—who do not want to be voluntarily imprisoned in an educational ghetto from kindergarten through college and would themselves draw some lines so far as the encouragement of parochial education is concerned. And yet there is a very broad consensus among Catholics that there is an element of injustice in the double burden for education which they carry, as taxpayers who support the public schools and as churchmen who support the parochial schools. The Protestant response is usually a denial that there is any element of injustice involved because if the Catholics wanted to, they could send their children to the public schools. Hence there is no discrimination against them.

I wonder if the effectiveness of the Catholic argument has not been increased by a partly new situation which can be described as follows. For the most part, Protestants think of a given public school system to which the parochial schools are added as an intrusion. But suppose we think of communities which are building their schools for the first time or re-building them and suppose that in the community planning it is taken for granted that there will be parochial schools and that, as a matter of such planning, duplication of space is avoided. Suppose also that the amount of saving to the community made possible by the Catholic expenditures for the parochial schools is dramatized by such planning. Will it not be more difficult for Protestants to continue to deny that there is any basis for the Catholic claim that there is injustice in their double burden of expense for education? I have no doubt that it will. And yet if non-Catholics come to admit that and carry through the logic that is implied in the Catholic claim, there is the danger that I have cited that the whole public school system might soon be weakened and the educational resources of the community dissipated. This is a real dilemma, and it is to be hoped that Catholics as well as well as non-Catholics may come to recognize it.

The provision of auxiliary services or so-called "fringe benefits" is the kind of compromise that has justification in order to meet a real human dilemma. These fringe benefits include transportation, health services, school lunches and text-books. Text-books may seem to go way beyond fringe benefits because they provide the content of education. The United States Supreme Court in an opinion written by Chief Justice Hughes in 1930 (*Cochran v. Board of Education*) approved the provision for parochial schools of the same text-books that are used in the public schools for non-religious subjects. I am surprised that in the discussion of this matter I seldom hear any emphasis on the fact that they have to be the *same* text-books. That encourages unity in the community. It also involves no more additional cost per pupil than would be involved if there were no parochial schools. Catholic parents have helped to pay for the books.[6]

The Supreme Court has permitted the provision of text-books and transportation on the ground that, while they do aid the school, their primary aid is to the student. The Supreme Court decision in the *Everson Case*, in spite of its opposition to aid to all religions on a non-preferential basis strongly expressed in the same decision, said that it was constitutional for the State of New Jersey to permit the public school buses to be used by parochial school children because to fail to do so might actually penalize Catholic children because of their religious belief if it was the intention of the state to supply school transportation for all children.[7]

This decision of the Court is permissive only. It leaves to the state the right to pass laws providing public transportation for all school children. It would seem to be highly arbitrary to deny to communities the right to supply such transportation. This is done in some cities by providing half-fare for all school children on the subways or city buses. Where special school buses are required, they could be public buses paid for apart from the school budget. In any case, the taxes of parents of parochial

[6] I once thought that the provision of transportation was more readily defensible than the provision of school books, but the following considerations cause me to change that view: (1) School books which are the same as those used in the public schools do not aid religious education. (2) The cost is equivalent to the cost of such books if the children went to the public schools which they have every right to do whereas in the case of buses not only extra seats but extra routes may be involved. (3) The use of these books in both systems of schools is in the interest of the unity of the community.

[7] "While we do not mean to intimate that a state could not provide transportation only to children attending public schools, we must be careful, in protecting the citizens of New Jersey against state-established churches, to be sure that we do not inadvertently prohibit New Jersey from extending its general state law benefits to all its citizens without regard to their religious belief." Majority opinion in *Everson v. Board of Education* (1947).

school children would help to pay for them. Such service is not an unfair favor to anyone.

Even those who oppose most strongly both the provision of text-books and the provision of transportation for parochial school children are willing to make some arrangement by which these children can receive health services and school lunches.[8]

This distinction between service to the children and aid to the school or the Church that conducts the school raises difficulties. It is in the public interest that the parochial school children have as good education as other children. Everything done with this in mind is a service to the children. One interesting problem may emerge if the state decides to insure that students in all schools get better instruction in science. An adjustment here might be the development of a kind of "released time" in reverse with the parochial school children going to the public schools for their teaching in science! Separation of Church and state does not mean separation of children and such a procedure would be favorable to the unity of the community.

The theoretical difficulty of finding an absolute line between aid to the child and aid to the school should not paralyze us completely any more than it has paralyzed the courts. Making this distinction enables the community to serve the parochial school children. It enables the community to make a concession

[8] Professor Butts, for example, distinguishes between any "auxiliary service" that "aids the child to receive instruction in religious schools" and any "auxiliary service that is designed to protect and promote the public health and thus requires the state to follow *all* children no matter where they are should logically be under the direct control and supervision of public health authorities." *Op. cit.*, p. 176.

Professor Butts criticizes the present School Lunch Act (1948) which pays funds directly from the Federal Government to parochial school agencies, but I assume that he would be open to some other arrangement that would keep the dispensing of food in the hands of state authorities. Leo Pfeffer is quite clear there should be no problem about "true welfare benefits" for "a child needs medical and dental care and hot lunches, whether he goes to a public school, a parochial school, or to no school at all." *Op. cit.*, p. 477.

to a felt injustice that has a substantial basis. It still prevents all-out encouragement to parochial schools. It offers an area of experiment that is on this side of multiple establishment. It is more favorable to harmony of the community than a rigid stand against any concessions even to meet the most obvious external needs of parochial school children.

NOTE

ON HIGHER EDUCATION

It is fortunate that the issue of religion in public higher education has not been considered in terms of the more rigid interpretation of the First Amendment. State laws and practices differ and the courts have not attempted to impose a national policy on them. There are a great many experiments in religious teaching in public institutions of higher education, some involving departments of religion or administrative aid to religious activities and others involving cooperation with schools for religious teaching near the campus very much along the lines of Jefferson's plan with acceptance of credits in religious subjects by the College or University. This greater freedom in higher education stems in part from the greater maturity of the students with less fear that they will be indoctrinated and from the fact that higher education involves no compulsion. Perhaps it is also a fact that on the level of higher education it is even more obvious than it is in the case of secondary education that a curriculum that ignores religion profoundly distorts the knowledge of culture.

See for a summary of the facts, Seymour Smith: "Religious Instruction in State Universities," *Religious Education*, May-June, 1958.

CHAPTER XVII

A Protestant View of American Roman Catholic Power

THE attitudes of Americans toward Church-State relations depends in considerable measure on their attitude toward Roman Catholicism. The chief concern that lies back of the convictions of non-Catholics is the concern for religious liberty and the chief threat to religious liberty is seen in the tremendous growth of Roman Catholicism as a cultural and political power in the United States.

There are two deep problems connected with Roman Catholicism that must be emphasized at the outset of any discussion. One is the *dogmatic intolerance* which is itself a part of the Catholic faith.[1] This dogmatic intolerance need not lead to *civil intolerance,* but there is a tendency for it to do so just as was the case when it characterized the major Protestant bodies. This dogmatic intolerance becomes all the more difficult for non-Catholics when it is associated not only with distinctively religious dogma, but also with elements of what Roman Catholics call "natural law" which are not accepted as divinely sanctioned moral demands by most non-Catholics. This is true of birth control, of some matters of medical ethics. It is true even of gambling under limited conditions, though this has to do not with a moral demand but with a moral permission! One symptom of the dogmatic intolerance that is most objectionable to non-Catholics is the strict Catholic regulation concerning the religious training of the children of mixed marriages.

[1] Whenever the word "Catholic" is used in this chapter it refers to the Roman Catholic Church.

There is an important qualification of the dogmatic intolerance that has received much emphasis in recent years, which was in fact dramatized by the excommunication of Father Feeney in Boston for denying that non-Catholics can be saved. This is a sophisticated interpretation of *extra ecclesiam nulla salus est* which enables the Roman Catholic to take a charitable and hopeful attitude toward the destiny of non-Catholics as individuals.

The other basic problem is the real tension between an authoritarian, centralized hierarchical Church and the spirit of an open, pluralistic, democratic society. There is abundant evidence that Roman Catholics in this country do sincerely believe in democracy and practice this belief, but I do not see how they themselves can deny that their polity poses a problem for democracy which is not posed by Churches which make their decisions in regard to public policy by processes of open discussion in which both clergy and laymen share. The polity of the Episcopal Church does give Bishops meeting separately a veto over many things, but it also gives the laity voting separately in the dioceses a veto over the choice of Bishops. I mention this as an example of one of the more hierarchical forms of polity outside the Roman Catholic Church. The Roman polity is itself a matter of faith and therefore religious liberty includes the liberty to preserve that type of polity. And if it is said that the Papacy creates a problem of peculiar difficulty because it is from the point of view of the nation a "foreign power," the answer that Protestants should be able to accept is that the Church as Church is supra-national and the religious liberty of all Christians includes their right to have relationships suitable to their polity with the universal Church.

American Protestants[2] are troubled over far more than these

[2] The books by Paul Blanshard, especially his *American Freedom and Catholic Power* (The Beacon Press, 1949), marshall many facts which both Catholics and Protestants should take seriously. It is unfortunate that Mr. Blanshard has presented his material in such a way as to confuse

abstract problems created by the Roman Catholic faith and ecclesiastical structure. They resent much that is done by the Roman Catholic Church in America and they fear greatly what may yet be done. This is such familiar ground that I need only outline some of the resentments and the fears. *The general thesis of this chapter is that, while many of these resentments and fears are justified, it is a mistake to project them in indefinitely extended form upon the future and to allow all of our thinking about Roman Catholicism and most of our thinking about Church-State relations to be controlled by them in that extended form.* After I have outlined the grounds for some justified resentments and fears, I shall mention other facts about Roman Catholic life that should play a larger part than they do in Protestant attitudes toward Roman Catholicism.

The Roman Catholic Church is not a majority Church in the country at large and, since immigration has been greatly limited, its rate of growth has not been quite as rapid as the rate of growth of the Protestant Churches, but its strength is so distributed as to give it great majorities in some cities and enormous political power and cultural influence in many states. It is extremely difficult for Protestants and other non-Catholics to live with Roman Catholicism as the religion of a large local majority. It has been difficult in the past for Roman Catholics to live with Protestantism as the religion of a large local majority. The centralized organization and the absolute claims of

---

criticism of many particular applications of Catholic teaching with what seems to be an attack on the freedom of a Church to have its own authoritarian structure as a matter of faith. Also he writes, not from a Protestant but from a secularist point of view, and thus sees no inherent problem in the relation of religion to public education. He is quite satisfied with the complete separation of school and religion. There is a tendency to exaggerate the monolithic character of world-wide Catholicism under papal direction, and Mr. Blanshard's projection upon the future of the indefinite threat of Catholic power to American democracy does not, it seems to me, do justice to the four considerations which I emphasize in the last part of this chapter. The book is the work of a very conscientious and well-informed prosecutor and should be used as such.

the Roman Church enhance the difficulty but Protestants must not forget that any small minority feels pressure that arouses resentments and fears under these circumstances. Part of the problem is a universal human tendency that does not depend on a particular ecclesiastical situation. However, it is the threat of a local majority that leads non-Catholics to emphasize the protections of religious liberty in the federal constitution. Catholics also have had occasion to appeal to these same protections but today their chief desire is to establish a somewhat flexible interpretation of the First Amendment.

Non-Catholics have grounds for resenting the tendency of Roman Catholics to use their power to impose on the community as a whole and upon its public institutions the Roman Catholic ideas of natural law. They see this in the birth control legislation in Massachusetts and Connecticut; they see this in the Catholic pressure to remove welfare agencies which have birth control clinics from local community chests elsewhere; they see this in the Roman Catholic objection to divorce laws which are much more flexible than the law of the Church; they see this in Roman Catholic efforts to have their principles governing censorship made public policy; they see this in the attempts to have non-Catholic hospitals adopt the Roman Catholic ideas of medical ethics in the field of obstetrics.

Non-Catholics have grounds for resenting and fearing the tendency of Roman Catholics, when they have the power, to seek control of the public school system to bend it in part to Catholic purposes. Parochial schools could operate as safety valves for the public schools, but this is often not the case. When Roman Catholics dominate the public school boards they sometimes discriminate against non-Catholic teachers. In extreme cases that have been much publicized they have operated public schools as though they were parochial schools. Perhaps more serious in the long run is the tendency of Roman Catholics in some places to oppose needed bond issues or appropriations for the public schools. This is not a surprising reaction to the double burden of education costs that they themselves bear, but it is very bad for education.

Non-Catholics have grounds for resenting and fearing Catholic boycotts of communication media, including the publishers of books, and boycotts of local merchants who have some connection with a policy which they oppose. Fear of Catholic boycott often operates as a reason for self-censorship. Newspapers are influenced by this fear, and it is very difficult to get news published that may be unfavorable to the Roman Catholic Church. No one can criticize the Roman Catholic Church or any other Church for seeking to discipline the theater-going or the reading of its own constituency. Boycotting that consists only of this self-discipline within the Church may be unfortunate in some of its effects, but it is not open to objection in principle. It is the punitive boycott directed against all that a particular agency may do that interferes with the freedom of non-Catholics.

Non-Catholics have grounds for criticizing in no uncertain terms the behavior of the authorities of the Roman Catholic Church in other countries, especially Spain and some of the Latin American countries. American Protestants are rightly concerned when their fellow Protestants are the objects of discrimination or persecution. Whenever American Catholics bring pressure on their government in favor of the Roman Catholic Church as against Protestantism in Latin American countries, American Protestants have a right to be disturbed and to bring counter-pressures as they have done.

The desire of many Catholics to have the United States send a diplomatic representative to the Vatican has become a symbol to most Protestants for the many things that they resent in the use of Catholic power. This issue is confused because it is obvious that in the world at large the representation of a nation at the Vatican is not interpreted as a sign that the nation involved shows favoritism to the Roman Catholic Church. Otherwise, there would not be representatives from many non-Christian countries, from Britain with a state Church that is not the Roman Catholic Church, or from France which is secularist and often anti-clerical in its politics. But it is only fair to recognize the fact that the very size of the Roman Catholic Church in this country and the absence of any state Church, the existence of which would prove that the Roman Catholic Church is not the favored Church, makes American Protestants feel that diplomatic representation at the Vatican is a great concession to one American Church in contrast to others. American Protestants emphasize the fact that the Pope is the head of one American Church rather than the fact that the Vatican is the center of a diplomatic service which is a unique institution of the old world that cannot be grasped by the American logic governing Church-State relations. Though I do not believe that this issue is as important as most Protestant leaders have made it, I have come to see that the meaning of representation at the Vatican to American non-Catholics in view of the actual religious situation in this country is natural, and the fact that this meaning exists here is more important than the fact that it does not exist in Britain or in Japan for there are objective reasons for the difference. Because of them, I believe that for the American government to be represented diplomatically at the Vatican is inevitably interpreted in this country as unfair to non-Catholics.[3]

[3] I do find it difficult to know what to say about this on the hypothesis that in a given situation, it may be important for peace or for the relations of the United States to parts of Europe, especially eastern Europe, to have some kind of relations with the Vatican as a center of diplomacy and information. I think that we should not approach this problem with an absolute veto in advance but should be open to some such arrangement as an *ad hoc* representative as was the case during the Second World War. If the issue does come up again in this form, I hope that Protestants will appoint a responsible group, partly lay, to test the truth of the hypothesis before a campaign of opposition is begun. But, I also hope that the issue will not arise!

There are four characteristics of Roman Catholicism which are usually neglected in American discussions of the problem of Catholic power and yet which may make a difference in our conclusions about it.

The first characteristic of Roman Catholicism which needs to be stressed is its great variations from culture to culture and from country to country. The vision of many American Protestants of a monolithic Roman Church, built somewhat on the lines of the Stalinist empire, that is controlled from the Vatican is very wide of the mark. Historically, it has proved itself capable of adjustment to the greatest variety of cultural conditions instead of being one kind of religious ethos exported from Rome. The difference between French Catholicism and Spanish Catholicism almost belongs to the study of comparative religion. Catholicism in western Europe is utterly different from Catholicism in Latin America. In Germany, France, Holland, Belgium, Switzerland, and England we see what Catholicism can be when it is religiously and culturally mature and when it has learned to live with strong Protestant and secularist competition. There is remarkable intellectual ferment in the Catholic Church in those countries. Catholic thinkers take considerable theological freedom, and they are especially free in their thinking about political issues. There is a long standing effort to overcome the political and economic conservatism which has been the great handicap of the Church in reaching the working classes. There is very much more discussion between Protestant and Catholic thinkers on a theological level than there is in this country. One interesting phenomenon is the fresh study of Luther and the Reformation by Catholic scholars which has shattered the old Catholic stereotypes. Dr. Kuehnelt-Leddihn in an article in the Jesuit weekly *America* summarizes this new Catholic literature on Luther and says: "It is evident today that Luther was not simply a 'neurotic who wanted to marry a nun,' and that he cannot be considered just an 'early liberal eager for more freedom, progress and enlightenment' either."[4] This freedom and diversity are encouraged by the differences between the various religious orders.

In August 1950 the Pope issued an encyclical, *Humani Generi,* which reflected anxiety in the Vatican concerning some effects of the freedom which had been assumed by European Catholics especially in France. Fortunately, this document named no names and did not identify the positions condemned so specifically as to prevent a continuation of much of the discussion which had stimulated the Pope's action. It did alarm and inhibit for a time, and the fact that this can happen makes Protestants wonder at the Catholic thinkers whose own minds are so free and yet who know that there are external limits beyond which they may not venture.

Just as the mature western European Catholicism differs from the Spanish type, so both differ from Catholicism in this country. American Catholicism has a degree of moral discipline and pastoral effectiveness that is notoriously lacking in Latin America. American Catholicism differs from western European Catholicism in that it has no rich cultural background. It has a strong feeling of cultural inferiority to American Protestantism as well as to European Catholicism. Intellectual ferment is exactly what it lacks.

The reasons for this are obvious as American Catholicism represents the tides of immigration that brought to this country millions of Europeans who had had few opportunities in their own countries. They had to start here at the bottom of the social ladder, and they have been moving up rapidly. Their situation is revealed by a statement of Archbishop Cushing of Boston at a C. I. O. convention that met in that city in 1947. He was explaining his special right to be there when he said that he did not know a single Roman Catholic Archbishop or Bishop in this country whose father or mother had been to col-

[4] *America,* March 2, 1957.

lege. When we realize how much status as well as education depends on going to college in this country this simple statement speaks volumes for the cultural and social handicap which Roman Catholicism has had to overcome. Roman Catholic journals frequently complain of the lack of intellectual and theological leadership in the American Church. One Catholic lay journal, *The Commonweal,* which does much of this complaining has won a place for itself as one of the finest journals of religious thought and of social and cultural criticism published in the United States. There are Protestants who acclaim it as the best Christian journal in America and who feel in complete rapport with it except when it is dealing with a rather limited range of ecclesiastical and theological subjects. A group of Roman Catholic laymen edit a quarterly, *Cross Currents,* which consists chiefly of reprinted articles by Europeans, both Protestant and Catholic. This enterprise is an effort to bring to American Catholicism the stimulus and inspiration that can come from the European Catholic intellectual ferment. Protestants, as they view the development of Catholicism in this country, have good reason to assume that as it becomes more mature culturally and theologically, it will have more flexibility of mind and that there will be greater tolerance and breadth in dealing with non-Catholics and with the public issues which concern Protestants most.

I should add here that Roman Catholicism needs not only the kind of maturing that takes time in a new country, but it also needs to have two other things. One is the strong competition from non-Catholic sources—Protestant, Jewish, secularist. It has had one or more of these types of competition in every one of the western European countries that I have named. The worst thing that can happen to Roman Catholicism is for it to have the very religious monopoly to which it feels entitled because of its exclusive claims! Protestants have a responsibility to confront Catholicism with a positive Protestant theology and that is happening today in many countries because of the recent theological revival. It is interesting that Karl Barth is taken with great seriousness by Roman Catholics in Europe and some of the best studies of Barth have been made by Roman Catholic scholars. It is perhaps a straw in the wind that one of the best reviews of Paul Tillich's first volume of *Systematic Theology* was written by a Jesuit scholar[5] in this country. But theological interaction between Protestantism and Catholicism in this country has not really begun.[6]

The other element that is very important in the environment for the development of Catholicism along the lines that I have suggested is the presence of a liberal democratic political tradition. This has greatly modified Catholic political attitudes and it is most fortunate that under the stimulus of democracy Roman Catholics can find the antecedents of democracy in their own tradition, especially in the great Jesuit political philosophers such as Francisco Suarez in the sixteenth and seventeenth centuries. They also discover antecedents of democracy in Thomas Aquinas. The combination of continuous encounter with non-Catholics on a basis of political mutuality and the influence of liberal democratic ideas enables Roman Catholics to avoid the *civil intolerance* that causes most anxiety among Protestants. Catholic clergy and laymen in this country have absorbed the American democratic tradition along with other citizens. If some of the clergy become the instruments of a rigid clericalism on political issues, they will find that they cannot deliver the votes of the laity as much as is often assumed. But the clergy themselves are not of one mind on the most important political issues, as I shall indicate later.

The second aspect of Roman Catholicism to which I shall

---

[5] Father G. Weigel in *Theological Studies* (Dec. 1953), pp. 573-585.

[6] Professor K. E. Skydsgaard of the University of Copenhagen has written a model of Protestant witness and argument in relation to Roman Catholicism. It reflects the better mutual understanding as between Protestantism and Catholicism in Europe to which I have referred, but at the central points in theology it is uncompromisingly Protestant. See his *One in Christ* (Muhlenberg Press, 1957).

refer is suggested by the fact, already mentioned, that American Catholics have had to win their way in this country against social and cultural odds. I do not know how one can estimate in any quantitative way its importance, but there is no doubt that much of the Roman Catholic aggressiveness that is most offensive to Protestants in this country is sociologically conditioned. It is a result of the sheer energy that it has taken for Catholics to improve their position in a new country and alien culture and it also reflects some social resentment for past disabilities on the part of people who have won social power. We forget today the long and bitter history of nativist anti-Catholicism but the memories of it do not die so easily among Catholics themselves. Quite apart from the deliberate and prejudiced anti-Catholicism, the present generation of American Catholics are still close to the bitter experience of belonging to ethnic groups that suffered from poverty and social discrimination. Only saints could avoid expressing social resentments as a result of this experience. Today changes are coming so rapidly and the economic and social and cultural opportunities for Americans of many ethnic backgrounds are so much alike that we can expect to see the particular sociological reasons for Roman Catholic aggressiveness to become less important. Religious reasons will remain and they should remain. No one can predict what the effect of these changes may be, but this consideration should prevent Protestants from projecting upon the future the indefinite extension of some of the tendencies which they fear.

Paul Blanshard recognizes that there is truth in this consideration. After describing the role of the Irish in American Catholicism he says:

"This Irish dominance explains many of the characteristics of American Catholicism. The Irish hierarchy which rules the American Church is a 'becoming' class. It represents the Irish people struggling up in a hostile environment, using the Roman system of authoritative power to compensate for an inner sense of insecurity which still seems to survive from the days when Irish Catholics were a despised immigrant minority. Boston is aggressively Catholic largely because it is aggressively Irish, and it is aggressively Irish because its people have not quite overcome their sense of being strangers in a hostile land."[7]

If this is the case, is it not natural to wonder if some of the aggressiveness will be lost as the Irish cease to have this sense of being strangers, when John Kennedy rather than James Curley becomes a symbol of the Irish leader in politics?

One of the most convincing pieces of evidence in favor of this judgment concerning the social dynamics of American Catholicism is found in Professor Kenneth Underwood's study in depth of Protestant-Catholic relations in one city which has had a large Catholic majority for some decades. Professor Underwood reports on the attitudes of both laymen and clergy from various parishes in Holyoke, Massachusetts. He finds that it is the parishes made up of recent immigrants who have not been much assimilated into American life where the most intolerant attitudes are found. It is those parishes where the rigid ideas of the priests are most readily accepted by the laymen. He says:

"The upper income, well-educated Catholic laymen are much less receptive to clerical guidance as to the practical social implications of moral and religious laws of the church than are the lower income, more poorly educated Catholics. The former tend also to be much more appreciative of the role of the Protestant Churches in supplementing or correcting Catholic action."[8]

Even on such an issue as the boycotting of Protestant merchants in the city when one of the Protestant churches had arranged to allow Margaret Sanger to speak on planned parenthood in its building, the Catholic constituency was divided.[9] Professor Underwood says:

[7] Op. cit., pp. 27-28.
[8] Protestant and Catholic (The Beacon Press, 1957), p. 94.
[9] This episode which took place in 1940 is fully described in the first chapter of Professor Underwood's book.

"The largest proportion of people who disagreed was found among well-educated Catholics in upper class business or professional positions in the community who interpreted the boycott action as the result of ways of thinking developed by an older generation of priests and laymen who were not yet aware that Catholicism was no longer an 'immigrant faith.' "[10]

A third fact about Roman Catholicism that needs to be understood by Protestants is that the Catholic Church is divided from top to bottom in this country and abroad on matters of principle in regard to religious liberty. There is a traditional main-line position that favors the Confessional Catholic state as the ideal type of relationship between Church and state. This view would limit the rights of religious minorities in a nation that has a very large Catholic majority. These limitations would have to do with public propagation of the non-Catholic faith rather than with freedom of worship or freedom of teaching inside the doors of the Protestant church. Under such circumstances there would be a union of state and Church and the state as state would profess the Catholic faith. This position is often called the "thesis" and the adjustments of the Church to religiously pluralistic nations, including the acceptance by American Catholics of the American constitutional separation of Church and state, involve a second-best position that is called the "hypothesis." Father John A. Ryan, the noted Roman Catholic liberal on all economic issues who is responsible for a famous statement on this subject, in a book now published under the title *Catholic Principles of Politics*, states the traditional thesis and then tries to soften it for Americans by saying:

"While all of this is very true in logic and in theory the event of its practical realization in any state or country is so remote in time and in probability that no practical man will let it disturb his equanimity or affect his attitude toward those who differ from him in religious faith."[11]

[10] *Op. cit.*, p. 97.
[11] Macmillan, 1940, p. 320.

So long as Protestants realize that there are authoritative statements of the so-called Catholic thesis of the Confessional State as representing the ideal possibility they will not be greatly comforted by Father Ryan's assurances, especially if they live in cities which already have large Catholic majorities. It is simply not enough for a Church which operates in the light of very clear dogmatic principles to make concessions on the issue of religious liberty for non-Catholics on a pragmatic basis alone, while its dogmatic principles still point to a Confessional Catholic state in which the religious liberties of minorities are severely restricted as the ideal.

It is important to realize that a very able and earnest attempt is being made by Roman Catholic scholars in this country, with much support from Catholics in western Europe, to change the principles as well as the practice of the Church in this matter. This attempt is associated chiefly with the work of Father John Courtney Murray, but it is gaining a good deal of support. His careful statement of his position is found chiefly in many articles in the Jesuit Quarterly *Theological Studies*.[12] In what follows, I shall attempt to summarize his main conclusions, but it should be realized that these conclusions which I mention here are abstracted from very complicated historical expositions and that they come in large part from Father Murray's analysis of the encyclicals of Leo XIII in order to show what is permanent and what is historically conditioned in those encyclicals. With apologies to Father Murray for much over-simplification of the kind that is alien to his own mind, I shall attempt to give the substance of his position in the following propositions:

The idea of a Confessional Catholic state belongs to an earlier period in European history and it has become an irrelevancy under contemporary conditions.

[12] See especially, March 1953; June 1953; December 1953; March 1954. Also, "Governmental Repression of Heresy" reprinted from the Proceedings of The Catholic Theological Society of America.

Anglo-Saxon democracy is fundamentally different from the democracy of the French Revolution which was totalitarian in tendency.

The state in this country is by its very nature limited and in principle the Church does not need to defend itself against such a state as was necessary in the case of the nineteenth-century European revolutionary states which formed the immediate background of Leo's political thinking.

There is no anti-clerical or anti-religious motivation behind the American constitutional provision for Church-State relations and the Church need not defend itself against this doctrine as such.

The Church in America has, as a matter of fact, enjoyed greater freedom and scope for its witness and activities than it has in the Catholic states of the traditional type.

It is important to emphasize the rights of the state in its own sphere, the freedom of the Church from state control, and the influence of Catholic citizens on the state.

It is impossible to separate religious freedom from civil freedom and there can be no democracy if the freedom of the citizen is curtailed in religious matters, for such curtailing can often take place as a means of silencing political dissent.

Error does not have the same rights as truth but persons in error, consciences in error, do have rights which should be respected by the Church and the state.

The church should not demand that the state as the secular arm enforce the Church's own decisions in regard to heresy.

It does more harm than good to the Church for the state to use its power against non-Catholics.

I think that all of these propositions fit together into a self-consistent social philosophy. They are presented by Father Murray as a substitute for the traditional Catholic thesis concerning the Confessional State. They have made considerable headway among both laity and clergy in this country. They correspond to views that are held in Europe and which have support in the Vatican itself. In December 1953, after this point of view had been strongly attacked by Cardinal Ottaviani in Rome in an address defending the Spanish conception of a Confessional

Catholic State as the ideal, the Pope in a speech to a convention of Catholic jurists somewhat ambiguously made room for this position. The fact that he said what he did in the midst of a trans-Atlantic controversy within the Church has encouraged American Catholics who hold this view to believe that the Pope is sympathetic with it. That is the most that can be said. American Protestants should realize that the Roman Church is not a vast international machine designed to overturn their liberties if this were to become politically possible, and that they have many allies in the Catholic Church who share their belief in religious liberty on principle.[13]

The fourth fact about the Roman Catholic Church to which I shall refer is that there are many points of disagreement on social policy among Roman Catholics: there is no one Catholic line on most public issues. There is agreement on birth control as a moral issue, but even on that there is no agreement as to what the state should do about it. Roman Catholics generally do not today advocate strict laws on the subject except in the two states in which those laws are already in force. On economic issues there is a broad Catholic pattern based upon the organization of producers' groups, but this is not obligatory and it gives rise to endless differences so far as application is concerned. In an earlier chapter I mentioned the Catholic doctrine of the just war and called attention to the fact that Catholics differ as to whether a war with modern weapons can be just. There is a deep difference as between Catholics in various nations on forms of government. Catholic doctrine makes room for governments based upon popular sovereignty but does not prescribe this universally. Even in regard to Communism there are great differences in temper between European Catholicism and much American Catholicism. It is an under-

[13] For an over-all view of this controversy I am indebted to Professor Tom Sander's thesis: *A Comparison of Two Current American Roman Catholic Theories of the American Political System with Particular Reference to the Problem of Religious Liberty.* (Columbia University Library.)

statement to say that the Catholic hierarchy did not act helpfully on the issue of McCarthyism, but they were deeply divided. There is no doubt that McCarthy had a strong hold on large groups of Catholics, especially Irish Catholics, but it is also true that some of the most eloquent opposition to McCarthy came from Catholic sources, notably such journals as *The Commonweal* and the Jesuit weekly *America*. American Protestants need not fear that Roman Catholics will usually throw their great weight as a religious community in the same political direction. This will tend to be even less a danger as Catholics move further away from the status of an immigrant bloc. In general we can say that natural law does not guarantee agreement on concrete issues. Natural law plus prudence equals flexibility.[14]

I have outlined briefly four aspects of Catholicism of which American Protestants should take account. Though they give no assurance as to the direction that Roman Catholicism may take in the next generation, they may help to release us from the exaggerated fears that are based upon past experience in this country alone. Protestants should put more rather than less emphasis upon positive elements of Protestant faith and doctrine. They should join the Roman Catholics in rejecting the superficial forms of religious harmony so often urged in the interests of national unity. But they can live with their Catholic neighbors in hope that much greater mutual understanding and the sharing of more moral and political purposes may become possible.

[14] Cf., Thomas Aquinas, *The Summa Theologica*, First Part of the Second Part, Article 1, Question 100.

"For some matters connected with human actions are so evident, that after very little consideration one is able at once to approve or disapprove of them by means of these common first principles; *while other matters cannot be the subject of judgment without much consideration of the various circumstances.*" (Italics mine.)

CHAPTER XVIII

Direct and Indirect Action of the Church Upon the State

THE American pattern of separation of Church and state has never meant that Churches should not seek to influence the policies of the state. Churches of most traditions have made a regular practice of speaking on public issues with which the state also was concerned and they have made great efforts to influence legislation. The difference between Churches has not been that some have done nothing about such public issues and others have done much; it is in the range of social interest that their activities have been displayed. There has always been a good deal of talk about the Church's keeping out of politics, but most Churches have had their own selection of political issues on which they have taken action, while they, in some cases, may have criticized other Churches on principle for meddling in public affairs.[1] Sometimes Christian leaders criticize others for becoming involved in politics, but their chief objection is really that they have been on the other side. There

[1] Something of the difference between formal statements and practice may be seen in the following passage from the Westminster Confession which is the official standard of the Presbyterian Churches U. S. A. and U. S. "Synods and councils are to handle or conclude nothing, but that which is ecclesiastical; and are not to intermeddle with civil affairs which concern the commonwealth, unless by way of humble petition in cases extraordinary; or by way of advice for satisfaction of conscience, if they be thereunto required by the civil magistrate." Section IV, Chapter XXXI.

We may remark that "that which is ecclesiastical" has come to include a wide territory and that there is some incongruity in associating Presbyterians with "humble petition" except as directed toward God!

is a kind of political action that goes with such strong tides within the Church that it is not noticed as political action at all. It is just behaving naturally! I shall not use space here to argue in favor of a decisive Christian concern for decisions which can only be made by the state by means of the machinery of politics, but I shall limit myself to a discussion of the types of action which are appropriate for the Church.

If we think of what the Church is in the light of my earlier chapter on the subject, we must realize that the Church in the range of its mission transcends while it includes the type of concern to which this book is devoted. It exists primarily to mediate the Gospel to all men, not in words only, but in the influence of life upon life. It is not a political movement though its mission is affected by many of the decisions which society makes in the sphere of politics. The Church by its very nature intends to include all kinds of people and that means people of all social groups, people whose bent of mind is conservative and people whose bent of mind is liberal or radical. It means that it includes and should include people in the various political parties. There may be parties in some countries which a Christian as Christian must shun, but that is exceptional and I need not say that it does not happen to be true of either major party in the United States. It would be a calamity if the influence of the Church ever became limited to one party and if there should develop a "Christian politics" of a partisan sort that caused people to identify the Church with the ambiguities and the fortunes of any political movement. This inclusiveness of the Church may be embarrassing in the short run because it is unable to speak out sharply as a Church on some issues at the point where a decision is about to be made, but in the long run the very inclusiveness of the Church, if it can be reflected in Christian bodies in which mutual influences from many social groups are real, can correct the narrowness of economic interest and the political self-righteousness which do so much to poison the life of a nation.

The Church as Church is limited in the kind of guidance it can give to its own members or to the community at large on political issues. Churches as organizations and Christian leaders whose chief area of competence is theology or Christian ethics should be self-restrained in these matters and not lay down the law on issues which are largely technical or which involve strategic judgments for which there is no Christian wisdom. Very fateful religious and moral issues are intertwined with these technical and strategic issues. This means that the Churches should encourage interaction between their clergy and theologians, on the one hand, and, on the other, lay experts and responsible participants in public affairs who have most wisdom on the technical and strategic problems.[2]

Both the World Council of Churches and the National Council of Churches have pioneered in this direction in recent years; it needs to be emphasized in all units of the Church. Lay participation at the point where the layman has the most knowledge and experience is a vast resource for the Church that has been on the whole neglected, but it needs to be kept in close relation with more distinctively Christian wisdom. Christian theology and ethics are sources of the Christian's understanding of God's purpose for human life and of the deepest truth about man's own nature. The Church, illumined by theology and ethics, has resources of inspiration and grace which, while they cannot provide short-cuts to social wisdom, can enable Christians to be sensitive to the effects of policies on people, to face reality with courage and with the sense of grace and forgiveness available through Christian mediation, to persevere in seeking next steps which are in line with God's will in the situation.

In some areas it is much easier than in others to see how these

[2] I have discussed this problem at greater length in my *Christian Ethics and Social Policy* (Scribners, 1946), Chap. 2.

Christian resources affect action. In a community where the most urgent social problem is racial integration, the Church locally is in a position to influence all parties to the conflict and the human aspects of the problem are immediately illumined by Christian truth even though baffling dilemmas remain. It is more difficult for the Church to influence the conflicts of nations because it does not have the same contact with all sides. A Church in one nation tends to encourage the moral complacency of its own nation or, in revulsion against that, to offer irrelevant idealistic answers that do not take account of the real dilemmas of its own nation. The avoidance of both temptations seems to me to set the boundaries of the Church's task in this field.

So far I have discussed the limitations of the Church in its resources for guidance concerning particular issues, but there is another type of limitation which has to do with what the Church should press for as a matter of public policy, assuming that it knows what is right according to its own standards. How much should it seek to have its guidance for its own members become the law of the state?

It is obvious that the Churches in America should not use their members as political pressure groups to get special ecclesiastical privileges for themselves as against other religious bodies. They should not seek legislation, even if they can influence enough votes to get it, which interferes with the religious liberty of minorities and they should be thankful that the courts stand guard at this point. They have to be alert in protecting their own liberty, in preventing any arbitrary action of the state that would hinder them in their mission. All kinds of new situations emerge—such as the access of Churches to new housing developments—which may call for pressure on public bodies by the Churches in the interests of their work as Churches. There is a large area here that calls for experienced awareness and vigilance on the part of many units of the Church. It also calls for a sense of fairness that refuses to take advantage of mere power to influence public decisions in the interests of a particular Church.

Are there limits to the moral and social issues on which the Churches, where they have a clear position, should seek to influence the action of the state either by pressure on public opinion or by a direct approach to government? The view I am defending here is that no Church, no matter how powerful, should bring pressure on the state to enact laws which are based upon principles that depend for their validity on its own doctrine or ethos. We can say the same about a limited group of Churches. I realize that this is a difficult position to maintain in borderline cases. We may say of many matters that there is a Christian inspiration growing out of the doctrine and ethos of Churches behind the conscience of the community, and there is no problem if the effects of this Christian inspiration are shared very broadly in the community. Also, Churches, as pioneers, should seek to educate the community on matters concerning which its conscience is dull or uninformed.

It is easy to cite illustrations of how Churches have gone out of bounds. This is true of the Roman Catholic Church in its efforts to maintain birth control legislation on the books of Massachusetts and Connecticut against the practices and against the conscience of almost the whole non-Catholic community. It is important to emphasize that this is for Protestants a matter of conscience just as it is for Catholics a matter of conscience. Protestants generally believe that it is their duty to limit the number of their children and that it is their duty to do this by methods which do not prevent the natural sexual expression of love in marriage.[3] Protestants usually reject the Roman Catholic teaching that of the two purposes of sexual intercourse, procreation and the expression of and nourishing of

[3] This relation of birth control to the Protestant conscience is well stated by Dean James A. Pike in *If You Marry Outside Your Faith* (Harper, 1954), Chap. 3.

love between husband and wife, the first is primary in the sense
that if it is frustrated by the use of contraceptives the second is
invalid. It is quite right for the Catholic Church to teach its
doctrine to its own members and to emphasize their own self-
discipline in the light of this teaching, but it is wrong for the
Catholic Church to encourage its members to go to the polls
and vote for a law that denies to non-Catholics the opportunity to act in the light of their own convictions.

It is now very widely admitted by Protestants that it was a
similar misuse of their influence on public opinion and on
legislatures that brought about the enactment of national prohibition of the sale of all alcoholic beverages. There is some
hindsight in my view here as I must admit that in the 1920's
I favored national prohibition. The control of liquor is certainly
a very necessary area of legislation, but the absolute prohibition
of alcoholic beverages makes no concession to the habits or the
convictions of large segments of the population. In this case, it
was the greater part of the Roman Catholic community that
was ignored in addition to the Jewish community, several Protestant denominations and many groups outside the Church. In
some homogeneous states it may have been justifiable for the
state to pass such a law even though it raised serious problems
concerning the limits of law where the daily personal habits of
people are concerned. But the mistake of National Prohibition
was to ignore those segments of the population which neither as
a matter of personal conscience nor as a matter of public policy
had any sympathy with the law. As a matter of enforcement it
is also important to note that the segments of the population
which were most opposed to prohibition were concentrated in
great cities or had their own ethnic or religious communities
and were thus insulated against what may have been at one
time the influence of a majority opinion in the nation in favor
of Prohibition. Protestants have learned a bitter lesson from
this experience because it was an example of an extraordinarily

successful Protestant crusade which ended in a catastrophic failure. Indeed, there are two lessons involved. One, already suggested, is that it is wrong to seek to make the ethos of one part of the community the basis of law. The other is that this was an example of identifying a moral judgment that there should be social control of the liquor traffic with a strategic judgment that total prohibition was the most effective way of securing such control. This mistake makes it very difficult to experiment today with other methods of control which might represent a broader national consensus and which might promise to be effective.

These examples illustrate negatively the general principle that Churches should not use their influence to secure action by the state unless such action is based upon broad considerations of justice and social welfare which appeal to the consciences of many outside the Churches. The reader can doubtless think of borderline cases which make judgment difficult, but Churches should be sensitive to this problem and exercise self-restraint. The distinction between sin and crime needs to be very clear in the minds of Church leaders, and they should be realistic about the limits of law in dealing with private life.

In most of the public issues with which American Churches have been concerned in recent years there has been much cooperation between Protestants, Catholics and Jews and people outside these religious communities. Many of them are issues on which each religious group is divided within itself. By and large the hardest problem which we confront in the sphere of Christian social action is created by the difficulty of expressing a consensus within any religious body. This is the special problem of Protestantism and it will condition much that is said about the strategy of the Churches in the remainder of this chapter.

Protestant Churches in coming to a consensus on the moral and religious aspects of public issues cannot do so by polling the whole constituency. Counting heads is not a way of determining Christian truth in theology or in social ethics. Even Churches with strongly democratic polities recognize this by their practice, though their theory may be confused. They give to the clergy a far larger representation in proportion to their numbers in all bodies beyond the local Church. This is at least a tacit recognition, even in Churches which would avoid clericalism at all costs, that those whose training and life work have caused them to concentrate on the distinctively Christian sources of wisdom should have a very important role in decisions. No Churches have yet found ways of assuring balanced representation of laymen from different social backgrounds and with varying forms of competence. At the Amsterdam Assembly of the World Council there was a large section of about one hundred thirty persons charged with the task of writing a report on economic and political issues. It was discovered that the section had in it no industrial workers and, more strangely, almost no active businessmen. This was against all intentions, but one difficulty is that sufficient leisure, if not a financial margin, is a selective factor when laymen meet under the auspices of the church.

Also, Christian social judgments need to come out of processes in which the one-sided social experience of one group of Christians is corrected by the experience of other Christians who live under quite different conditions. Our social judgments are so largely determined by the place that we occupy in society, by the outlook of our nation in international affairs and by our economic status or occupation in domestic affairs that to take a poll of Christian opinion among people who have been through none of these processes of self-correction cannot provide an adequate basis for a Christian judgment.

The experience of Churches in regard to the race problem in the United States illustrates this point with great clarity. Every representative body of Christians from beyond the local level has expressed unambiguously the conviction that there is a contradiction between Christian faith and ethics and the practice of involuntary racial segregation. This has been said by the Assembly of the World Council of Churches, by the Assembly of the National Council of Churches, reaffirming a similar statement by the Federal Council of Churches, and by the national denominational bodies, even by those which have their strength in the south.[4] I know of no Christian thinker or leader with more than very narrow regional influence who does not share this conviction about segregation, and yet local Churches, where the segregationist pattern is established, seldom express this ecumenical consensus with any clarity.[5]

This situation illustrates a general tendency that may seem rather shocking, but it is a sign that there is no Christian way to wisdom that does not take account of the sinful distortion and the finiteness of our minds. The best chance for a Christian judgment to emerge from such situations comes when partial or one-sided views are expressed in such a way as to correct each other, and so prepare for better mutual understanding and a more objective approach.[6]

Judgments which come out of such processes have a validity which the result of a poll of the total constituency cannot have. The total constituency needs to be exposed to the results of such processes and to respond to them. Actually, the ethical teaching which helps to form the minds of the clergy and the

[4] Four times the General Assembly of the Presbyterian Church in the U. S. (the Southern Presbyterian Church) passed resolutions in favor of desegregation, and each time by a larger majority even though the issue had become more divisive with each year.

[5] There has been a succession of statements by groups of ministers in southern communities who represent the ecumenical position on race.

[6] For ten years, first in the Federal Council of Churches and now in the National Council of Churches there has been a Department of the Church and Economic Life which has been organized on this principle with representation of business and management, labor, various segments of agriculture, and with economists and theologians and pastors. This has been the best experience of this type of mutual correction that I have ever known.

content of Christian education have been determined in large measure by these processes. I am advocating no closed clique of clergy and of the comparatively few laymen "who get around" as the ultimate Protestant authority! All the openness possible and on as many levels of interaction as possible is to be encouraged; and all of the processes involved should be under the authority of the revelation given in Christ.

I shall now outline briefly types of action of the Churches upon the state which are appropriate and suggest priorities among them. In all that follows in this chapter I am thinking chiefly of the impact of the Churches upon the state through their impact upon society.

The most important type of impact of the Church on society or the state is indirect. By "indirect" I mean either that the Churches are not conscious of a primary intention to influence economic or political decisions, or when they are concerned about such decisions they influence society or the state through the activities of their members as citizens. The Church has at least three kinds of indirect influence.

(1) The first is the long-term influence of the Church on the spirit and ethos, the moral sensitivities, and the value systems of the community. Respect for all persons, the value given to the family, the moral disciplines of the individual, the existence of a sense of social responsibility without absolutizing the community or the state, the openness of society to transcendent truth and goodness, the tender attitudes toward the weak, the mediation of new possibilities of life to offenders against society, the reconciling of enemies—these are some of the effects of the long term influence of Christian faith. The influence of the Wesleyan revival on the moral feelings of the British people, the effect of the disciplines of the Catholic Church on Europe emerging from the dark ages, the impact of Puritanism on the development of moral disciplines in personal life and on the growth of individualism are all examples

of this kind of indirect, long term influence. Influences of this
kind may in time become corrupted. They may be one sided;
they may create moralistic rigidities; they may become secularized. A fresh Christian influence is often needed to counteract
the third-hand effects of a one-sided Christianity which has
been secularized. Yet, when all is said, this long-term influence
is the most important social work of the Church. It nurtures
the conscience in the community on which all other methods
depend.

(2) A second type of indirect influence is the by-product
of action by the Church when it seeks to be true to itself
even though it has no political purpose in view. The effort
of the Church to maintain its own freedom to witness to the
Gospel often helps to keep the door open for the freedom of
men generally. This is also one of the long-term effects on
society to which we have referred, for it was the determination
of Christians to preserve their own freedom—from the state
and from one another—that had much to do with the development of freedom of expression in the course of generations in
the Anglo-Saxon tradition. But we have seen more recently the
consequences of the Church's struggle for freedom under the
Nazi regime. The Church proved to be the toughest of all
social institutions for the state to control and so acted as a
brake on totalitarianism. Another example of this indirect effect
of the Church's action is seen in cases where Christian fellowship across lines of social conflict melts hostilities and makes
political reconciliation possible. This was one factor in the
reconciliations across national lines that came so quickly after
the Second World War. It is sometimes a reality in local industrial conflicts and in overcoming racial prejudice. These
things should not be said without the realization that religious
differences have often hardened social conflicts. However, in
the case of the Churches that belong to the ecumenical com-

munity their influence is chiefly on the side of social and political reconciliation.

(3) A third type of indirect influence by the Church on society and the state is through the teaching of its members about the meaning of Christian faith for the great public issues of the time. There is a vast amount of Christian social education within the Churches which is intended to affect public decisions through the work of the members of the Churches in their various economic vocations, in their influence on public opinion and in their political activities as citizens. This teaching may often be necessary to correct distortions of the public mind resulting from the one-sided forms of Christianity to which I have referred. There is a characteristic distortion of every type of Christian faith! Often this distortion, when the Christian sources that could correct it are forgotten, becomes a pervasive influence in the public mind. Some kinds of Protestant individualism and some forms of conservatism providing the rationalizations for existing conditions as ordained of God are examples. The Churches can teach about the goals and criteria which should influence decisions and they can help show the human consequences of what is being done and of what may be proposed. They can help to illumine the special temptations which affect the minds of Christians in the various roles that they occupy in society.

The Churches in emphasizing the responsibility of their members to act in their various vocations and as citizens in society should do more than teach and exhort. They should also help their members to discharge this responsibility. One kind of help is the provision of occasions for those who face similar problems in their vocations to come together and to discuss those problems in the context of the faith. Also, it is desirable for Christians who generally hold the same social views to form groups of this kind, and they should have the encouragement of the Church so long as they do not claim to commit the Church to their position. It is desirable for the Church to bring together Christians of differing political tendencies so that they can struggle with one another's convictions in an atmosphere created by the Church. There are many types of official, semi-official and voluntary groups that the Church should help to initiate as they are needed for these purposes.

The distinction between direct and indirect action by the Churches is not an absolute one. As we move toward the more direct forms of action, the emphasis is upon decisions that are made by official church bodies for the purpose of influencing public policy either through public opinion or through direct approaches to agencies of government. These more direct forms of action are far less important than the indirect forms of influence which have been discussed. They are less frequent and they are more precariously based and their impact is usually less significant for the life of society. Yet, if the constituency of the Churches is aroused by the processes of education there will be a strong demand that the Churches take additional steps intended to influence public policy more directly. The form of these steps may often be indistinguishable from the indirect forms of action already mentioned. For example, the famous letter from the Presbyterian General Council (U. S. A.) to the Presbyterian Churches in 1954 about the consequences of the anti-Communist hysteria connected with McCarthyism was addressed to the Churches. Yet, it was published in full in the *New York Times* and had considerable influence outside the Churches. In the period in which the United Nations was being established there was an enormous amount of activity of the Churches to create a public opinion favorable to the United Nations. Most of this activity was, in form, directed to the constituency of the Churches, but it was on a scale which was so great and it was given so much publicity that it was obviously directed also to the general public and to the agencies of government. It represented such a clear consensus of articulate opinion in the Churches that it would be difficult to distinguish between the statements or the educational processes directed by Church councils to the Church and those directed to the public. The over-lapping of the constituency of the Churches and the general public in this country make the distinction in practice somewhat artificial so far as actual policy recommendations are concerned. Yet, technically, it is often better for councils of the Church to speak to the Churches rather than to the public even though it is expected that the public will overhear. The reports of most of the ecumenical conferences and assemblies are in this form.

There is one form of direct action which has been well tested and which is least vulnerable to criticism. It is the arrangement officially by the Churches of processes which enable a responsible group to speak for itself to the Churches or to the community. Actually, this is the way in which the World Council Assemblies and the conferences of the National Council of Churches on world order and on economic affairs (the various conferences associated with Cleveland, Detroit and Pittsburgh) have been set up. There have been various commissions officially created and financed by the Churches and empowered to speak for themselves. The statements that they make do not have the authority of the Churches behind them. Members of the Churches who disagree are not committed to them. They have only the weight that is given to them by the authority of the persons responsible and by the intrinsic merit of the statements. If convictions are expressed in this way which are controversial, there will be some resentment felt by those who disagree. Usually those who disagree are willing to tolerate the process and, if they are wise, they will do so because they realize that this is one way of securing corporate Christian guidance, even though it is not infallible and even though one may not always agree with it. It is better to have various corporate expressions which have intrinsic authority and for which careful preparations are made than to be left with only casual, individual expressions of conviction.

There are two other types of direct action. One is the decision of a representative Church body which commits a denomination, or an ecumenical organization, to a particular position on a public question.

In the case of denominations with more centralized polities there is no question about the official character of the decision. The rights of minorities to differ with the majority should be emphasized and no such action in the major denominations is binding on the consciences of individual members and yet the denomination as a whole does take a position that enables it to speak to the nation and to the state.

In denominations with congregational polities there is a different situation because among them any ecclesiastical body speaks only for itself although it does have weight because it is a representative body in its make-up. There are ambiguities here and those who belong to such denominations are familiar with them. It is significant, however, that the polity of such denominations is similar to that of the ecumenical bodies which have no authority over the member-denominations and speak for them with the same kind of ambiguity.

There has been much criticism of this form of direct action on the ground that pronouncements and resolutions by Church councils are too casual and uninformed. It would, in fact, be better for the Churches to be silent than to speak as casually as they sometimes do in resolutions on extremely complicated subjects passed by majority vote without adequate discussion. The only pronouncements or resolutions which are worth the paper they are printed on are those which are the culmination of a carefully organized process of consultation so that they represent the kind of consensus which I have described in an earlier part of this chapter.

The second of the two types of direct action to which I have referred depends upon the first. When a denomination, or an ecumenical body, or a group of local Churches, come to a consensus their representatives may at times bring that consensus to the attention of the agencies of government. This may involve testimony before legislative committees, communications to the President, meetings with representatives of executive departments, or the equivalents of these actions on the level of local or state government. Technically, this may or may not be "lobbying," but if it is, it is appropriate provided it is above board and is based upon careful processes for reaching a consensus. Often it is more effective for the Churches to suggest that their members use their individual influence with their own political representatives.

I want to emphasize again that the indirect forms of action are more important than the direct. Direct action is a kind of overflow from indirect action. If it is not that, it is artificial and does not represent the kind of consensus that justifies it. Whatever may be anyone's judgment about the relative importance of these forms of direct action, the American Churches will insist on them from time to time. Their effectiveness depends somewhat upon economy in their use—if the Church acts and speaks too often there will be diminishing returns. But, if the Churches never act or speak directly this is likely to be a sign not of restraint, but of their not caring enough.[7]

[7] The real situation would be obscured if I did not also point out that one way in which in practice the Church speaks is through individual leaders in or outside of the pulpit who have considerable weight. When a group of such leaders speak or act together, what they do may not be official but it is one of the ways in which the Church does have impact upon society and the state. Archbishop Temple was extremely cautious about the Church's ever commiting itself as Church to any position which is controversial, but he perhaps did not realize how much his own habit of speaking freely on issues did provide a Christian voice that meant that the Church did not, in the public mind, remain silent. Of course, there is often misunderstanding here as to how representative any such person is and this calls for restraint, but this kind of witness helps to save the Church from the silence of indifference when issues are too complicated for an official word.

[Three books have influenced me so much in my thinking about the subject of this chapter that I want to mention them:

William Adams Brown: *Church and State in Contemporary America* (Scribners, 1936)

F. Ernest Johnson: *The Church and Society* (Abingdon, 1935)

J. H. Oldham and W. A. Visser t'Hooft: *The Church and Its Function in Society* (Willett, Clark, 1937).]

CHAPTER XIX

The Christian Citizen and Politics

A MAJOR form of the Church's impact on the state is its influence upon its members who express their Christian convictions in their political activities as citizens. Politics are the machinery through which society makes decisions. These decisions often have great religious and moral meaning. They are often extremely fateful in their effects upon the welfare of the nation and the world. It is unfortunate that there is a tendency, especially among Protestants, in this country to look down upon politics as a rather dubious field of activity. To withdraw from politics is to withdraw from an essential area of Christian responsibility.

Politics are an area of moral ambiguities, not primarily because of the forms of corruption which often accompany them, but because when decisions are finally made, the real alternatives are very much limited. These alternatives in terms of movements, candidates and policies are limited because each has to represent a possible consensus in the community or the nation. The political parties must keep close to what is achievable—to what the public will accept and to what the external historical situation will permit. There are areas of freedom here but there are limits and it is for this reason that it is wisely said that politics are the art of the possible. Also, political movements are concerned about gaining power, the power to put a program into effect, the power to serve the interests of those who control the party or who are attracted to it. Necessary as political power is, it is pursued with mixed motives and it does tempt people to seek it for its own sake or, more accurately, to enable them to serve their own interests over-much or to satisfy their vanity. These are the moral ambiguities of politics and they are in large measure inescapable. The serious abuses of power can be transcended by individuals, but the limitations of available alternatives with attendant moral frustrations remain.

There is also in political life, perhaps less among the professionals than among the rank and file enthusiasts for a party, a strong tendency to deal self-righteously with opponents. At least, there are periods, chiefly in the fall of election year, when otherwise sober and self-critical people lose all moral sense of proportion as they contemplate the alternatives between which the nation must choose. This type of political partisanship may become egregiously unfair, bitter and divisive as was the case in the struggles over the New Deal in the 1930's and as it was in the struggles over problems of subversion and over China policy in the 1950's.

These ambiguities of political life make it impossible to think in terms of "Christian politics" in the sense that at any given time Christians should be expected to support one party or one political line. It is the responsibility of Christian citizens to use their intelligence to find the best movements and policies and candidates to support. Because of the technical and strategic issues that affect judgments about policies and for which there is no Christian guidance, Christians can be expected to differ. Also, there are deeper social preferences, based upon differing emphases on order or freedom, on indignation over existing evils or on fear of evils that changes might bring which cause the most devout and morally sensitive Christians to differ. So far as the emphasis on present or possible future evils is concerned, it makes a great difference how near the present evils are to one's own experience.

In some other countries there are Christian political parties.

They are not usually ecclesiastically controlled parties and membership in them is not considered obligatory for all adherents of any Church. These parties are sometimes Protestant, sometimes Catholic and sometimes mixed, but the most important example of a mixed party, the Christian Democrats in West Germany, is dominantly Roman Catholic. Holland has been the country where Protestant parties with a Calvinistic ethos have flourished and it is significant that in the 1940's a large part of the Protestant leadership broke away from the two Protestant parties to join with labor groups and secularist Socialists to form a Labor Party. They did this because the Protestant parties were too conservative on economic issues and on the colonial problem connected with Indonesia. This was a very remarkable example of how a Christian Party loses its reason for existence and how Christians of another generation must escape from it into a secular party in order to fulfill their Christian vocation.

Christian political parties and Christian political movements in general misrepresent the true situation: they give the impression that Christianity implies a particular political program whereas it does not do so. They drain off from secular parties the Christian influence which they need. They tend to give a false sanctity to the inevitable compromises of politics. By combining religion with politics, they are likely to add to the bitterness of a political conflict the fanaticism and self-righteousness of a religious conflict and this combination threatens to create a deep spiritual chasm in the national community.[1]

[1] The Amsterdam Assembly of the World Council of Churches (1948) considered this matter of Christian parties and Section III made the following statement:

"One problem is raised by the existence in several countries of Christian political parties. The Church as such should not be identified with any political party, and it must not act as though it were itself a political party. In general, the formation of such parties is hazardous because they easily confuse Christianity with the inherent compromises of politics. They may cut off Christians from the other parties which need the leaven of Chris-

To say that there should be no Christian party does not mean that Christians with the guidance of the Churches should not at times unite to oppose a political party, for example, a party dedicated to racial hatred, to white supremacy or to anti-Semitism, or a party with clearly totalitarian aims. In practise such parties would doubtless develop strength among members of Churches, but the Churches on all but the local level would oppose them. The Roman Catholic Church sometimes goes too far in this negative Christian politics. In Europe it is guided in this by its strong opposition not only to Communism, but even to democratic socialism that is suspected of being Marxist in inspiration and by such religio-political questions as those affecting Church schools.[2]

In this country the major parties have no consistent ideology. The most decisive political struggles among us are the struggles within each party to determine its leadership and direction.

---

tianity, and they may consolidate all who do not share the political principles of the Christian party not only against that party but against Christianity itself. Nevertheless, it may be desirable in some situations for Christians to organize themselves into a political party for specific objectives, so long as they do not claim that it is the only possible expression of Christian loyalty in the situation."

That last sentence was included because of the strong convictions of some German delegates that their country at the time needed a party that would have the positive inspiration of Christianity.

[2] In 1957 the Roman Catholic hierarchy in West Germany before the national elections sent a pastoral letter to be read in Churches which by implication strongly supported Chancellor Adenauer and his Christian Democratic Party. The letter did not explicitly ask adherence to that party or condemn all Social Democrats as such. The *New York Times'* interpretation at the time said: "The pastoral letters could be read to permit communicants to vote for Social Democratic candidates, provided the individual candidates could be regarded as Christian and had proved this by supporting legislation favored by the Church. A fact that militates against this possibility is the feeling prevalent in the Church hierarchy here that Social Democrats are not true Christians but Marxists and free thinkers." (Sept. 8, 1957) Actually there is now much Protestant support for the Social Democrats and they have moved away from their traditional Marxism, but this interpretation indicates that the Catholic Church remains cautious about drawing an absolute line.

The overlap as between the parties in outlook and policy is remarkable and often the chief differences between prominent leaders of the two parties are over very marginal issues of strategy and these as seen in the light of regional differences.

There is difference of opinion as to whether or not it would be better to have parties controlled by more consistent philosophies and purposes. That is the kind of issue about which there is certainly no Christian judgment. I think that there is great value in the inclusive parties since it means that the major struggles go on within each party and when there is a change of party the policies of the new administration have a broad acceptance. The two-party system, in any case, is likely to mean ideologically inclusive parties and to move far away from it is likely to lead not only to extreme factionalism but also to stalemate and paralysis. The American parties may be too inclusive, one on the race issue and the other on economic issues and foreign policy, but even this is probably better than the results to be expected if rational political planners had the power to create two new parties according to a more consistent pattern. One of the two parties would probably be denuded of all that now makes it a tolerable instrument of government!

At any given moment it may seem objectionable to have parties which cannot take unambiguous positions on major issues, but in the long run there is much to be said for the kind of political machinery which does not create deep chasms between majority and minority. Both parties have to come to a moderate position if each is to be held together as a party. Professor Schattschneider argues this very well. He says that "a large party must be supported by a great variety of interests sufficiently tolerant of each other to collaborate." Also he says that, while "a homogeneous party might be oppressive," "the tentative aggregates of miscellaneous elements collected within the loose framework of a major party are unthinkable as instruments of tyranny."[3]

[3] E. E. Schattschneider, *Party Government* (Rinehart, 1942), p. 85.

One of the common illusions among American Protestants is that it is sufficient to emphasize the decisions that are made on election day after the alternatives have been determined by earlier decisions within the political parties. The parties choose the candidates and the parties provide the organized support for policies and programs. Christian citizens should be concerned about the influences which control the parties and about the honesty and effectiveness of party organizations and party leadership as well as about the results of elections. The effectiveness of parties within the Congress and state legislatures as bodies with some coherence in spite of their inclusiveness is of great importance and yet it seldom receives any attention by Churches. The health of the American political system depends in the long run on the health of the political parties. Congressman Eugene J. McCarthy who has given a great deal of thought to the role of the Christian in politics says quite rightly of the position of the independent voter or the nonpartisan citizen that "these forms of political activity can be enjoyed only because others are actively engaged in party politics."[4]

There is a common feeling that political parties and the type of political life that is lived close to party organizations must always be so much involved in compromise or so close to corruption that a Christian citizen would do well to assume the role of the independent voter.

Undoubtedly, the independent voters do have a wholesome influence on our political parties: they keep both parties worried. Their existence is a corrective factor and there are many people who by temperament or vocation probably should be independent voters. There is a special problem connected with American parties which supports this tendency; this arises from the fact that in many states the voter feels kinship with one party on the national level and with the other party on the

---

[4] This is from an extraordinarily wise and, in a Christian sense, sensitive article, "The Christian in Politics" (*The Commonweal*, October 1, 1954).

local level. I doubt if independent voting needs encouragement, for there is no likelihood of there being any lack of independent voters in the near future. Today the encouragement should be the other way, and idealistic Christians should come to realize the enormous importance of party organizations as instruments for creating a consensus that is necessary for decision and action. Also, they should see that while the independent voters do have some influence on party organizations from the outside, they are limited in their choice to candidates and programs that are determined as a result of intra-party struggles. These struggles go on continuously within the parties and the independent voters leave the most difficult and the most unappreciated work to the faithful party members in local clubs and committees. I think that Protestants should reverse their prevailing attitudes here and emphasize the enormous importance of the vocation of Christians in this patient activity within party organizations.

Something needs to be said about compromise and corruption. They are often joined and one form of compromise is living with corruption in the same party. Party leaders, if they are to get anything done, can hardly be crusaders against corruption on all levels at once and national political leaders of high character and purpose will depend in part upon support from local bosses the sources of whose power will not bear much examination. There are many degrees of this and the earlier paternalistic political bosses whose corruption consisted in looking out for people whose needs were otherwise neglected are being displaced by labor organizations and by the welfare activities of the state.

It is important to avoid identifying corruption and compromise though sometimes they are related as has been suggested. There is one type of compromise which is the adjustment of convictions and interests for the sake of a consensus. Compromise in this sense is necessary for politics and for all forms of negotiation or cooperation. Those who can never compromise in this way are the people who claim a monopoly of wisdom. If they were to have their way, society would be dissolved by a stiff-necked individualistic factionalism which would be the more destructive if each faction were sure of its own righteousness. Any large political movement which has a chance of gaining power and of realizing any of its purposes must be an alliance of many groups all of which must compromise in this sense. There are times when great matters of the common welfare with the help of strong leadership can cement a political movement; this may obscure, but it does not destroy, elements of compromise by individuals.

The external observer may often find it difficult to distinguish between these necessary compromises which are marks of a good humility that concedes something to the other person's judgment and interests, and compromises which are dictated by a selfish expediency that may involve betrayal of an essential loyalty. The two kinds of compromise are often blended in the same person, but no combination of self-criticism and moral integrity can remove the need of the first kind. One sees the necessity of it most vividly when a legislator must vote "aye" or "no"—not "aye, but" or "no, but"—on a particular bill or amendment,[5] often with little time to decide as a parliamentary situation develops.

I have put the emphasis on the legitimate form of compromise because much conventional Christian teaching has failed to recognize its necessity. It is impossible to set down rules in the abstract about the limits of compromise but Christian politicians and other citizens who keep morally sensitive will discover these limits. There are times when one should choose a course that will lead to personal defeat rather than soft-pedal

[5] Jerry Voorhis, *Confessions of a Congressman* (Doubleday, 1947), p. 233. Mr. Voorhis says after the clerk begins to call the roll it was "too late for 'on the one hand—but on the other hand' discussions. It would be another aye or no—one hundred percent one or the other."

a major issue or follow the popular trend. An outsider may not know when the time has come to take the difficult stand and the person himself can be easily self-deceived about it. But the accent should not be on keeping oneself unspotted, but rather on how one can most adequately serve the real welfare of the community. There are differences of vocation here and some Christians should probably put their emphasis on prophetic leadership in the interests of moral clarity and others should work quietly to level down obstacles to moral achievement. Those who are cast for the first role should respect those whose best contribution can be made in the second.

Political corruption, when it pervades a society, makes good government impossible; it leads to all kinds of favoritism in the enactment and enforcement of law; it makes society helpless before any group that can pay for protection against the law. Corruption breeds cynicism about government, and this encourages more corruption. In this country the cruder and more obvious financial corruption is marginal; it is most common in some departments of city government and it is subject to waves of popular indignation and periods of reform. The larger the unit of government in this country, the more antidotes to corruption there seem to be. Sporadic corruption in the federal government, always slight in relation to the gigantic sums of money that change hands, comes immediately under the searchlight of the criticism of the opposition party.

When we seek to judge the moral climate of politics it is well to realize that when a politician or public official receives a bribe it is generally someone who is not a politician or public official who pays it. Some private business interest is willing to pay for privilege or protection. The more respectable the private interest, the less it needs to descend to overt corruption to get its way. On the higher levels of government, especially in the Federal Government, the standards of political life are more exacting than those in the business community. The "conflict of interests" law is rigorously applied to federal appointees. Legislators have much more leeway, but with them the danger of favoritism comes less from actual corruption than from the social influences which are natural when people share a common background of associations and interests. The deepest source of corruption is the pressure of all sorts of private interests upon government at a time when the power of government to help or harm those private interests is very great. When private business with its own standards of conduct and with its lavish expense accounts touches government it creates so many temptations that the wonder is that there is so little corruption in government. At any rate, it ill behooves the world of business to take a self-righteous attitude toward the world of politics and for the Churches to share that attitude.

I have been speaking about the moral risks and costs of politics in the narrow sense of activities within partisan political organizations, and I have emphasized the positive contribution of partisan politics. It hardly needs to be said that the Christian can never be an absolute partisan. He can have no part in the partisanship which breeds bitterness and untruth, which leads politicians to raise false issues or to trifle with grave matters of policy for a political advantage. True partisanship requires much moral patience; it must accept a strange assortment of bedfellows. But it should remain self-critical and in sight of the purpose of the whole process. It should seek to make the party a more consistent instrument of that purpose.

There are two common errors, both of them related to the neglect of political parties, in the American Protestant attitude toward politics.

One of these errors is the tendency to see parties and candidates in terms of a single issue. This often is a moralistic issue in the narrow sense as it has to do with matters of personal behavior that are in an area with which the Church is most familiar. The crusade for Prohibition was the most obvious example of this tendency. Protestants often judged candidates only on this one issue and neglected all of the broader issues of social justice and of foreign policy. Much has been learned from this experience and I doubt if national Church bodies are likely now to encourage Christian citizens to take such a narrow view of their political responsibilities. There is a danger that some form of the Catholic issue may dominate much Protestant politics and create a similar distortion.

The other major error is the tendency to stress the personal character or piety of a candidate without taking into account the forces which support him or the wisdom of his policies. The personal character of our leaders in public life is of great importance, but the primary emphasis should be placed upon integrity in the discharge of public responsibilities. The error appears when the private character or religious habits of a candidate become a front for interests and policies which are not examined. A man of the highest personal character, known to be devout in his personal life but whose views of policy are mistaken and who is supported by narrow interests which use him the more effectively because of his high character, may be a bad choice compared with a man who, while dependable in his integrity, is less acclaimed for private virtue or piety, but whose convictions about policy are sounder and whose supporters are in their interests closer to the public interests. It seems hardly necessary to say it and yet there are times in religious circles when it still needs to be said that neither personal virtue nor sincere piety are any guarantee of social wisdom. They are often combined with serious blind spots on problems of justice, if the person's experience has not given relevant education to his conscience. I have no patience with the cynicism that is indifferent to the role of morality in politics, but emphasis should be upon the relevance of the morality, upon a more than conventional moral sensitivity, upon the interests which control the political movements which are voted into power, upon competence as well as character.

There are other dimensions of the Christian life in relation to politics. I have in mind here less the goals that are sought than the spirit of the Christian citizen and the resources by which he lives. He should be able to transcend partisanship without denying its proper place, to avoid bitterness and unfairness. He should not expect to find the perfect policy, but he should have the patience to seek the best available one with a mind that is open to new ways in which he may help to counteract the evil in it. He should be self-critical and aware of the bias in his own judgment that comes from his own social background and thus able to sense the moral limitations in all sides of a political conflict. He should be helped by his faith to combine contrition with resolute action. Always he should be aware of the consequences of his decisions in the lives of people and show a special concern for the weak and defenseless. He need not feel alone, not only because in the hardest and loneliest places he can know the divine companionship, but also because at all times he is a member of a Christian community which relates him to the sources of vision, of power, and of forgiveness.

INDEX

INDEX